IT PROJECT MANAGEMENT

STUDY GUIDE

Best Practices, Tools and Techniques

J ROSS PUBLISHING

FIRST INDIAN EDITION 2017
REPRINT 2023

ISBN : 978-93-8655-151-1

REPRINTED UNDER A LICENCE FROM AGREEMENT PUBLISHER: J ROSS PUBLISHING, 300 ROAD, #305, S PINE ISLAND PLANTATION, FL 33324 (USA)

FOR SALE IN INDIA, NEPAL, BANGLADESH, SRI LANKA, PAKISTAN, BHUTAN & MALDIVES ONLY.

Distributors:

BPB PUBLICATIONS
20, Ansari Road, Darya Ganj
New Delhi-110002
Ph: 23254990/23254991

BPB BOOK CENTRE
376 Old Lajpat Rai Market,
Delhi-110006
Ph: 23861747

COMPUTER BOOK CENTRE
12, Shrungar Shopping Centre,
M.G.Road, BENGALURU–560001
Ph: 25587923/25584641

DECCAN AGENCIES
4-3-329, Bank Street,
Hyderabad-500195
Ph: 24756967/24756400

MICRO MEDIA
Shop No. 5, Mahendra Chambers, 150
DN Rd. Next to Capital Cinema, V.T.
(C.S.T.) Station, MUMBAI-400 001 Ph:
22078296/22078297

Published by Manish Jain for BPB Publications, 20, Ansari Road, Darya Ganj, New Delhi-110002 and Printed at Manipal Technologies Limited, Manipal

Table of Contents

Foreword

In Stephen King's chilling novel, *IT*, a demonic clown terrorizes a small town in Maine before being confronted and ultimately overcome in the sewer system by the Losers Club. Unfortunately, for too many organizations, the thought of their internal IT function conjures up the same terms: demonic, clowns, terrorize, and sewer system.

In *Mastering IT Project Management*, Murali Chemuturi contends that you do not need to be a member of the Losers Club to overcome the challenges presented by IT. He demonstrates that you only have to apply proper project management principles to plan and execute IT projects successfully. This book provides a full spectrum, step-by-step, how-to approach that arms both novices and gurus with best practices, tools, and techniques that allow them to emerge victorious while avoiding the sewer system altogether.

Full spectrum—Mr. Chemuturi has included chapters that cover the feasibility study, sizing the components, planning, execution, project control, and project closure.

Step-by-step—This book contains literally hundreds of enumerated lists. Everything from setting up a configuration management system, to factors to consider for the make versus buy decision, to the types of metrics to be collected for IT projects can be found. In fact, I challenge the reader to open the book to any random page and *not* find a list (including this one)!

How-to—A number of sample forms and reports are provided such as a feasibility report template, a quality assurance plan template, a sample risk management plan, a group review process flowchart, etc.

But the book isn't just a two-dimensional survey of the IT project management landscape; it also provides a third-dimensional contour by discussing what works and what doesn't and by providing insight into current and emerging best practices.

This is Murali Chemuturi's fourth, and hopefully not his last book, appropriate for a master's program:

- *Mastering IT Project Management*
- *Mastering Software Project Management*

- *Mastering Software Quality Assurance*
- *Software Estimation Best Practices, Tools & Techniques*

With final apologies to Stephen King, I'd like to conclude by proclaiming that *Mastering IT Project Management* will *Stand* as one of Mr. Chemuturi's *Shining* accomplishments; one that will most certainly help you *Carrie* out your *IT* projects much more successfully.

Pat O'Toole
CMMI High Maturity Lead Appraiser
Burnsville, MN

Acknowledgments

When I look back, I find that there are so many people to whom I should be grateful. Be it because of their commissions or omissions, they made me a stronger and better person and both directly and indirectly helped to make this book possible. It would be difficult to acknowledge everyone's contributions here, so to those whose names do not appear, I wish to thank you all just the same. I will have failed in my duty if I do not explicitly and gratefully acknowledge the persons below:

- My parents, Appa Rao and Vijaya Lakshmi, the reason for my existence, especially my father, a rustic agrarian, who by personal example taught me the virtue of hard work and how sweet the aroma of sweat from the brow can be.
- My family, who stood by me like a rock in difficult times, especially my wife, Udaya Sundari, who gave me the confidence and the belief that "I can," and my two sons, Dr. Nagendra and Vijay, who provided me with the motive to excel.
- My two uncles, Raju and Ramana, who by personal example taught me what integrity and excellence means.
- The staff of J. Ross Publishing, especially Drew Gierman, my publisher, Steve Buda, and everyone else involved in bringing this book to the public.

To all of you, I humbly bow my head in respect and salute you in acknowledgment of your contribution.

Murali Chemuturi

Prologue

Murali Chemuturi's book, *Mastering IT Project Management: Best Practices, Tools and Techniques,* is an indispensable resource for IT project managers, business analysts, and anyone who wants to understand managing projects in the IT environment.

This book provided me with a valuable reference for a comprehensive analysis, structure, and clear solution for developing a complete feasibility study. It outlines a critical approach in product/project right sizing, with emphasis on project planning, techniques, and quality, in every phase of product development.

It is hard to find a single source reference that contains a holistic approach with relevant examples, charts/tables, and hardware. This reference addresses the importance of inspection/reviews and details how to accomplish and analyze critical performance measures, budget controls, and cash flow. The author provides a holistic resource that IT managers can use as a quality reference that has quantitative examples one can tailor to their projects.

Murali Chemuturi has succeeded in communicating the necessary components one must have operating in the IT organization and related infrastructure. The author has provided examples of best practices in project management by definition, as shown in Chapter 1. He also offers steps in conducting the feasibility study that are helpful as most do not know where to start. The steps are a good checklist for anyone executing a study. Chapter 5 focuses on planning the project in IT. It has been my experience that many projects do not have a plan—they simply start—and the project becomes a failed statistic. Overall, this book is a must have for every IT organization as a usable reference and guide for a successful project.

David Carrier, Ph.D., PMP, LEAN/DFSS, ITIL, SSBB, CSM

About the Author

Murali Chemuturi is an information technology and software development subject matter expert, hands-on programmer, author, consultant, and trainer. Since 2001, he has consulted on IT and training for organizations in the United States and India via his company, Chemuturi Consultants. Chemuturi Consultants offers a number of products to aid project managers and software development professionals such as PMPal, a software project management tool; and EstimatorPal, FPAPal, and UCPPal, a set of software estimation tools. Chemuturi Consultants also offers a material requirements planning software product, MRPPal, to assist small- to medium-sized manufacturing organizations to efficiently manage their materials.

Prior to starting his own firm, Mr. Chemuturi worked for over 40 years in various engineering and manufacturing management positions and in IT and software development. His most recent position prior to forming his firm was Vice President of Software Development at Vistaar e-Business Pvt., Ltd.

Mr. Chemuturi's undergraduate degrees and diplomas are in Electrical and Industrial Engineering and he holds an MBA and a Postgraduate Diploma in Computer Methods and Programming. He has several years of academic experience teaching a variety of computer and IT courses such as COBOL, Fortran, BASIC, Computer Architecture, and Database Management Systems.

Mr. Chemuturi authored two books, *Software Estimation Best Practices: Tools and Techniques for Software Project Estimators* and *Mastering Software Quality Assurance: Best Practices, Tools and Techniques for Software Developers,* published in the United States by J. Ross Publishing. He coauthored another book with Thomas M. Cagley Jr. titled *Mastering Software Project Management: Best Practices, Tools and Techniques,* also published by J. Ross Publishing.

He is a senior member of IEEE, a senior member of the Computer Society of India, a Fellow of the Indian Institute of Industrial Engineering, and has published numerous articles in professional journals.

This book has free material available for download from the Web Added Value™ resource center at *www.jrosspub.com*

At J. Ross Publishing we are committed to providing today's professional with practical, hands-on tools that enhance the learning experience and give readers an opportunity to apply what they have learned. That is why we offer free ancillary materials available for download on this book and all participating Web Added Value™ publications. These online resources may include interactive versions of material that appears in the book or supplemental templates, worksheets, models, plans, case studies, proposals, spreadsheets and assessment tools, among other things. Whenever you see the WAV™ symbol in any of our publications, it means bonus materials accompany the book and are available from the Web Added Value Download Resource Center at www.jrosspub.com.

Downloads for *Mastering IT Project Management* consist of:

1. A sample schedule for a typical IT project
2. Electronic versions of valuable templates displayed in Appendix I of the book
3. A personal effectiveness (PET) software tool

1

Introduction to IT Project Management

Introduction

Information technology (IT) is now all-pervading. Just 20 years ago, we were talking about a paperless office and we seem to have arrived at it; at least records are not being maintained in paper form anymore. Some reports, receipts, and acknowledgments are still being issued in some places and they too are being replaced by e-mails. In days gone by, computers were large and relegated to a corner in the administrative building/area of the organization primarily serving finance functions or finance department needs. Now computers have become much smaller with the iPad generation taking less space than a scribbling pad. Nearly every employee has a PC on their desk unless the person is working on a production shop floor. Information handling has truly and completely shifted to computers.

All of this has not been achieved without sweat and tears. Organizations like IBM, Apple, Microsoft, and Compaq have worked miracles (well almost!) to make computers affordable for everyone. While the first computer, ENIAC (less powerful in terms of processing power than today's iPad) was operated by PhDs, school-going kids are now using computers (itself a miracle). With the explosion of the Internet and cheap hardware and software, almost every conceivable information-processing task in the organization is being carried out on computers.

This places a new onus on organizational management which has to provide computers to all information-handling employees and then offer continuous support to users. In the initial stages of the computer revolution, the growth of computers in organizations was haphazard. It grew in clusters wherever a group or department could justify computerization (automation and mechanization were other terms used in those days) in terms of costs and benefits. Such groups or departments were provided with computers along with other paraphernalia. It resulted in different departments having different computer systems and application software that did not talk to each other. The situation was untenable and additional investment became necessary to make all the computers speak to each other and all software products in the organizations exchange data with each other. In those days, the IT infrastructure did not find a place among strategic decision making mainly due to still-evolving technology and because IT was not perceived as strategic infrastructure. Now, we have a sufficient body of knowledge gathered over the last 20 to 30 years of implementing end-user computing (as it was called in its nascent days) from which we can derive principles to plan IT infrastructure efficiently and effectively.

There are two components to implementing IT infrastructure in an organization: (1) making the technical decisions for each component and (2) managing its implementation. In this book, I focus primarily on the management portion of the project. But I concede that it is really impossible to completely avoid any discussion of engineering activities altogether while discussing the management aspects. Therefore, I will be discussing engineering aspects where appropriate as they become necessary for a discussion on management.

Components of IT Infrastructure

Before we move forward on the management of IT projects, let's review the rudimentary components of IT infrastructure. Building IT infrastructure needs multiple pieces of discreet equipment. These are described below:

1. Computer hardware:
   a. *Servers—primary servers and mirror servers.* Servers are larger computers with special software. A server could look like a client machine, especially when running the Microsoft Server operating system but it is different in hardware construction. The primary differentiator between a server and a workstation is the ability of the server to support multiple concurrent users and multiple concurrent tasks. It would have better hardware for I/O (input/output) operations and communication and contain much more RAM (random access memory) and disk capacity than a normal

PC. Sometimes the server may have more than one CPU (central processing unit) when we desire a fault-tolerance feature. In fact, it has become common to have multiple CPUs in servers. A mirror server is identical to the main server in terms of hardware and software, except that it will be standing by as long as the primary server is running and only takes over whenever the primary server fails. It would be seamless so that users would be unaware that the primary server failed. A mirror server ensures that the network is never off-line. We will discuss more on servers in Chapter 4.

b. *Client machines/workstations.* Most organizations use PCs as workstations today. These can be terminals in the case of mainframes and, in engineering environments, the workstations can be graphics CADD (computer aided design and drafting) machines. The workstation can be a system of a PC, printer, scanner, POS (point of sale) machine, credit card terminal, and so on. When a PC is used as a terminal it runs terminal emulation software.

2. Networking hardware:
   a. *Gateways.* Gateways connect two computer networks running under two different protocols. A gateway is a communicator between two networks. It is akin to a translator between two people speaking two different languages. We use it to connect our organizational computer network with a provider of bandwidth.
   b. *Routers.* A router literally routes Internet/Intranet traffic to different workstations within or outside the organization. It mainly resolves network addresses and keeps data packets flowing on the network to their destinations.
   c. *Switches.* Switches distribute bandwidth to all the machines in a network by switching between the workstations dynamically. They are used within organizations over local area networks.
   d. *Hubs.* Hubs also distribute bandwidth to all the machines in the local area network but they do this by dividing bandwidth between machines. They do not switch the bandwidth between machines but divide it.
   e. *Modems.* Modem is an acronym meaning modulator-demodulator. A modem receives low-voltage computer signals and converts them to higher voltage signals suitable for telephone networks to facilitate transmissions. It also receives signals from public telephone networks and converts them back to digital signals suitable for computers. Modem usage has decreased as high-speed Internet

networks are becoming more widely available. Modems may still be used in remote locations where the only network available is via the telephone. In cities where the Internet is supplied on a TV cable network, a modem suitable for coaxial cable is used. Presently, the Internet is also supplied on telephone lines in two ways, namely, dialup and DSL (digital subscriber line). In both cases modems are used.

f. *Cabling.* Cabling is the setting of electric wires that connect the hardware in the network. The cables contain special features to protect the electrical signals from external noise. They can be standard, electric coaxial, or optical fiber. Optical fiber cables offer better data transmission speeds and better protection against external noises than coaxial cables.

3. Peripheral devices:
   a. *Printers.* Printers are basically of two varieties, namely, bulk printers and small printers. Bulk printers in the past were printing one line at a time and were called line printers, but today's bulk printers are capable of printing eight lines or more at a time. They usually print only textual information but some of them are also capable of printing graphics and are used at the organizational level for producing high-volume printouts. Bulk printers use continuous stationary and can produce up to 132 characters per line normally and up to 255 characters per line using a smaller font. Small printers print page by page and are used as personal printers. These printers use discreet office stationary and are used for low-volume printouts. These normally do have excellent graphics capabilities and can also print in color. They can even print photographs to a resolution of 1200 by 1200 dpi (dots per inch). These are usually used at workstations, and high-resolution photo printers are used centrally.
   b. *Plotters*:
      i. *Drawing plotters*. Plotters produce map/engineering drawing outputs on small to large size paper. The maximum size handled can be one meter in width and of necessary length. These devices are used in cartography or engineering drawing or design offices.
      ii. *Photo-plotters.* Photo-plotters are used in printed circuit board (PCB) designing offices. PCBs are used in all electronic instruments and have electronic circuits etched on them with

great precision. This process of etching on the PCB requires artwork. An electronic circuit diagram is drawn either by hand or on a computer. Artwork is prepared from this circuit diagram using a graphic workstation with a software package like Red CAD or P-CAD. Photo-plotters print the artwork with great precision on the selected medium, normally photo film. While photo printers print on paper, photo-plotters expose photo film using a thin beam of light to produce the artwork.

c. *Digitizers.* Digitizers offer a flatbed on which we can move a pointing device like a digital pen or mouse and create drawings or paintings on a screen. They are used to transform hand sketches into engineering drawings. Digitizers are also widely used to draw freehand drawings on computers. They are a vital component in the movie making of animation/cartoon films and are also used for converting engineering drawings from paper to digital form. Digitizers come in a variety of sizes ranging from A4 to A0.
d. *Very high-resolution video terminals.* These are used in the medical field to view x-rays, sonograms, body scans, etc. When we set up IT infrastructure in hospitals, we need to consider these terminals. They are of very high resolution and with vivid color resolution to enable true rendering of internal parts of the body.
e. *Credit card terminals.* These machines help us collect money from credit cards. They are used in all types of retail stores and can consist of a card swipe terminal and a signature capture screen.
f. *Scanners.* Scanners capture images from paper and place them onto computers. They can convert characters (alphabets and numerals) into digital (ASCII or EBCDIC) form in combination with an optical character recognition software product. Scanners come in a wide variety of sizes and resolutions. They are used in most organizations to digitize pictures and all types of written documents with no electronic counterpart.
g. *Closed-circuit cameras.* These are used for security purposes and can be connected to computers to record the captured pictures and to facilitate faster retrieval when needed. Most organizations install them for security purposes so consider the hardware and digital storage space necessary when setting up IT infrastructure in an organization.
h. *Audio devices.* These may not be needed in bulk in an organization but they are being used for teleconferences and may be needed in

conference and meeting rooms. Many organizations conduct webinars using these devices. Sometimes video is also used, but even then audio devices are required so everyone in the room can listen to the audio comfortably.

   i. *Videoconferencing devices.* In geographically disparate organizations, videoconferencing has become the normal way to meet. Videoconferencing has eliminated the need for travel to attend meetings. The specialty of these devices is that they can detect voice and focus the camera and microphone in that direction to ensure better reception of picture and sound. All major organizations use videoconferencing and therefore video devices need to be considered when setting up IT infrastructure in an organization.
   j. *Biometric devices*. Slowly, biometrics are entering the corporate scene for restricting entry into organizations or creating a secure space within an office space. Fingerprint and iris readers are commonly used biometric readers.
   k. *Backup devices.* There are many types of backup devices, including CDs, pen drives, conventional tape cartridges, USB mass storage media and disks, external hard disks, and online storage.
4. Power supply equipment:
   a. *UPS (uninterrupted power supply)*. UPS provides backup power to important computer systems. When the public power supply system fails, UPS takes electric power from the storage batteries, converts it to alternating current (AC) and supplies it to the connected computer systems. Important machines like servers and networking hardware are supported with UPS so that no transaction is terminated halfway through and data integrity is protected. UPS comes in a wide range of capacities and is able to support a single PC as well as the entire network. Today, UPS has become an indispensable part of IT infrastructure.
   b. *Alternators.* An alternator is an electric generator producing AC power. In countries with an erratic public power supply like India, alternators have become a must have. These are typically not needed in advanced countries where public power supplies are reliable.
   c. *Batteries.* Batteries are used for providing backup power to the infrastructure and are used along with the UPS.

d. *Emergency lighting.* This is required in server and communication rooms for power-out times. It may be used at other computer locations where emergency lighting is a requirement. We need to consider all places where emergency lighting is needed. Various types of lighting are available from torch lights to normal bulb lighting, which take over automatically when the power trips.

e. *Spike busters.* A spike is a sudden and steep increase in supply voltage that lasts for a very short time, perhaps just milliseconds. Normally, spike busters are built into UPS systems or sockets. We need to ensure that protection for the systems against spikes is available as part of the power supply network.

f. *Surge protectors.* A surge is an increase in supply voltage that usually lasts longer than a spike. These surges can really destroy computer hardware so protection of equipment is key.

5. Software:

a. *System software.* This software administers the hardware and is the software layer closest to the hardware. All other software products work through this layer. It consists of the operating system at the workstation level and the server operating system at the server level, and is normally supplied with the hardware. When we select the hardware, we have selected the system software. It is also possible to select this system software first and then select the hardware later. There is a two-way dependency between the hardware and system software. There are some system software products like UNIX/Linux that can work on a variety of hardware platforms, but most others are tied to a specific hardware platform.

b. *Database software.* Every computer-based system works on data. It used to be that data were stored in flat files that offered no facilities for data manipulations. The application software undertook all the data manipulation functions. A DBMS (database management system) separated data from programs by providing data definition and manipulation facilities. Presently, an RDBMS (relational database management system) is the most popular form of DBMS. While some RDBMSs are available on multiple platforms, others are platform dependent. Some of the popular ones are DB2, Oracle, SQL Server, Progress, Unify, and Informix. An RDBMS needs to be loaded on the common server or a dedicated server.

c. *Web server software.* This software acts as an interface between the server and the World Wide Web. Any request sent over the World Wide Web is intercepted, interpreted, and responded to by this software product. Web server software needs to be loaded on the common server or a dedicated one. The web server software determines the load (the number of concurrent connections that can be made to the website) and therefore, it has a direct effect on the response time felt by the users on the website.

d. *App server software.* The application server provides specialist services to the application software. Some of the app servers provide rules engines, business processes, and so on, that can be called by the application software avoiding the necessity to develop those functions from scratch. An app server can be on a separate machine or on the common server itself.

e. *Security software.* These products ensure security of the IT infrastructure from attacks and include:

    i. *Antivirus, anti-malware, anti-spyware.* With applications moving to the Internet, the incidence of malicious attacks on systems have increased multifold. Attacks come in the form of viruses (software that attaches itself to other software products or files and causes some malicious action), worms (independent programs that enter the system and cause damage to the data and programs), spyware (programs that snoop around computers, collect information, and then transmit it to some predefined destination), and malware (programs that are of an unspecified nature but are intent on causing damage to the data and programs on computers). There are thousands of these in circulation. Some organizations have specialized in preventing these attacks and supply solutions to protect against attacks as well as prevent their entry into systems. These programs can work at the workstation or the server level. This protection is mandatory in systems using Microsoft platforms and a careful assessment must be made to select the right solution for the organization.

    ii. *Firewalls.* These software products try to prevent any unauthorized entry into the network. Some firewalls are tied to the operating system tightly and some are available as commercial off-the-shelf (COTS) products. They must be applied at both the server and workstation levels.

iii. *Website filtering software.* With so many websites available on the World Wide Web and some of them malicious and undesirable (such as pornographic sites), every organization needs a filtering software product to prevent employees from accessing unauthorized websites. Firewalls do possess this capability to some extent but specialized products are also available. The need for this product depends on the selection of the firewall. If the firewall is fully capable of filtering, we may not need this variety of software.

iv. *Usage control software.* This software assists in ensuring that sensitive functions of the application are used carefully. Facilities include restricting the usage of sensitive functions by the IP address, by the user ID, the time of usage, or any other organization-specific restrictions. If the restricted function is requested from an unexpected IP address, or at an unexpected time, or from an unexpected user ID, it would alert security authorities, seek additional authorizations, and take evasive/restrictive action so that organizational interests are protected.

f. *E-mail software*:

i. *Exchange software.* E-mail has become all-pervasive and an indispensable part of corporate communication. An e-mail server can be hosted within the organization or outside of it. If the e-mail server is hosted inside the organization, the exchange software needs to be installed within the organization. There are many alternatives available in the market. Some keep e-mails on the server at a central location and others allow them to be downloaded to individual workstations. The advantage of keeping them at a central place is that all e-mails can be regularly backed up and stored, and if the user resigns they can be passed on to the next person. Besides enabling audit trails, keeping all e-mails at one location allows strict control on the usage of this vital organizational resource (however, this certainly would take up a lot of storage space). By allowing the download of e-mail to workstations, server space would be economized.

ii. *E-mail client.* This software usually comes along with the exchange software but can also be independent, especially when we use a public domain e-mail exchange such as Gmail. E-mail client connects to the exchange and downloads e-mail at preset intervals of time and allows all the e-mail facilities such as reply, forward, delete, and so on. There is a wide variety of e-mail client software so we can select the optimal one appropriate for our organization.

g. *Administrative tools*:
   i. *User management tools.* This utility is commonly available with the server operating system but specialized tools are also available. They will assist us in adding a new user, setting and modifying user security rights, deleting users, and verifying usage by the user.
   ii. *Configuration management tools.* Configuration management tools protect the integrity of the software product in production and also control the changes being made to the software product. They ensure that only those programs that are tested and approved for production usage are allowed into the production system. When a change is requested, they will strictly enforce a system of approvals and check-in and check-out. These tools are normally bought from outside vendors but also come along with some operating systems. These are essential, especially in data centers.
   iii. *Build management tools.* In some cases, the software needs to be rebuilt every time a component undergoes modifications. Build management tools assist us in preparing the build easily. A build consists of many software components like screen layouts, reports, back-end programs, database triggers/procedures, and so on. A build management tool keeps track of every component and highlights missing components and errors in them. These are essential in web-based systems.
   iv. *Recordkeeping tools—audit trails.* Whenever something goes wrong, records come in handy to track the information and find the errors and loopholes. In these days of web-based applications, users are located all over the world. Any one of the world's citizens can cause havoc on our systems or steal vital information. We need to equip ourselves with tools to locate what happened, when it happened, and from where the attack came. These tools maintain records of all transactions and provide facilities for rules-based retrieval of information to pinpoint the issue. These have become essential, especially for data centers giving access to the World Wide Web.

v. *Monitoring tools.* While the system is in operation, the monitoring tools keep watch on all the usage and trigger alarms when suspicious activity takes place. This would enable us to prevent major damages or loss to our systems.

h. *Application software.* Application software is the heart of the IT infrastructure. It serves business functions and handles revenue. It is normally developed exclusively for an organization, but can also be implemented with or without customization with proven COTS products such as SAP and SIEBEL and can be developed in-house or outsourced. The application software is essential; without it the IT infrastructure is simply a cost center.

i. *Special software* (BI, Data Warehousing, EAI, etc.). Over and above the application software, these special software products give us the power to subject data to various analyses and draw intelligent inferences from this analysis. Evaluate the necessity for such tools on a case-by-case basis.

j. *Mobile platform.* With the capabilities of mobile phones increasing at a tremendous pace, mobile platforms have made inroads into business operations. Within a few years, they may altogether replace PC-based workstations. Even now, many senior executives are using smart phones to connect to organizational servers and carry out official activities from afar. Therefore, we need to equip ourselves with a mobile platform that can interact with our IT infrastructure as well as send/receive information to mobile phones.

Classifications of Organizations

Nearly every organization needs IT infrastructure, but the needs of different organizations require different types of IT infrastructure. We can classify business organizations based on the size and type of business conducted. Based on the type of operations carried out, the organizations from the standpoint of IT infrastructure are classified as follows:

1. *Business organizations* that carry out business other than providing IT services include manufacturing, construction, and services organizations. IT for them is a service supporting their business functions. Data need to be stored over longer periods of time and would include a data center in addition to end-user computing.
2. *Software development organizations* whose mainline business is to develop software for other organizations are not data processing

organizations. Completed but yet to be delivered software components, test data, and software that is under maintenance are stored in this type of organization.

3. *Business process outsourcing (BPO)* organizations that support other organizations in performing their business functions would not hold any data but would connect to the data centers of the client organizations to perform assignments.
4. *Bulk data-processing* organizations are also BPOs in a sense, but their needs are different from BPOs because the main work is preparing bulk data, processing the data, and transmitting the information either in electronic or paper form to individuals or institutions. Therefore, these organizations would have a different type of IT infrastructure.
5. *Call centers* receive calls and support organizations' customers or make calls to acquire customers for an organization. The data held here are not business data but master data about prospects and customers of multiple organizations about the calls received, made, and the resolutions achieved. These data are not of a permanent nature and would be retained for a much shorter duration. Alternatively, if data is accessed from the data centers of the client organization, they would hold no data at all.
6. *Hospitals* are special business organizations in the sense that there is a data center with facilities for advanced analysis and for use in diagnostic procedures for patients. Computers have made significant inroads into medicine. Computer aided tomography scans, computer-based ultrasound scanners, and many instruments that are now interfacing with computers include x-ray machines, MRI (magnetic resonance imaging), fetal monitoring systems, ECGs (electrocardiographs), EEGs (electroencephalographs), 2D echo graphs, and pathological laboratory instruments. Computers are also being used to aid keyhole surgery. We need typical computers but also high-resolution graphics terminals for use by doctors. Hospitals also need specialized software for medical uses. The IT infrastructure would be high-end, high-cost, and high-reliability systems.
7. *Malls* are also special organizations in the sense that they do have data centers that are most likely located at the central office. When a retail chain opens a new mall, it needs to be equipped with IT infrastructure that is compatible with the headquarters' infrastructure. But the technology might have changed since the infrastructure at headquarters was set up. So, it is possible that different malls in the chain may have different IT infrastructure, but they still need to interact with

each other as well as with headquarters. Another notable feature is that the IT infrastructure in the mall needs to be heavily interacting with POS systems and credit card machines, which necessitates high-speed bandwidth to clear transactions in real time.

8. *Graphics and design organizations* use graphics workstations for engineering design, product design, or moviemaking. With movies increasingly using computers for special effects, these organizations are sprouting in large numbers. Manufacturing organizations are opting for outsourcing the production portion and retaining the design function so the demand for these design organizations is increasing. In developed economies, large corporations have become more like marketing setups using their long-standing reputation and are outsourcing research to universities, design to design shops, and manufacturing to overseas shops. The result is that we have many specialized design shops equipped with graphics workstations and relevant software. The IT infrastructure and the engineering and modeling software needed in these organizations are very specialized and costly. The networking and bandwidth take a backseat in these organizations and the power of the workstation assumes primary importance. Networking is for information sharing rather than for driving the work.
9. *Transport organizations* are certainly business organizations but their business units are traveling! They need to track their moving vehicles and the data entry locations are spread across the globe. The data may come in from their own offices, public Internet cafes, mobile phones, and by landline phones. Data may be character data, picture data, or voice data. The infrastructure would have to cater to all of these and perhaps convert from one data type to another.
10. *Government/public organizations* include federal, state, county, and local government organizations and departments. They may also include corporations run by the government directly. These organizations are similar to business organizations with the exception that security becomes much more important. The data perhaps need to be stored externally with the possibility for online retrieval. We need to incorporate all means of hardware and software to ensure that each transaction can be traced long after its occurrence, integrity is protected, and access controls are at their strictest. Different departments need different types of infrastructure. They may need data processing machines, graphics machines, and all types of software.

11. *Other miscellaneous organizations* do not fit any of the above classifications. The IT needs of these organizations can be done on a case-by-case basis.

What impact does the type of organization have on IT project management? Well, the type of organization has more of an impact on the type of infrastructure selected than does the type of project management methodologies used by the organization. We ought to have an idea of the type of organizations in which IT infrastructure would be set up to be able to effectively manage IT projects.

Understanding Project Management

We have reviewed the IT infrastructure that forms the backbone of IT projects and the types of organizations in which we execute IT projects. Now, let's understand what a project is and then discuss IT projects specifically. A project is *a temporary endeavor with a preset objective adhering to the specifications of the customer regarding functionality, quality, reliability, price, and schedule and conforming to international/national/customer/internal standards for performance and reliability*.

The following inferences are drawn from the above definition:

1. A project is a temporary endeavor and not an ongoing venture.
2. A project has a definite beginning and a definite ending.
3. No two projects will be identical but could be similar.
4. Each project needs to be separately approved, planned, designed, engineered, constructed, tested, delivered, installed, and commissioned.
5. A project may be stand-alone or a component in a larger program.
6. A project is executed in phases with an initiation phase, one or more intermediate phases, and a closing phase.
7. Many projects have a transition phase (handover to a customer transitioning from an existing system to the new system).
8. A project may continue through the maintenance phase.

Historically, one-time endeavors were managed on a case-by-case basis, but recently have been influenced by the development of the Polaris missile by the U.S. Department of Defense (DOD), which was handled as a project. The USDOD used a methodology named PERT (Program Evaluation and Review Technique) to manage the venture. Today, nearly every type and size of business uses the project management methodologies developed in the intervening period between the Polaris project and now.

Setting up an electronic data processing (EDP) facility was the initial IT project back in the 1950s–1980s. Normally, it was set up by the supplier of hardware. It was a large room or hall as the case may be that housed all the IT equipment. The introduction of the PC by IBM in 1981 heralded the era of end-user computing, which caught on very quickly. This enlarged the scope of IT projects from a one room/hall facility and included end-user workstations within its domain. Now, computers have become ubiquitous and IT projects encompass the entire organization. This has increased the complexity and calls for treating it as a separate project with a well-defined methodology.

We can derive the definition for an IT project from the above discussion on project management. Thus, an IT project is *a project that sets up IT infrastructure in an organization, encompassing all locations and departments to handle selected/all information processing procedures in the organization.*

The key terms in the above definition are:

1. *Project.* Defined earlier in this section.
2. *Sets up IT infrastructure.* IT infrastructure includes hardware, software, networking, and all of the processes necessary to run it effectively and efficiently. Setting up includes sizing, selection, procurement, installation, and commissioning of the IT infrastructure.
3. *Organization.* The organization is a business entity consisting of multiple departments and locations. We discussed the types of organizations in the previous section, *Classifications of Organizations.*

We have just defined a *project* in general and an *IT project* in particular. Let us now understand the definitions of *management* and *project management* before we attempt to define IT project management (ITPM).

Management in its simplest form is getting things done. The activities performed by managers to get things done are planning, organizing, staffing, coordinating, and controlling. The subject of management deserves better treatment, and Appendix A delves deeper into the topic.

Project management is *the application of knowledge, skills, tools, techniques, and resources to the project activities to meet or exceed stakeholder needs and expectations. It is the discipline of planning, organizing, staffing, coordinating, and controlling project activities to ensure that project deliverables conform to specifications, and are on time and within budget.*

We will be discussing the activities of planning, organizing, staffing, coordinating, and controlling in greater detail in the following chapters.

The remaining key terms are:

1. *Application of knowledge, skills, tools, techniques, and resources.* We need to possess the knowledge of project management and the skills for executing project activities, utilizing the tools and techniques available

to deliver the expected results. The resources are people, equipment, money, and methods.

2. *To meet or exceed.* The minimum objective is to meet the requirements but we should strive to exceed expectations, which are unexpressed needs.
3. *Stakeholders.* A project has multiple stakeholders, including the customer, end users, the project team, the management of the organization executing the project, the quality assurance team, the marketing department, and any appropriate statutory agencies. We need to meet or exceed the needs and expectations of these stakeholders through effective and efficient project management.
4. *Discipline.* Discipline connotes selecting, or defining, a set of standards for a human endeavor and adhering to them during the course of such endeavor.
5. *Planning, organizing, staffing, coordinating, and controlling.* These are the management activities that are applied to the project activities.
6. *Conform to specifications.* The project deliverables must conform to the specifications mutually agreed upon with the customer.
7. *On time and within budget.* It is not adequate just to deliver but it must be done on time and without escalating the costs. Both are important because any delay will affect other activities and increased cost will reduce the availability of resources for other activities.

Now that we have discussed the definition of project management, we are ready for the next topic of what constitutes an IT project.

Activities to Be Performed in an IT Project

IT projects come in a variety of hues. A *full-cycle IT project* would include:

1. *A preliminary study to ascertain the IT needs of the organization.* This study collates the information processing needs of the organization including textual information, graphical information, loads, number of workstations, servers, networking, Internet bandwidth, application software, DBMS, and so on. This document will form the basis for all further engineering activities of the IT project.
2. *Determining the capabilities of software and hardware to fulfill the IT needs of the organization.* This activity is also referred to as *sizing* and is discussed in Chapter 4 in greater detail. Completion of this activity results in freezing the specifications for all hardware and software needed for the project. Using these specifications, procurement action for all the components would be initiated and completed.

3. *Determining the strategy for acquiring the software.* System software is procured along with the hardware. We can buy COTS products for the database and app server, but application software needs to be developed. We have the alternatives of customizing a COTS product, developing the software in-house, or outsourcing it completely. Based on the strategy, we need to initiate action to ensure that all software is acquired by the time the hardware is procured and installed.
4. *Procuring the selected hardware.* We need to prepare detailed specifications, ask for quotations from short-listed vendors, finalize the vendor and place purchase orders, receive deliveries, inspect/test the hardware, and install the hardware and commission it.
5. *Preparing various sites.* Site preparation includes laying out networking cables, providing electric power sockets at each workstation, and preparing server rooms, including electrification, air conditioning, networking cables, installing the furniture to hold all the hardware, and setting up access control equipment. We must also procure the networking hardware.
6. *Carrying out a cost-benefit analysis.* We need to determine an appropriate strategy to build up master data files/tables and arrange to prepare the data (including quality control of data entry) to ensure their accuracy in master files/tables.
7. *Laying networking cables and installing the networking components.* We may have to pass through public areas for laying networking cables. This would necessitate obtaining the necessary permissions and could be time consuming. It is important to test the communication to all cable terminations to ensure that the network would be functional when commissioned.
8. *Installing and commissioning the hardware.* This activity would include putting the hardware in place, providing electric power, connecting it to the network, and testing the hardware to ensure it is functioning as specified. This will also include preparing the hard disks, making required partitions, and organizing libraries/directories/folders, and so on. This will ready the hardware for going on stream.
9. *Accepting the software and installing it.* First we need to install the system software other than the operating system, which normally comes preloaded. This means the configuration management tools, administration tools, database server, app server, and web server. Then configure them to work under any organizational parameters, which includes IP address, number of users, and number of concurrent connections, and so on.

10. *Testing the system and removing defects if any*. We need to test the system with all the hardware, system software, and networking and application software to ensure that all components are interfacing with each other without any issue and that everything is as designed and expected.
11. *Developing processes and rolling them out*. Develop various processes necessary to operate, troubleshoot, and administer the infrastructure; subject the processes to organizational quality control activities; implement them on a pilot basis; review and implement the feedback; then roll out the processes and subject them to the rigor of a configuration management system.
12. *Preparing training materials to train the end users*. To this end, we need to prepare the training materials to include the teaching aids for faculty and take-home material for participants. This would include the functional facilities of the system, how to obtain help when needed, rudimentary troubleshooting, and so on.
13. *Training the end users*. If end users are numerous, they may have to be trained in batches and/or by the activity they perform. Engagements can include classroom training and hands-on sessions. Therefore, we may need to set up a temporary training environment so employees may experiment during these sessions.
14. *Preparing operations and troubleshooting manuals*. To aid the system administrators in administering the infrastructure, we need to prepare the operations and troubleshooting manuals, subject them to quality control, and roll them out.
15. *Training the systems administrators in the operation and troubleshooting of the system*. This is needed to efficiently manage the infrastructure, troubleshoot it, and provide assistance when requested. The main objective of this training is to ensure that the system administrators are equipped to maintain the uptime of the infrastructure as close to 100% as possible.
16. *Setting the configuration management system*. This would include installing the configuration management tools, if acquired; defining check-in, check-out, and change management procedures; and subjecting all data and application software to the rigor of the configuration management system. This is a crucial activity in ensuring the integrity of data and programs.
17. *Rolling the system into production*. Switching over the infrastructure into production would involve pilot runs, parallel runs, cleaning the system of experimental data, if any, and lastly, discontinuing the earlier system. We need to closely monitor system usage for errors in results, incorrect or malicious usage, and attempts at misusing the

system during initial stages. Take expedient action to plug any loopholes and make the system sturdy. Then, initiate actions to move the infrastructure into maintenance mode and hand it over to the infrastructure maintenance team.

18. *Moving the system to maintenance mode*. This would involve determining the strategy for maintenance (in-house or outsourced maintenance, procurement and stocking of spares, and availability of maintenance around the clock), handing over the equipment to the maintenance team, training them on the processes for system maintenance and troubleshooting, handholding for a brief period of time, and so on.

Different organizations may go through different sets of activities—either dropping a few of the above activities or adding a few more. But the above set is typical in setting up IT infrastructure in an organization. All of these activities are engineering (technical) activities. These are not management activities although they all need to be managed.

Now, if the organization is executing the project completely in-house, obviously all of these activities have to be performed in-house as well. In most cases, the organization outsources the performance of some or all of these activities to one or multiple agencies. For example, the hardware sizing and selection may be outsourced to one group, software development to another, and data preparation to yet another with the overall project being managed in-house. In some cases, even the overall project management may be outsourced. This takes advantage of the benefits that accrue from receiving specialist assistance.

Phases of an IT Project

The execution of an IT project has six phases:

1. Project feasibility study
2. Project acquisition
3. Project initiation
4. IT project planning
5. Project execution
6. Project closure

We will discuss these six phases in a little more detail below.

Project Feasibility Study

This is the first step to be taken when an IT project is being contemplated. As soon as the organizational senior management considers installing a new

IT infrastructure or augmenting the existing one, a feasibility study is commissioned. If the organization has an information systems (IS) department with competent personnel, they would carry out the study. More often than not, it would be entrusted to an external consultant to take advantage of the availability of cross-functional and cross-organization expertise. The feasibility study should determine a go/no go decision to proceed further. We discuss this study in greater detail in Chapter 3.

Project Acquisition

On receipt and acceptance of the feasibility report, the organizational management should consider all aspects and make a decision to either drop the project proposal or to move forward. When the decision is to move forward, it should accord technical and financial approval for the project. If the project is to be executed by in-house resources, the project would begin. If the IT infrastructure is to be set up using a vendor organization, we need to obtain a proposal and issue a purchase order before work can begin. The project may be executed in a combination of internal and outsourced modes. Project acquisition is discussed in greater detail in Chapter 3.

Project Initiation

Since setting up IT infrastructure is a strategic decision, great care should be taken in the all important project initiation phase. A project that is initiated well is halfway down the path to success. Initiation includes activities such as selecting the project manager, selecting and allocating resources, preparing the project dossier, and handing over the project to the selected project manager. Information about earlier projects executed within the organization is located and made available to the project manager, as are best practices and pitfalls to avoid, gathered from both internal and external sources. This includes compiling the best practices and pitfalls from internal and external sources so that the project can take advantage of the best practices and avoid the pitfalls. In short, the organization must provide all of the support the project manager needs to ensure the success of the IT project. This aspect is detailed in Chapter 4.

IT Project Planning

Planning is very important for any human endeavor and is especially important in a project dealing with so many different aspects needing multidisciplinary expertise. There are a number of plans and these are detailed in Chapter 5.

Project Execution

This is the phase in which the rubber hits the road and the project starts rolling forward. All planned activities are performed to ensure the success of the project. This phase consumes project resources and by the end of this phase, the IT infrastructure would be ready for use. This phase implements the plans approved in the project planning phase and is discussed in greater detail in Chapter 6.

Project Closure

Project closure is the mopping up of the completed project. It releases the resources allocated earlier. The project manager documents the project experience and presents it to colleagues and senior management. The project records are archived. A reconciliation statement is prepared for the resources planned and actually expended. Relevant records are handed over to the maintenance team. Handholding assistance would be provided by the project manager and a few resources to the maintenance team for a brief period. Then the project manager is either designated as the manager for the maintenance team or released. This completes the project (more detail is in Chapter 10).

Types of IT Projects

Here are the main types of IT projects:

1. Implementation of new IT infrastructure
2. Enhancement of existing IT infrastructure
3. Upgrade and update of existing IT infrastructure
4. Migration of existing IT infrastructure
5. IT infrastructure maintenance

Let's now discuss the attributes of each of these types.

Implementation of New IT Infrastructure

In this project, the slate is clean because there is no existing infrastructure. Maybe the organization is new or has been using manual methods for handling information, or the organization wishes to replace the entire existing infrastructure. We need to go through all the activities enumerated earlier in this chapter, known as a full-cycle IT project.

Enhance Existing IT Infrastructure

This type of project is considered when the organization is expanding and the existing IT infrastructure needs to be augmented to handle the increasing load. The existing infrastructure is retained and additional infrastructure would be added.

Upgrade and Update of Existing IT Infrastructure

When the organization is in existence for a considerably longer time and the IT infrastructure has become aged and is unable to function well in the changed technical environment, this type of project is undertaken. The infrastructure is adequate to handle the business processes, but needs to be upgraded because technical support for the hardware/software no longer exists. Perhaps the infrastructure is not able to interface with the new technology being used by our partners or the public, or the response time has degraded significantly, or the load on the system has peaked beyond the maximum capacity of the existing infrastructure. When our infrastructure comes to that level, we need to upgrade it to remain effective in that business context. In this project, either the hardware or software or both may be upgraded. Normally, the class of hardware and software are retained but upgraded to be able to handle increased loads and to function in the present technology environment.

Migration of Existing IT Infrastructure

The suppliers of IT infrastructure often release newer and much more powerful versions of their software (more frequently) and hardware (less frequently). While the hardware is more stable with a life of about ten years, software is getting metamorphosed every three years and has a maximum life of seven years. The last two years of the software product life have been fraught with dangers of incompatibility, less support, and malicious attacks from malware. Since the advent of the Internet and the World Wide Web, IT infrastructure is exposed to anyone anywhere to attack and exploit. Over the last two years of a product's life, system software vendors do not normally release security patches to plug vulnerabilities exposed by hackers. Thus, we are more or less forced to upgrade our software. When we upgrade our system software, it needs more RAM and hard disk space. So, we need to either upgrade our hardware or replace it. These scenarios necessitate migration of hardware/software to the next versions.

Now, what is the difference between an upgrade project and a migration project? The projects are similar except for the *need* of the project. In an upgrade project, we are upgrading due to increased load on the system. In a migration project, we are upgrading because the infrastructure is becoming obsolete.

IT Infrastructure Maintenance

Hardware and software maintenance is mandatory. Companies typically have entered into an annual maintenance contract only for hardware. Now, even software, which does not deteriorate with usage (it does not have moving parts nor suffer from wear and tear), needs maintenance. Consider these scenarios:

1. The browsers are upgraded and they render the interface in a different manner. We need to improve our software to be compatible with the new release of the browser.
2. The middle tiers (DBMS, app server, or any other software) release new versions or patches to existing versions and these necessitate maintenance of our software.
3. New viruses are released into the network regularly, and besides upgrading the antivirus software, we may need to update the software too.
4. The operating system on the server or the workstation releases a service pack or new version that necessitates maintenance of our software.

Maintenance work is sporadic and intermittent so keeping stock of all the spares that may never be used and software developers waiting for a maintenance work request could be costly and tedious. Therefore, many organizations are outsourcing this work and entering into routine software maintenance contracts.

Organizations that outsource maintenance of its IT infrastructure should have at least two contractors on site, one for hardware and one for software. And, we may need to have arrangements with more than two parties. Consider the following scenarios:

1. The hardware vendor does not provide support calls for maintenance but has partners to undertake the work on its behalf. We then need to have a contract with the hardware supplier for spares as well as its partner for service.
2. There needs to be a separate contract with the network specialists to maintain our network.

3. If software development was outsourced, a contract with the developers is a must.
4. If a COTS product was customized for our application software, we need to have a contract with the COTS product vendor for updates to the product as well as its implementation and customization partner.
5. There should be a similar scenario with the suppliers of middle-tier software.
6. We also need to have contracts with the suppliers of utilities for anti-virus, anti-malware, and anti-spyware so that our protection is always up-to-date.

Some organizations, unable to monitor so many contractors, award the overall maintenance to one agency and that agency would divide the work between multiple providers. The numbers of these types of organizations are increasing due to increasing demand. Just be aware that if you contract with a maintenance agency, this process now needs to be treated as a project.

Distinguishing IT Projects from Other Projects

How do IT projects differ from other projects, especially from software development projects? Is software not the vital component in setting up the IT infrastructure in an organization? If we take software development out of an IT project, what else is remaining?

It is natural to ask these questions and it is essential to answer them before moving on to other topics of ITPM. Let's look at the features that distinguish IT projects:

1. IT projects need a multidisciplinary approach for hardware, software, middleware, and networking. Software development needs expertise in a single discipline—software development.
2. In an outsourced management situation, IT projects do have multiple contractors while software development projects rarely have more than two contractors—one for user interface development and another for software development.
3. Software development projects are just one component in a program while an IT project is a self-contained full program. An IT project is not a component but is a program/project in itself.
4. Software development rarely needs procurement activity whereas procurement is a very important activity in an IT project.
5. Schedule has little significance in the planning of software development projects where the effort estimation is of paramount importance.

In IT projects, scheduling is of paramount importance in synchronizing delivery of multiple components or in synchronizing the completion of multiple subprojects.

6. The deliverables of a software development project have one objective: to deliver working and defect-free software. IT projects have to deliver the fulfillment of business objectives.

Thus, IT projects are more complex than software projects. Suffice it to say that software is itself a component of an IT project.

Conclusions

In this chapter we were introduced to IT projects. We also looked at the components of IT infrastructure. The types of organizations where IT infrastructure needs to be implemented were also categorized. We defined and discussed project management in general and IT project management in particular and enumerated the activities to be performed in a full-cycle IT project. We also delineated the phases of an IT project and detailed the types of common IT projects. Now, we are ready to move on to the appropriate ways to manage IT projects.

2

Approaches to IT Project Management

IT project execution has two components—engineering and management. The engineering part consists of all technical activities that are performed to execute the project. Engineering in IT projects deals with sizing the components of the IT infrastructure and preparing the technical documents that guide the agencies concerned with implementing the infrastructure. Management facilitates the engineering aspects of the project so it is efficiently completed on time and without defects.

The two aspects of engineering and management, although being independent of each other, do still influence each other. Therefore, each needs some tailoring to suit the other. Project management has multiple objectives but the prime one is to *build the deliverables*. Other objectives include the efficient and effective management of: schedules, productivity, quality, resources, morale, stakeholders, and profit. The project manager (PM) needs to be a manager first and knowledgeable about the engineering methodologies second.

Project Management Approaches

There are basically four approaches to managing projects. They are:

1. Ad hoc approach
2. Process-driven approach
3. Schedule-driven approach
4. Hybrid of ad hoc and process-driven approach

Let's look at each of them in detail.

Ad Hoc Methods-Based Project Management

Ad hoc methods are not based on any documented methodologies. The methodology depends on the involved parties including the PM, the customer, and the project team. PMs are given almost absolute control within a flexible policy framework as long as the stakeholders are happy with project execution. In organizations that adopt ad hoc methods, management typically dictates policy and then modifies it as convenient. Management reflects the personality of the leaders of the organization. This style is classically defined as hero-driven management. Success is achieved more out of a PM's personal ability than from well-directed effort and knowledge. But these methods are more commonly used than one might imagine. The logic behind supporting ad hoc methods is as follows:

1. It is better to entrust the assignment to an expert in the field and give operating freedom to him/her to obtain best results.
2. There is no guarantee that the results would be any better by following the process rigorously. There are many failures in projects following a process-driven approach.
3. This approach has the least amount of overhead and is therefore more profitable.
4. There is one individual who bears complete responsibility and accountability for results. A process releases stakeholders from accountability.

The advantages with the ad hoc approach are:

1. It fits a dynamic environment. When the environment is fluid with unforeseen changes being requested midway through the project execution, this approach would enable faster response.
2. It allows the leader to have absolute control. Since there are no or few documented policies/processes dictating what to do, the leader has almost total freedom in responding to situations in the way the leader deems necessary.
3. It is perceived to allow very fast response to environmental changes. The leader, unbridled by any process compliance requirements, can act fast in response to environmental changes.
4. It can be the lowest cost and most profitable methodology with a well-seasoned PM. The overhead for implementing the process is minimized resulting in reduced cost.
5. It is perfect for pinning the blame for failures on one person. As the responsibility and accountability is person-based, in case of failure, the PM automatically is the culprit.

6. Heroism for personnel management is the standard. When a project is successful, the single point of accountability, the PM gets the accolades too.
7. The principle of *unity of command* can be implemented. (This concept is explained in detail in Appendix A.) Unity of command can be a great motivator for people involved in the project as they know whom to please with their performance.
8. Reduces process overhead activities such as process definition, process maintenance groups, measurement, and analysis to nearly zero.

The disadvantages with the ad hoc approach are:

1. It creates uncertainty in the working environment. As there are little to no defined processes to guide resources, they would not know what to do in the absence of allocation and direction from superiors.
2. It fosters a leader centric environment rather than an environment driven by organizational and project goals. A defined process would guide the team toward organizational culture, values, and goals. In its absence, the leader's culture, values, and goals would become the team goals.
3. All authority is centralized. If the leader is lost for any reason including resignation, injury, or transfer, we lose the project as there is no defined process to empower the remaining resources.
4. It is not predictable due to being person-driven. The person who can achieve grand success can also engineer grand failures. A process would have systematic measurement, analysis, and progress reporting. In its absence, all measurement, analysis, and reporting would be person dependent (bringing in all the biases of the individual) resulting in a less predictable outcome.
5. Project monitoring is focused on monitoring people rather than the project as a whole.
6. Organizational capacity for handling multiple projects concurrently and guiding them toward success is limited by the leader's capability to handle concurrent projects.
7. The growth of the organization is limited by the capacity of its leaders.
8. These methods tend to promote personal loyalty to leaders than to the organization. Therefore, sycophants tend to multiply and ultimately the environment deteriorates due to an unhealthy ego-driven environment.
9. Developing leaders from within the organization is nearly impossible as everyone works in their own cocoon.

10. Failures are inevitable in any human endeavor, and if it happens for an organization using this ad hoc approach, it cripples the organization in ways from which it may not recover. Failure can have a severe impact.

All in all, this approach may produce some grand successes, but overall, it is not sustainable. Despite the risks, this approach to project management is adopted by a significant number of organizations.

Process-Driven Approach

Organizations using this type of approach are characterized by a set of defined processes for all activities. Individuals must be knowledgeable in the processes that concern them to be effective and efficient in the organization.

An organization that adopts a process-driven approach to project management recognizes that the onus is on both the organization and the individual PM for ensuring continued project success. The organization facilitates the execution of projects by providing the processes, tools, knowledge repository, training, and expert assistance as needed to help the project teams. The organizational infrastructure enables project teams to successfully execute projects. In addition to facilitation, the organization also has the responsibility of project oversight, measurement, benchmarking, and effecting improvements in processes and tools to continuously keep the organization well honed.

Each PM is responsible for executing the projects while diligently conforming to defined processes provided by the organization. PMs are also responsible for plowing their project execution experience back into the process by providing feedback, suggestions, and support for organizational initiatives. In process-driven organizations, both the organization and the PM work shoulder to shoulder in a close-knit manner. The goal of this approach is to achieve uniformity in project execution across the organization regardless of the PM involved. One often quoted benefit of this approach is that it enables free movement of people from project to project without any visible impact on project execution.

The advantages with a process-driven approach to project management are:

1. A process-driven approach minimizes the person dependency within project management. The process provides the details and the PM supplements them with his/her experience and insights to prevent issues and increase the chances of success.
2. It enables the beginner in project management to perform like an expert and an expert to excel. A beginner takes cues from the process

and a seasoned PM uses them as references. Thus a minimum level of performance is ensured.

3. It allows the experience gained from project execution to be put back into the process and thus every successful project execution enriches the process. Defined processes would include procedures for capturing feedback, analyzing it, and dovetailing it back into the process. This would make the capture of feedback a routine task.
4. It equips everyone with the best practices culled from project execution.
5. It monitors projects rather than people.
6. It involves the organization in project execution. The organizational expertise, not only from the process but also from senior executives and peer PMs, is brought to bear on project execution and supports continued organizational success.
7. It facilitates measurement resulting in fair performance appraisals; thus making it possible to bring about real cultural improvement in the organization.
8. It builds the basis for predictability in project execution.
9. It enables all-around participation and iteratively drives the organization toward excellence.
10. It reduces the turnaround time for the recruitment of people as the process shortens the learning curve for new hires.

The only flaw, if it can be called that, of this process is the additional overhead in documenting project execution in the form of plans and reports. However, this would really only impact the PM and not other members of the project team. All in all, a process-driven approach facilitates single-person independence in project execution while enabling process improvement and uniformity in project execution across the organization. These are characteristics that tend to lead to organizational excellence.

Schedule-Driven Approach

Many organizations follow this approach, including those outside the spheres of IT and software development. In this approach, a rigorously detailed schedule is prepared and each activity is detailed with an estimation of the human, equipment, and time resources needed to complete the tasks. The characteristics of these projects are:

1. The norms of estimation would be deterministic; that is, there is a large body of knowledge available for projects from previous ones,

and norms are meticulously maintained and derived from strict procedures.
2. Every individual allocated to the project team is knowledgeable about his/her role and are motivated to perform it effectively.
3. The PM is an expert in the program evaluation and review technique/ critical path method and prepares the schedule conforming to that technique.
4. The schedule is reviewed and agreed upon by all the stakeholders of the project.
5. All stakeholders would use only the schedule as the reference point for all interaction with the project team.
6. The execution methodology is known to all stakeholders through standard operating procedures/policies.
7. The activities of configuration management or quality assurance are internalized and project specific planning is not necessary.
8. The emphasis is more on meeting deadlines than other aspects.

It is not unusual for organizations adopting a schedule-driven approach to project management to prepare plans other than the schedule for training or deployment, but the schedule is the primary planning document. This approach has been quite successful in sectors other than IT and software development. In the construction industry and made-to-order manufacturing, this is the most widely used approach to project management.

The merits of the schedule-driven approach are:

1. It would involve less planning documentation and therefore planning overhead is greatly reduced.
2. There is one common document of reference for all stakeholders keeping all of them on one page regarding project execution. This results in less confusion and more clarity.
3. There are excellent tools like Primavera and Microsoft Project that will enable easy definition and monitoring of the schedule at an economical cost.
4. The large body of knowledge that has already been developed around this approach in other sectors can be utilized profitably in monitoring the project progress.

The disadvantages of the schedule-driven approach are:

1. By excluding other plans, we tend to overestimate the resource requirement to guarantee meeting the schedule, which may lead to a more expensive project than necessary.

2. The emphasis is on schedule monitoring and this can lead to consumption of more resources.
3. It tends to neglect other aspects of project management in preference to the schedule, such as quality assurance.

Hybrid of Ad Hoc and Process-Driven Approach

This approach has been gaining ground in recent times. In some organizations, the process is so tightly defined that it does not leave any room for the PM or the project team to show initiative on project execution. When the process is framed within a steel structure, it is possible that people are demotivated as they become mere cogs in the process wheel. This hybrid approach recognizes the quick response capability of the ad hoc approach and the predictability of the process-driven approach as well as their corresponding issues. However, organizations that utilize a hybrid approach do have a defined process and are generally process-driven. All personnel in the organization would be trained on the process, thus internalizing the process-driven approach. By providing appropriate tailoring guidelines, the organization is ensuring that projects are executed most efficiently and effectively by allowing a required amount of freedom to the PMs and project teams.

These two approaches are combined in the following manner to allow maximum leverage for the organization:

1. For smaller projects (projects consuming less than three calendar months), this approach permits the project to be executed without conforming to organizational processes. The PM and the project team are given much greater freedom than in the case of the process-driven approach. But since the PM and the project team are exposed to organizational process, some of the process-driven approach would still be implemented in the project. But by reducing the documentation overhead, the project could be executed faster.
2. For medium-sized projects (projects consuming between three and nine calendar months), a skeletal process would be implemented. The organizational process library would contain guidelines on how to tailor the process based on project duration. Therefore, these projects would implement a scaled-down process with less documentation and process rigor allowing greater freedom to the project team.
3. For larger projects of more than nine calendar months, the full process will be applied and full process rigor would be implemented. No ad-hoc(ism) is permitted.

One concern would be the efficacy of the tailoring guidelines. If defined well, the organization would work efficiently and effectively. If defined poorly, the organization could stagnate and see a litany of failed projects. Therefore, take care to define the process as well as the corresponding tailoring guidelines pragmatically.

What Is the Right Approach for Project Management?

An organization's IT infrastructure is characterized more by its diversity than homogeneity. Therefore, it is not advisable to attempt to prescribe one right approach. Here are some factors that will help determine if an organization will thrive with an ad hoc approach:

1. The organization is small.
2. The number of PMs in the organization is relatively small (two or three). The small number of PMs will make it easy to even out differences between methodologies with the help of progress-monitoring meetings. Such organizations need not have a set of documented project references and the senior manager can act as a resolution mechanism in cases of differences of opinion.
3. The number of concurrent projects is five or less. As with the small number of PMs, the small number of projects makes it easier to eliminate variances in project execution.

All organizations that evolve in an organic manner start small and typically begin with an ad hoc approach to project management. As they grow and take on more and more projects the workload increases putting pressure on human resources. As pressure builds two things can happen: (1) the organization buckles under the pressure and moves toward stagnation, failure, and closure or (2) the organization moves toward a process-driven approach. When organizations embrace a process-driven approach, they adopt process improvement principles and develop processes to cover project management first. Then, they deal with other organizational areas in a drive to mature processes. This seems to be a natural progression. However, it would be better if organizations embrace a process-driven approach proactively when they are at the take-off stage rather than having to be forced to do so by the complexity created through the sheer volume of work.

The schedule-driven approach is being applied in many organizations. Although I do not disparage this approach, it is more advantageous to adopt a process-driven approach with more emphasis on the schedule. Focusing on the schedule only and neglecting other aspects of project management has proven to be detrimental to organizational interests in the long run. Schedule is perhaps the most important aspect to be monitored but productivity, quality, morale, and cost are equally important aspects that deserve attention. Neglecting these aspects in preference to schedule can cause project failures. (Note: This book deals with the subject of project management from the standpoint of an organization that approaches it utilizing a process-driven approach.)

Is the Process-Driven Approach Right for You?

Some organizational activities are already process-driven. Financial accounting must adopt a rigorous process through statutes in almost every country. Strict internal controls and external verification through audits are made mandatory for any company that raises funds from public markets. Statutory bodies act as watchdogs over organizations as well as the auditors.

The human resources department also follows a process-driven approach. This comes as a result of wanting to ensure fairness to candidates approaching the organization and a supply of the right human resources for the organization. In addition to recruitment, unionization of workers and other statutes enacted to ensure fair working conditions resulted in pressure to adopt a process-driven approach.

In the two examples above, each department has the objective of ensuring fairness while still delivering results. When it comes to delivering results in projects, the aspect of fairness is not audited by any statute. Thus, it is optional to adopt a process-driven approach for reasons of fairness, which leads many organizations to forego it. Some organizations of this ilk even go to the extent of stating that any process-driven approach is a restriction of their freedom to act creatively. "Results at any cost" and "by hook or by crook" are the terms one often hears in organizations that practice ad hoc project management. Another classic statement indicating an ad hoc project management approach is a senior manager telling subordinates, "I do not know/care how you do it, but I want it done."

An organization that adopts an ad hoc approach can produce heroes by chance, but a process-driven organization makes everyone in the organization a hero/heroine! An organization that adopts an ad hoc approach survives on heroics of its employees, but a process-driven organization runs like a well-oiled machine without the necessity for wide-scale heroics. A process-driven approach is a means to assure project success—first time, every time—and ensures organizational success in the short and long term.

What Process and How Much?

Once we decide to adopt a process-driven approach, the next questions that we need to address are the type of processes to adopt and how deeply they should penetrate into organizational functioning. While deciding the type of process, we have a popular process standard framework, namely, ISO 9000 from the International Organization for Standardization (ISO). There are many other maturity models but ISO 9000 is the most popular standard for managing IT projects. Capability Maturity Model Integration from the Software Engineering Institute at Carnegie Melon University is geared more toward developing software products than implementing IT infrastructure in an organization. ISO covers the entire organization and advocates defining, implementing, and internalizing a process within an organization. This means a process-driven project management in the organization consisting of:

1. Processes for carrying out the activities that would result in delivering products/services to customers
2. Processes for ensuring that quality is built into the deliverables
3. Processes for defining and maintaining organizational processes
4. Processes for measuring and analyzing process performance
5. Each process having a set of procedures that explain the step-by-step instructions for performing various activities, standards and guidelines, formats and templates, and checklists for carrying out the activities efficiently and effectively

In short, a process-driven approach would contain defined methods for carrying out work, as well as checks and balances to ensure that the processes are internalized in the organization.

A simple framework for project management includes:

1. Project acquisition
2. Project initiation
3. Project execution
4. Project closure

Project management commences with project initiation after the project is acquired. Project acquisition is an organizational level activity. Project management is a project level activity carried out by the PM. Therefore, we ought to have project management processes at the project level as follows:

1. Project initiation:
   a. Review and revise preliminary estimates
   b. Identify and acquire necessary resources

   c. Finalize service-level agreements (SLAs) between various stakeholders of the project
   d. Prepare project plans
   e. Conduct induction training for team members
   f. Project kickoff
2. Project execution:
   a. Work management
      i. Management of in-house work
      ii. Management of outsourced work
      iii. Installation/integration/implementation management
   b. Quality management
   c. Productivity management
   d. Team management
   e. Customer management
   f. Measurement and analysis
   g. Project monitoring
   h. Reporting and escalation
   i. Project delivery/handover of the infrastructure
   j. User training
   k. Documentation
3. Project closure:
   a. Release project resources
   b. Document best and worst practices as well as lessons learned from the project
   c. Identify reusable components and document their design and usage
   d. Update skill database
   e. Update knowledge repository with best and worst practices, lessons learned
   f. Conduct project postmortem
   g. Conduct knowledge sharing session
   h. Release project manager

In addition to these processes, which are the core of project management, the organization has a role in ensuring the success of projects and hence, project management should also have the following organization-level processes:

1. Project acquisition process:
    a. Request for proposal (RFP) scrutiny (feasibility study for internal projects)
    b. Cost estimation
    c. Proposal preparation and submission
    d. RFP follow-up
    e. Obtaining the order (obtaining budget approvals for internal projects)
2. Project management office process:
    a. Project initiation:
        i. Identification of PM
        ii. Allocation of resources for the project
        iii. Finalization of SLAs between various stakeholders of the project
        iv. Project kickoff
    b. Project execution:
        i. Project monitoring
        ii. Exception reporting
        iii. Measurement and analysis at the organization level
    c. Project closure:
        i. Take over project records
        ii. Coordinate knowledge sharing
2. Measurement and analysis process:
    a. Measurement procedures
    b. Analysis procedures
    c. Metrics reporting procedures
3. Training process:
    a. Identification of organizational training needs
    b. Bridging the skills gap uncovered during training requires analysis
    c. Maintaining a skills database for all human resources of the organization

   d. Maintaining a training material repository as part of the organizational knowledge repository
   e. Taking ownership for maintaining the organization at the cutting edge of the organization's chosen area of expertise
4. Knowledge repository process:
   a. Identify components of the organizational knowledge repository
   b. Design, build, and maintain the organizational knowledge repository
   c. Periodically carry out cleanup of the repository
5. Process engineering group process:
   a. Define and maintain organizational processes
   b. Process and quality audit processes
   c. Roles and responsibilities
6. Engineering processes:
   a. Requirements process
   b. Design process
   c. Testing process

All of these processes, with the exception of the engineering processes, will be discussed in detail in subsequent chapters. Engineering processes describe the technical side of the IT project. A detailed description of engineering processes is out of the scope of this book. However, we will discuss the influence of these methodologies on project management.

3

Feasibility Study and Project Acquisition

Why Do We Need a Feasibility Study?

Is it necessary to conduct a feasibility study before deploying IT infrastructure in an organization? The short answer is yes. Conducting a study sets the tone for the project and, specifically, achieves these goals:

1. To determine the information needs of the organization/branch/department where we propose to deploy the IT infrastructure
2. To determine the hardware and software requirements necessary for the proposed project
3. To determine and enumerate the possible benefits from deploying the IT infrastructure
4. To determine the costs of the proposed IT infrastructure and set a budget for the project
5. To determine the scope of the proposed project and set the parameters for determining the success or failure of the project

The organization proposing to deploy IT infrastructure needs to conduct this study whether or not they execute the project in-house or outsource it. While many of the costs are certain, the corresponding benefits can be difficult to measure in practice. In some organizations like software development organizations, business process outsourcing (BPO) organizations, call centers and the like, it is possible to ascertain the benefits because IT infrastructure in those organizations is meant to generate revenue. IT is the cost of doing business for those organizations. But in other business organizations in which IT is to support other revenue earning activities, and not meant for earning revenue, it is very difficult to ascertain the savings. Savings are always evasive in real terms. I am reminded of the anecdote: A husband in New York City came home panting from the office and told his wife that he saved 50 cents by running behind the bus instead of taking it. His wife chided him, "You should have run behind a taxi. That way you could have saved $12." So much for savings! So, when all the capital investment appraisals and analyses are carried out and all figures are available, the one set of questions management would ask are: "Can we continue to function without this investment? Can we get any benefit out of this investment? Do we have the needed money?" The first two questions need management acumen to answer. The third question can be answered objectively, at least the "needed" part. Does the organization have the money to pay for the investment? A credible vehicle is needed to ascertain the total investment and this is where a *feasibility study* comes into play.

The First Decision: In-House or Outsource the Study?

The first decision surrounding deploying IT infrastructure in organizations is who is best suited to conduct the feasibility study? Should we ask our in-house experts to conduct the study or outsource this study to a specialist organization? Further, we need to answer another important question: Who are the right experts to carry out this study—IT experts or management experts? Let us examine both alternatives.

Let us first evaluate the IT experts. Presently, most universities house computer science under the Mathematics Department. Those universities are pushing the knowledge frontiers in IT in general and software algorithms in particular. Hardly any university is conducting courses in cost estimation or management as part of the computer science curriculum. Even where those courses are offered, they are relegated in importance compared to other core computer science courses. Exposure to management concepts for graduates of computer science is very limited, if at all.

Well, organizations do have chief information officers (CIOs) and they have been managing the information systems (IS) function ably. They grew from programming work and have been trained in management concepts. Technical staff would be needed to make technical decisions and choose specific types of hardware and software, but have limited capacity when it comes to determining costs and benefits. Here are the main takeaways regarding the suitability of using IT staff to carry out a feasibility study:

1. Junior IT staff are not generally trained in management concepts necessary to conduct a feasibility study.
2. New(er) organizations may not have full-fledged IT staff to carry out the study.
3. CIOs are eminently qualified to conduct this study but their time is costlier because of their seniority. The study would be a secondary assignment for them because they would have other primary assignments, namely to fulfill the information needs of the organization.
4. IT consultants have been traditionally engaged on technical assignments dealing with delivering a working software product as well as using that product to process data and deliver information. Therefore, they are usually not the best choice.

Thus, we can safely conclude that junior-level IT staff and the very highest-level IT staff (the CIO) are not the best choices for conducting the feasibility study.

Let us now look at management experts. Management courses have been offered by universities for a long time. These individuals are exposed to management concepts that include evaluating investment proposals from both financial and technical standpoints. They are not trained on one aspect of management but in all branches of management and on the organization as a whole. Most financial institutions involved with financing capital investment projects employ management consultants for project appraisals, including IT investment projects, rather than IT specialists. Therefore, they are best suited to carry out a feasibility study.

However, senior IT staff with more than five years of experience who have grown to management positions in the IT function are certainly exposed to management concepts. Such individuals are also appropriate for carrying out feasibility studies. They may perhaps need some training/orientation on conducting feasibility studies. Thus, we can use either management experts or senior IT staff engaged in managing the IT function to conduct the feasibility study.

Now let us return to the question: in-house or outsource? First, let us enumerate the prerequisites necessary for conducting the feasibility study with in-house senior IT staff:

1. The organization must have a fully staffed IS department; this is possible when we are expanding the IT infrastructure rather than setting it up for the first time.
2. The department ought to have qualified, experienced senior staff carrying out management functions and thus are exposed to management

concepts. Most organizations do have data processing staff and maintenance teams but not senior IT staff who can conduct a feasibility study because of their high cost to the organization. Some companies have such people when software development is done inside the organization.

3. Such staff must be released for carrying out the study, which may mean not being available for their usual tasks for a period of a month or more. When the staff has regular tasks to be performed in the organization, it is difficult to spare them for a month. However, if the workload of the feasibility study is too limited to outsource or if the workload of senior IT staff just happens to be light for a brief period of time, they can be profitably utilized to perform the study.
4. It is common to develop interdepartmental rivalries, prejudices, and biases within an organization. IS staff would have biases against end-user departments and those end users tend to have biases against IS staff. The selected individuals ought to be above biases both from their side as well as from the end-user's side.

If we have such a staff member, he/she could be used to conduct the feasibility study with in-house resources.

Now, let us look at the prerequisites for in-house management experts performing a feasibility study:

1. All the management experts available within the organization are normally allocated to one of the organizational functions and specialize in that area. Organizations normally do not have management experts just for the sake of offering expertise to other staff. The one expert managing multiple departments is normally the CEO or close to such a level in the organization. So, normally organizations do not have in-house management experts with cross-functional expertise.
2. When in-house senior managers elicit IT requirements, end users are inhibited from giving free and frank information because of the difference in seniority.
3. When an expert with responsibility for one of the organizational functions carries out the study, it can be difficult to rise above the interests of his/her own department and show equal concern for other departments.

All in all, unless you are hard pressed for money or your organizational culture prefers an in-house endeavor, I would suggest that the feasibility study be outsourced. Here are the advantages:

1. There are organizations that specialize in conducting feasibility studies. We can derive the benefit of their organizational processes and expertise in terms of the duration and effective cost of the study.
2. The outside experts are free from interdepartmental prejudices and biases and would be better positioned to produce an objective report.
3. End users would be more forthcoming in providing information and their requirements as they are free from rank-related inhibitions.
4. The outside experts can draw from the knowledge repository of their organization to fill in information gaps and produce a comprehensive report.
5. Being exposed to several similar organizations, the outside experts would be able to bring the best practices of the industry into the report.
6. Experts from consultancy organizations would have an opportunity to work on multiple assignments on different functional specialties as part of their regular work. Therefore, they would possess the cross-functional expertise vital for producing a credible feasibility report.

So, my recommendation is to outsource the assignment of conducting a feasibility study to a specialist organization. One thing to be noted here is that the study would be conducted by a team of experts. Compilation of information may be carried out by junior members, but data analysis would be performed by adept senior team members. Then the team may need to take the assistance of experts from hardware, software, and networking to prepare the recommendations for the proposed infrastructure. Thus, it is a collaborative effort carried out by a team.

Steps in Conducting the Feasibility Study

Normally, a feasibility study is conducted to assess the viability of a proposal. It is also used to ascertain the costs and benefits for an accepted proposal or to evaluate alternatives. A feasibility study is used in a variety of business scenarios and contexts. It may range from setting up a business organization to buying a piece of capital equipment. The scale and extent of the study would vary with the business context. For setting up IT infrastructure in an organization, the steps would be:

1. Define the scope of the proposal. Where in the organization is the proposed infrastructure to be set up?
2. Elicit and gather information processing requirements.
3. Analyze and establish information processing needs.

4. Define the proposed IT infrastructure.
5. Determine the necessary support infrastructure.
6. Define the organizational structure for managing the proposed infrastructure.
7. Define the deliverables from the proposed infrastructure.
8. Define the security arrangements for the proposed infrastructure.
9. Estimate the cost of the proposed IT infrastructure.
10. Estimate the cost of the proposed support infrastructure.
11. Estimate the annual maintenance costs of the proposed infrastructure.
12. Estimate the operational costs for running the proposed infrastructure.
13. Define the upgrade path and replacement criteria for the proposed infrastructure.
14. Prepare the report.
15. Carry out quality control activities and implement the feedback in the report.
16. Present the report to management and receive feedback.
17. Implement the feedback and submit the report.

Now, you can see that I omitted the cost-benefit analysis that is traditionally part of a feasibility study. We carry out a cost-benefit analysis between the available alternatives to enable the selection of the optimal alternative. We do not question the benefits from implementing the IT infrastructure in organizations because the alternative of carrying out business transactions manually on paper is obsolete and unviable. IT today is simply the cost of doing business. More detail on the above steps follows.

Define the Scope of the Proposal: Where in the Organization Is the IT Infrastructure to Be Set Up?

The first step is to define the scope for the proposed infrastructure in the organization. It may encompass the entire organization or it may be limited to one or more departments. We have to understand the coverage carefully and define the need for central server machines. If we are augmenting/extending the existing infrastructure, we may be able to utilize the existing central servers. In such cases, we only need to concern ourselves with the workstations. We need to identify:

1. The departments of the organization that should be part of the project
2. The items not in the scope of this project, such as central server machines

With the scope of the project set, the next stage is to document it. Initially, this can be in an informal document which must be sent for customer/appropriate authority approval. This document is crucial for setting the tone for the remainder of the study. If the scope is incorrect, the entire project could go off course. Obtaining approval from management is key before moving forward with the study.

Elicit and Gather Information Processing Requirements

You must collect top-level requirements from end users either through direct personal interviews or by examining existing records. For each business process, you must detail:

1. The number and nature of transactions handled for the process
2. Data volumes
3. The periodicity/frequency of process operations
4. Exceptions processing
5. Special reports expected including trend, analysis, and exception reports, etc.

It is not necessary to go into the finer points of process steps as they will be part of the requirements at the engineering phase of software development. Assess the workload and data volumes to determine the hardware and networking necessary for executing the process effectively. Do this for every business process falling within the scope of the project.

Analyze and Establish Information Processing Needs

In this step we consolidate all the information collected and arrive at the overall statistics for data volumes and workload. Data volume that needs to be kept online and stored off-line is determined, as is the workload in terms of the number of transactions processed per day at peak load volumes and the times of such loads.

We derive the number of workstations in the following manner:

- Time required to perform one business transaction (P minutes)
- Total number of business transactions expected per day (Q)
- Number of workstations necessary (P ÷ Q)

We derive the data volumes in the following manner:

- Data received and stored per transaction (A bytes)
- Number of transactions per day (B)
- Data received and stored per day (A × B)

Perform these computations for each business process and derive the total workload and data volumes per day. From this, the data volumes per year can be derived, thus:

- Number of days in a year:
    - 365 if the system is in operation around the clock on all days where it can be used by customers from their homes, such as ticket reservation systems or online purchasing systems
    - 251 if it is strictly an in-house processing system reducing 52 weekends and 10 holidays from 365
- Data volume per year = data volume per day × number of days in the year

We may adjust the volume upward or downward using a contingency factor that depends on our knowledge of the functional domain. For example, online stores have peak loads before important shopping holidays like Christmas and Independence Day.

Using these data, we can decide on the disk capacity as well as the random access memory requirements on the servers. Next, document the information processing needs compiling all the information collected and any analysis that was performed. Use the elements suggested in Figure 3.1 formatted into a template for establishing these needs. Have a separate document for each business process (which can mean many documents). They can be reviewed by peers and end users to ensure accuracy of the captured information. Ultimately, they should be added as appendices to the feasibility report.

Information processing needs:

Compiled by: Date:

Information details:

Brief description of the business process:

List the possible days for peak loads:

Period for which the transaction data needs to be online:

Period for which the transaction data needs to be stored off-line:

Any other relevant information:

Figure 3.1 Elements for establishing the information-processing needs template (template exhibited in Appendix I)

Define the Proposed IT Infrastructure

From the information compiled about the business processes, we need to derive the capabilities of the IT infrastructure necessary to handle information processing needs. In this step, we obtain the capabilities of various components of the IT infrastructure but not the actual infrastructure components. We do that in the "sizing" of the components to be discussed in detail in Chapter 4.

Determine the Necessary Support Infrastructure

Support infrastructure is needed in addition to IT infrastructure components. These are:

1. Electrical power sockets for workstations, servers, printers, etc.
2. Backup power arrangements including uninterrupted power supply systems, generators, and storage batteries.
3. Furniture to hold the IT infrastructure components:
    a. Racks for housing network switches
    b. Server cabinets for keeping the server machines
    c. Climate control equipment for server rooms
    d. Seating facility for IT personnel
    e. Space for all the above
4. Communication equipment including telephone, videoconferencing facilities, fax machines, etc.
5. Security equipment to screen physical entry and access to servers and networking equipment. These may include card swipe equipment, biometrics equipment, etc.

We need to determine the requirement for all this equipment and document capabilities.

Define the Organizational Structure for Managing the Proposed Infrastructure

Now, we need a structure and personnel for operating and maintaining the proposed IT infrastructure. Determine the organizational structure and enumerate all the positions essential for the IS department, including positions for:

1. A head of the department to take ownership of all infrastructure and other resources and be accountable for the results

2. One person to look after each of the functions, namely:
    a. Configuration management—maintaining the integrity of the data and programs in the production system that are used in day-to-day activities by end users
    b. Operations—job scheduling for periodic batch processing jobs (day-end, week-end, month-end, quarterly, half-yearly, and annual processing), backup and restore data, user management, security management, etc.
    c. Hardware maintenance
    d. Software maintenance
    e. Network management
    f. Quality control of IS department activities
    g. Process definition and improvement
    h. Help desk to assist users to effectively use the system
3. If any of the above activities are handled in-house, provide for staff based on the workload for each activity

It may be possible to combine some of these positions. However, they must be fit into an organization chart to define:

1. The roles and responsibilities for each position
2. The job description for each position
3. The key result areas for each position
4. The key competencies necessary for each position
5. Educational qualifications and training required for each position
6. Induction training necessary for each position

This document would be used for recruiting and training personnel to use the IT infrastructure effectively.

Define the Deliverables from the Proposed Infrastructure

Based on the information compiled, we need to define the outputs from the system. The system, of course, would process business transactions but it would also produce some outputs in hard or soft copy formats. For ease of reference, these are documented in logical groupings. Most of these would be specified by the end users and management and there may be additional outputs that have not been produced before. These deliverables include:

1. Periodic reports
2. On-demand reports

3. Inquiries
4. Analysis reports
5. Consolidation reports
6. Trend reports
7. Forecasting reports
8. Exception reports
9. Electronic data transfers
10. Audit trails

Define the Security Arrangements for the Proposed Infrastructure

The type of security the system requires also must be defined. If the system is accessible for use only on the organizational network, the security needed would be less severe than if the system is accessible over the Internet. The following security measures should be considered:

1. *Security against malware threats like viruses, worms, spyware, and adware.* This is the basic security necessary for all systems including desktop applications. This security may be applied at the workstation level or at the server level. If there are a significant amount of workstations, it may be economically and operationally more advantageous to have server-level security.
2. *Security against intruders.* When we allow our system to be accessed over the Internet, even if it is our private network, it can be intruded by determined hackers. Since data transmission is in the public domain and cyberspace, it can be intercepted with the right electronic equipment and programming expertise. We need to install two-tier security software against intruders—intruder prevention and intruder detection and tracking. A firewall is a must but even the best of firewalls can be hacked. It is reported that some countries are officially sponsoring electronic snooping to steal data and information. Some evil geniuses also developed bots (automatic programs) that can intrude systems, steal information and transmit it to a defined location, and cause damage to data and systems. Therefore, we need to put measures in place to detect the entry of an intruder the moment our security is breached and track the individual. Since the intrusion is electronic, we cannot arrest the individual red-handed because he/she may be sitting 10,000 miles away. Security measures that capture the IP address, determine the location from where the intrusion occurred,

and collect evidence for lodging a complaint with the appropriate authorities are vital.

3. *Security against internal misuse.* It is prudent to protect systems against misuse by authorized users. There have been many cases where a disgruntled employee has stolen company information and caused damage to the system. Therefore, strict access privileges are needed to prevent intentional misuse.

Specifications must be defined in the feasibility report so they can be designed into the system.

Estimate the Cost of the Proposed IT Infrastructure

The information available at this stage of the project is not really complete to carry out a deterministic estimate. Although requirements have been specified, alternatives have not yet been explored. Decisions about specific software, hardware, networking, and security measures would not be completed at the time of the feasibility study (these are made during the sizing stage). So, we should not attempt giving a deterministic estimate at this time. We need to give what is referred to as a "budgetary" estimate. This would be used to set a tentative budget in financial terms and then would be frozen after the sizing exercise is completed. It would be better to arrive at the minimum as well as the maximum expenditure needed; a range with the actual expenditure falling within it. The estimate would be a gross estimate lacking in detail but we do need to carry out a cost estimate for each of the components of the proposed IT infrastructure and include it in the feasibility report.

Estimate the Cost of the Proposed Support Infrastructure

We also need to have an estimate of the cost of the support infrastructure cited above. A specific alternative selected would impact the support infrastructure, but only to a minimum extent. Even then it is always good practice to provide a range of minimum and maximum expenditures that would be needed. The cost estimate of the proposed support infrastructure should be in the feasibility report.

Estimate the Annual Maintenance Costs of the Proposed Infrastructure

All equipment needs maintainance and there are three types of maintenance that should be conducted:

1. *Preventive maintenance.* Carried out in order to prevent breakdowns. This includes periodically cleaning and tightening electrical terminals, lubricating moving parts, if any, topping off batteries, dusting off machines, etc.
2. *Breakdown maintenance.* This is carried out to restore an asset to its working condition when it stops delivering the expected level of performance.
3. *Condition-based maintenance.* This is another type of preventive maintenance. Instead of doing preventive maintenance periodically, it is carried out based on the condition of the asset. The condition of the equipment can be assessed based on the number of hours in operation or using sophisticated condition-monitoring devices.

On top of estimating equipment maintenance costs, a strategy of who will be performing maintenance (in-house, outsourced, or a combination of both) should be in the feasibility report.

Estimate the Operational Costs for Running the Proposed Infrastructure

Apart from maintenance expense, we need to estimate the costs necessary to keep the system running, including:

1. Salaries of the staff required to keep the infrastructure in operation; the total cost for all human resources.
2. Consumables required to make use of the system. These include printer cartridges, ribbons, continuous stationary, discreet stationary, and spares for equipment maintained in-house, etc.
3. Energy expenses toward electrical power spent by the infrastructure and on environmental control for the server areas.
4. Cost of Internet bandwidth for connectivity.
5. Communication expenses toward the cost of telephones, faxes, audio/video conferencing, etc.
6. If any premises are rented, then the cost of rent. Extra space may need to be secured for keeping disaster backups.

We need to arrive at the operational expenditure required so that the impact of setting up the proposed IT infrastructure on the profit of the organization can be assessed. It will also help us make adequate budgetary provisions at the beginning of every year.

Define the Upgrade Path and Replacement Criteria for the Proposed Infrastructure

We need to recognize the high rate of obsolescence and the short life of hardware and software. Therefore, define the limits of hardware and software and when to upgrade. When applications are put on the Internet, they are impacted by environmental changes. Events like browser upgrades, web server upgrades, middleware upgrades, operating system upgrades, upgrades for standards like HTML, and new classes of malware could impact our infrastructure and necessitate an upgrade. We may need to upgrade our infrastructure or add fresh components. Therefore, we need to determine and include recommendations for upgrading the infrastructure as a response to various events, along with guidelines as to when to replace the system. Some events may not be foreseeable, which is an important aspect often overlooked in feasibility reports. We need to be sure to include an evaluation process in our recommendations for such eventualities.

Prepare the Report

Once we have determined all the above aspects from the information compiled, we can prepare the feasibility report. The elements of a suggested template are provided in Figure 3.2.

Carry Out Quality Control Activities and Implement the Feedback in the Report

Once the feasibility report is ready, it ought to be subjected to quality control activities, namely, the peer review and managerial review processes.

A peer review can be conducted by a group of technical personnel specialized in hardware, software, networking, and management of the IT infrastructure. They should thoroughly review sections of the report in which they are proficient to ensure:

1. Implementation of the report would fulfill the objectives of the proposed project.
2. The proposed hardware, software, and other components are appropriate for the purpose.
3. The cost estimates are credible.
4. The proposed organizational structure is right for managing the infrastructure effectively.
5. The report is error free from the standpoint of the organization's standards and guidelines for documentation, formatting, and so on.

<Title page>

Feasibility report

For *<name of the project>*

Revision history:
<End of *Title page*>

<Table of contents page>

<Content Pages>

1. Scope of the project
2. The goals set for the proposed project
3. Information processing needs to be fulfilled by the project
4. Deliverables from the proposed infrastructure
5. Proposed IT infrastructure
6. Proposed support equipment
7. Organizational structure for managing the proposed infrastructure
8. Security arrangements for the proposed infrastructure
9. Cost estimate for the proposed IT infrastructure
10. Annual maintenance cost for the proposed infrastructure
11. Operational costs for running the proposed infrastructure
12. Suggested upgrade path and replacement criteria
13. Project management strategy

Appendixes

Figure 3.2 Elements for feasibility report template (template exhibited in Appendix I)

Their feedback would be presented to the leader of the feasibility study team. Once the feedback is implemented and verified by the review team, it should be subjected to managerial review.

Managerial review would be carried out by the authority approving the report for further consideration. Here, we should not misconstrue this approval as the go-ahead for the project. This approval of the report is to authenticate it for consideration by appropriate authorities for implementation. Normally, organizations do have committees for approving capital expenditure consisting of senior executives from finance, operations, human resources, and other relevant departments. They would consider competing demands for capital expenditure and would approve projects that would benefit the organization the most. The approving authority for the report is authenticating it for consideration by such a committee. The approving authority would review the report looking for defects and possible problem areas. This review would not go into as much detail as the peer review. It would ensure that all activities were carried out diligently, the report was peer reviewed, and that all feedback was satisfactorily implemented.

Project Approval

Once the feasibility report passes through the peer and managerial reviews, it would be submitted to the organizational capital expenditure committee to:

1. Consider competing projects and select the best alternatives to sanction for capital investment
2. Ensure that only the right investment projects are approved
3. Consider the "opportunity cost" of the rejected projects and ensure that the approved projects make up this cost
4. Ensure that alternatives are considered and the recommended alternative is positioned to best serve organizational interests
5. Ensure that the proposed expenditure is optimal from the initial cost, operating cost, maintenance cost, and, ultimately, replacement cost perspective

However, if the organization where the proposed infrastructure to be implemented happens to be a software development or BPO organization, or a firm where IT infrastructure is vital for doing business, IT infrastructure projects are not compared to other competing projects. In such cases, only objectives 4 and 5 would apply. But it still has to go through committee!

Normally, when there are competing demands for capital investment, the committee uses capital budgeting techniques. These are:

1. Return on investment (ROI)
2. Payback period
3. Discounted cash flow techniques:
    a. Net present value (NPV)
    b. Internal rate of return (IRR)

Although a detailed discussion of these techniques is out of the scope for this book, let us look at each of these techniques briefly.

Return on Investment

In this evaluation, we estimate all the benefits that would accrue to the organization—both tangible and intangible. This exercise is conducted for all the projects and then the one that gives us the optimal benefit is selected. In using this technique, we would not consider profit alone, but also gross revenue. The decision criteria would be (1) the gross revenue and (2) the amount of capital expenditure proposed to be incurred. The ROI is considered to be positive if the total benefit (gross revenue) exceeds the cost (amount of capital expenditure) and only ROI positive projects are considered. This technique works well when the economy is stable and inflation is either zero or hovers around zero. In an inflationary economy, this would not give correct projections because the value of money is eroded.

Payback Period

Every investment is expected to pay back the investment. This technique requires computing yearly revenue from the project and the number of years (or other time periods) in which the expenditure is recouped. The economic life of the investment should be longer than the payback period. Only then is the investment viable and profitable. In all such investment proposals, the ones with the shortest payback periods and longest economic life, post-payback, would be selected. This too is a simple technique like ROI and works well in a stable economy with zero or near-zero inflation.

Discounted Cash Flow—Net Present Value

This technique takes into consideration the fact that we are living in an inflationary economy, meaning monies we receive in the future would not have the same value as the money spent today. So, projected future cash inflows are adjusted to present value using a discounting rate. The discounting rate may be equivalent to a projected inflation rate, a borrowing rate, or a rate considered by management to be necessary for the adjustment of future cash inflows to present value. The sum of projected future cash inflows adjusted with a discounting rate would be compared to the present expenditure on the project. If the sum of discounted cash inflows is higher than the present cash outflow, the NPV is said to be positive. When comparing competing projects, the project having the maximum positive NPV would be selected. Microsoft Excel has an easy-to-use formula for computing the present value of future cash inflows that can be used to arrive at the NPV of an investment.

Discounted Cash Flow—Internal Rate of Return

This technique assumes a stable economy free from inflationary pressure but recognizes the fact that most investments are made with borrowed capital.

That is, we pay interest on the capital borrowed and the inflows must pay back not only the principal amount but also the interest thereof and leave some surplus for profit.

In using this technique, we compute the rate of return based on the projected future cash inflows. This rate of return is referred to as the IRR. Then we compare the IRR to the rate of interest we pay. If the IRR is higher than the projected interest rate, the IRR is said to be positive. When selecting from a set of competing projects, the project with the highest positive IRR would be chosen (again, Microsoft Excel can help with this).

An important aspect to be noted is that the above techniques evaluate the proposals only on a quantitative basis using assumed cash inflows. If the difference between two proposals is marginal, it is difficult to go with the marginally better proposal because the actual cash inflows could be different from the projected inflows. Marginal differences are insignificant as a different set of assumptions may result in a different set of projected cash inflows. When we evaluate the same set of proposals with all the above techniques, they may not produce the same conclusions.

It is important to note that qualitative aspects play a much more important role in decision making about capital investment. These factors include the future outlook for the technical stability of the investment, new discoveries coming in that area, the credibility of the projected cash inflows, and so on.

Decision makers take objective analysis *and* qualitative factors into account to approve or reject an investment proposal. Once approved, a provisional budgetary allocation of funds would be made for the project. Why provisional allocation? The actual allocation would be made after the cash budget for the project is prepared, which we will discuss in Chapter 5 (*Planning in IT Project Management*).

Strategies for Executing IT Projects

For the organization implementing the IT infrastructure, a budgetary allocation of funds signifies project acquisition for the in-house IS team. The next step is to decide on the strategy for executing the project. An IT project is multidisciplinary and, at a minimum, four specialties stand out:

1. Hardware implementation (along with system software)
2. Application software development
3. Networking
4. Support infrastructure implementation

Now the organization has to make the first decision on how to execute the project. There are alternatives:

1. Execute the project totally with in-house resources.
2. Execute the project with a single contractor on a turn-key basis.
3. Coordinate the project in-house but execute the project with multiple contractors.

Let's discuss each of them in a little more detail.

Execute the Project Totally with In-House Resources

Under this strategy, the organization would employ appropriate staff to execute the project. They would be on the rolls of the organization as full- or part-time employees. All technical decisions are made in-house and all work is carried out by in-house resources.

The advantage is that the work is under the direct control of the organization implementing the project, and the work carried out would be conforming to organizational quality standards. This is also the least-cost alternative as it is free from the overhead and profits of contractors.

The main disadvantage is that *extra* staff may have to be laid off after the completion of the project because (1) more staff is needed in implementation than in maintenance and (2) the resources used for implementing the infrastructure would not be suitable for maintenance or operation. If the strategy for maintenance is to be handled in-house, then some of the resources may be useful. If maintenance is outsourced, then even fewer resources would be useful after the project is completed. In such cases, we need to lay off most of the implementation team after the project is completed. Alternatively, we can hire temporary staff and execute the project without worrying about layoffs afterward.

However, the overwhelming reason why this strategy is not used is that it necessitates having in-house specialties that are not normally found in most organizations. It is not feasible to build them internally for short-duration projects since once the work is completed, they would have nothing to do.

Execute the Project with a Single Contractor on a Turn-Key Basis

This strategy awards all activities to a single contractor who specializes in IT infrastructure implementation on a turn-key basis. (When the contractor hands over the infrastructure in these contracts, they would be ready for operation in every aspect. The organization has to just *turn the key* to open the facility to start using it. That is why these all-activities-encompassing contracts are referred to as *turn-key* contracts.) The organization has to provide all specifications and the contractor would perform all activities to make the facility a reality.

The advantage to this type of arrangement is that the principal organization can be free from all the hassles of evaluating alternatives and making strategic decisions. With appropriate points for approval, the project can be controlled effectively. The money payments are progress-based and hence financial risk is minimized.

The disadvantage is that it is the highest cost alternative. The contracting organizations in this field typically specialize in large projects and they too would engage subcontractors for various activities. So the cumulative overhead and profits (of the principal, main contractor, and subcontractor) would escalate the overall cost.

This alternative is used normally by organizations in the IT/BPO sectors.

Coordinate the Project In-House but Execute the Project with Multiple Contractors

This is the most popular strategy utilized by organizations implementing an IT infrastructure. Normally, at least some activities are contracted out so overall control is exercised by the principal organization and various subcontractors are engaged for carrying out different activities, including:

1. Application software development
2. Hardware sizing, supply, installation, and commissioning (including system software)
3. Design, supply, install, and commission support infrastructure

Additionally, a project management and quality control consultant may be engaged to monitor the project. The project management consultant would coordinate and keep management of the principal organization up to date with necessary information. This consultant also would act as the interface between the principal and contractors in all technical and financial matters. The quality control consultant would ensure that all relevant quality control activities are diligently performed by the contractors and would carry out inspection/testing of the completed structure before accepting and handing it over to the maintenance team.

The main advantage of this strategy is the ability to utilize specialists for each part of the project at an optimal cost. The disadvantages are the additional overhead to monitor and control both the progress and quality of the project deliverables.

Each organization should carefully weigh the pros and cons of the strategies and select the one that best suits their unique requirements. Once the right strategy for executing the project is selected, requests for proposals (RFPs) should be prepared and sent to vendors requesting them for the required services.

Project Acquisition

This activity is carried out by firms that specialize in implementing IT infrastructure in other organizations. For them, the above activities conducted during the feasibility study and project approval are outside their scope. Their activity starts when an RFP is received and ends when the infrastructure is implemented and handed over to the customer.

One question here is pertinent to answer: Would there be any difference in the project acquisition process based on the specialization of the contractor? The answer is no. Specialization comes in during the engineering part of project execution. The project acquisition process goes through the activities of RFP, proposal, negotiations, and the purchase order. Receipt of the purchase order is the culmination of the project acquisition process. Now, let's look at each of these activities in a little more detail.

Request for Proposal

The RFP is the first activity in project acquisition. An RFP is raised by the organization seeking the specialized services of the vendor. There is no suggested format for raising an RFP. Normally an RFP would contain the following information:

1. *A preamble section.* This section would contain information about the principal organization, the project name and its brief description, last date for submission of the proposal, date for opening the bids, and date for awarding the contract. It would also contain details about how to submit the proposal, to whom it should be submitted, and with whom, if necessary, to follow up on the proposal.
2. *Details of the work.* This section would contain a detailed description of the work covered by the RFP. It would contain all the technical, logistical, and administrative details, and the standards and guidelines for the work. It is common to include a person to contact in case clarification about the details in the RFP is needed. Normally, a meeting would be conducted to clarify all doubts from participating vendors. The transactions of such meetings are recorded and posted on a website as addendum to the RFP or e-mailed/posted to all participating vendors.

3. *Selection criteria.* This section details the criteria (price, technical competence, experience in similar contracts, certifications, and so on) used for the selection of the vendor. These criteria would be normalized using a weighting system of importance to the organization to arrive at a final decision.
4. *Escalation mechanism in case of dispute.* In certain cases, a vendor may dispute the selection of the winner. Normally, the aggrieved vendor can approach the senior executives of the principal organization to resolve the dispute or, in extreme instances, seek out the court of jurisdiction.
5. *Penalties.* In most cases, RFPs are sent to preselected vendors. But in some cases, especially from public institutions and government departments, they post a public RFP either in the press or on a publicly accessible website. In such cases, to prevent frivolous participation a monetary deposit would be required to participate in the tender. Similarly, to discourage non-serious vendors to quote a very low price and take the order but not with the intention to execute, penalty clauses would be inserted in the RFP. Also, in time-sensitive projects it is common to impose penalties for delay in execution. All such penalties would be included in this section. However, it may not be needed in the case of every RFP.

The RFP would be conveyed to the vendors through the mail, e-mail, or would be posted on a website with links forwarded to select vendors. Sometimes RFPs are advertised in the press too. Another aspect to be noted is that most RFPs ask for two-bid proposals. The first one would contain only the technical proposal and the second one would contain financial details of the technical proposal.

The Proposal

The proposal is the set of documents submitted by the vendor organizations against the RFP. Normally two documents are submitted as a proposal:

1. Technical proposal
2. Financial proposal

It is possible that the two could be merged into one, but many professional organizations insist on two-bid proposals so that technical aspects can be separated from financial considerations. The principal organization would evaluate all technical proposals first and select the ones that best meet their technical requirements. Then, they would open the corresponding financial proposals and select the lowest financial bid among them. The problem is that the process is often not so straight forward. In these days of monopolistic competition, vendors propose different types of technical solutions to show that their offering is superior to others. For the same needs, one vendor may offer a mainframe solution, another a minicomputer-based solution, and yet a third a microcomputer-based solution! All will say that their solution meets the organization's needs effectively. This makes it difficult to compare different technical solutions on an even footing. Each value proposition is assessed, based on the combination of technical and financial bids, and the vendor offering the best value is selected. In cases where the decision is still not so clear, negotiations may be carried out to clarify issues and arrive at the best alternative.

The technical bid proposal, being the first to be opened and evaluated, is crucial for the vendor to win. Unless the technical bid meets or exceeds the specifications set by the RFP, the financial bid would not even be opened. The following sections should be part of a technical proposal:

1. *Preamble.* Would be similar to the preamble of the RFP. Additionally, information about the vendor organization would also be included, highlighting its history, specialization, and experience in the relevant field.
2. *Scope of work.* The scope of work as offered would be described here. This section should normally be identical to the scope of work described in the RFP. Sometimes, the offering may not be exactly identical to what is requested. Therefore, this section should describe the scope of work as offered. What is stated here is what will be delivered. We need to understand clearly what is asked and then explain what is offered to ensure the client can correlate their needs with the offering and agree that specifications are met.
3. *Approach and methodology.* The approach to the assignment and methodology for executing it are explained here. International, national, and industry guidelines and internal consulting firm quality standards should be included if necessary. The project execution life cycle is explained so that the customer understands the approach to the project and its execution to ensure success. This section should also contain the procedure for handling change requests placed by the principal.
4. *Responsibilities.* Vendors need to clearly delineate the responsibilities in the project activities between customer and vendor and enumerate all activities as part of the proposal:
   a. There are three levels of responsibilities—the principal's, the vendor's, and shared (primary/secondary) between the principal and the vendor.

b. Sometimes the responsibility needs to be shared between principal and vendor equally.
c. Sometimes the principal would have primary responsibility with the vendor second (e.g., approvals).
d. Sometimes the vendor would have primary responsibility with the principal second (e.g., raising invoices for payment).

5. *Assumptions and support needed from the customer.* Vendors need to enumerate all the assumptions made in preparing the proposal. If the project execution needs any support from the principal, it is included here. Certainly the vendor needs support in terms of entry, common facilities, approvals, and so on from the principal. All these aspects need to be included in the proposal.
6. *Schedule of project execution.* The proposal needs to include the schedule of project execution. A very detailed schedule is not necessary but major milestones need to be included.
7. *Terms and conditions.* What constitutes technical success of the project belongs here. There can also be a number of things that can go wrong technically to affect project execution, including a disruption in supplies, supplied equipment being different than planned, sites not being ready due to delays in other contractors' work, and so on. These also need to be in this section.
8. *Exclusions.* Sometimes the RFP can be confusing and the scope of work described in the foregoing sections may leave in some ambiguity. All such ambiguities need to be spelled out here. This is done by enumerating the exclusions from the project. Consequential liability is applicable in countries like the United States but not in countries like India. If the contracts span across countries, we need to note this issue very carefully. Whatever is part of the scope of work and not included in the exclusions' list would be deemed to be included. So, vendors need to exercise diligence in describing the scope of work and exclusions.

The financial proposal would contain the following sections:

1. *Professional fee.* This section would indicate the professional fee or charges for executing the assignment. It may be a single figure or an itemized set of figures for all the services provided. It depends on the requirements of the principal or the practices of the vendor organization. This would be the sum of money the principal needs to pay in addition to items that will be charged at their actual cost to the principal.

2. *Items that will be billed at actual cost.* There are a number of things that would be billed at their actual cost (travel, supply of specialized high-cost equipment, etc). Vendors need to list all such items in this section, and include the procedure for determining and billing for work carried out against change requests placed by the principal.
3. *Methodology for billing.* In long, drawn-out projects, it is common to periodically bill for services rendered by the vendors. Sometimes it is based on measuring the work completed and sometimes it is by the reaching of a milestone. Whatever methodology will be used for submitting bills needs to be included here.
4. *Methodology for billing for works executed that are not part of the contract.* Sometimes the vendor will have to execute some work for the principal that is not in the contract. When such out-of-scope work is executed, a procedure for invoicing is necessary.
5. *Payment schedule.* The schedule of payments expected by the vendor needs to be included in this section. It may include an advance required to mobilize resources for executing the project and the periodic bills that would follow.
6. *Taxes.* It needs to be made explicitly clear if the project is eligible for taxation. The tax rate and whether it is included in the professional fee or would be separately billed should be noted in this section. Although taxes are an item to be billed at actual cost, vendors still need to separately deal with them because it is not a cost item but an amount that has to be paid to a government entity.
7. *Penalties.* Explicitly mention two items in this section: whether penalties proposed by the principal are accepted/rejected by the vendor and any penalties for delayed payments by the principal. If not mentioned here, the principal cannot be asked to pay interest on delayed payments.
8. *Price escalation.* For long, drawn-out projects, a price escalation is very likely due to inflation or other reasons. If vendors need to raise their prices to neutralize the impact of price escalation during the course of project execution, it needs to be mentioned in this section along with criteria for when the price escalation becomes applicable.
9. *Issue Escalation.* An escalation mechanism to resolve disputes should be included. Usually this starts with senior executives but could go to an arbitrator or even the courts if the dispute is serious.
10. *Force majeure.* This section describes the actions when things beyond vendor control, such as floods, fires, strikes, strife, wars, and natural

calamities, disrupt operations and prevent the fulfilling of the contract. It would include the waiting period before taking action, the remedies available, any penalties that could be levied, and so on.

11. *Validity period of the proposal.* The period for which the amounts quoted in this proposal are valid and a timeframe for finalizing the proposal. If the decision is delayed beyond the time limit set in this section, the principal needs to obtain a fresh financial proposal.
12. *Other terms and conditions.* Each vendor organization would have a host of other miscellaneous terms and conditions included in the proposal. These would contain the use of customer names in marketing collaterals, disclosure of information contained in the proposal, non-solicitation of staff, confidentiality clauses, etc. All of these would form this section.

The proposal is a very important aspect of project acquisition and when the project is awarded, it will be the primary document for reference in any legal matters, along with the RFP, purchase order, and the acceptance letter of the purchase order documents. Therefore, careful diligence must be exercised when preparing the proposal. Normally a senior management committee reviews and approves the proposal before it is submitted to the customer.

Negotiations

As noted in the previous section, negotiations may occur mainly to clarify technical and financial aspects. The principal would try to increase the technical liability while at the same time reduce or maintain the financial liability. The ideal situation is to arrive at a win-win settlement for all, or at the very least, reach a settlement that is fair to all.

Purchase Order

A purchase order is the legal document a principal would place on the successful vendor. It would contain the service requested, the fee applicable thereof, and other terms and conditions. For scope of work and other technical aspects, it may refer to the RFP or the technical proposal and record the deviation, if any, in the purchase order itself. The purchase order would be the primary document in legal matters. Normally, purchase orders are formatted by legal experts in view of their legal liability.

Acceptance of Purchase Order

Unless the vendor formally accepts the purchase order, it would not take effect. The vendor's liability begins only after accepting the purchase order. This is also a primary legal document. It should be signed by an authorized signatory of the vendor organization.

Contract

Today, in most cases, the system of a purchase order and its acceptance is being replaced by a contract signed by both parties. A contract is a self-contained document that would contain all aspects of the project including both the technical and financial aspects. When a contract is signed, the RFP and the proposal would not be called into legal disputes unless the contract contains a reference to those documents. All countries have their own contract law and the court of jurisdiction mentioned in the contract would take precedence in determining the applicable law.

Cost Estimation

The professional fee and other financial stipulations that form the financial proposal would be arrived at through cost estimation. The topic of cost estimation is not covered in this book because it is a big subject deserving separate treatment. However, one thing should be mentioned here; pricing is different from cost estimation. Cost estimation determines the range of the expenditure that is incurred to execute the project. After cost estimation, the vendor would be able to arrive at the minimum and maximum expenditure that would be needed for executing the project. Pricing aims to win the contract and beat the competition if there is no differentiator on the technical side while maximizing profits over an acceptable period of time. The price would be decided by the management of the organization submitting the proposal.

This book has free material available for download from the Web Added Value™ resource center at *www.jrosspub.com*

4

Sizing of IT Components

Introduction to Sizing

Sizing is the term used in the IT industry that represents all of the actions taken to determine the capacity required of a component in the proposed IT infrastructure, which can be a piece of hardware or software or a combination of both.

Merriam Webster's dictionary defines *size* as "to make (something) a particular size—example—'The jeweler sized the ring to fit the finger;' to consider (something or someone) in order to form an opinion or conclusion; and to arrange or classify (things) to size—usually used as *sized*." All of these definitions are relevant in the IT context. We do all these in sizing IT components and carry out the following activities as part of it:

1. Try to fit IT components to our requirements.
2. Consider all available IT components to form an opinion about their capability to meet our requirements.
3. Arrange all the available alternative IT components in the order of their capacity to meet our requirements.
4. Reconcile our needs with the systems/components available in the market to determine the most optimal choice for our organization.

These actions allow us to freeze the specifications of the IT components that are appropriate to our project at hand. We discuss the sizing of hardware and software in the following sections.

We can outsource all these sizing activities to a specialized organization or perform them in-house. Wherever they are performed, they must be completed in order to finalize IT components for the project.

Software or Hardware First?

Traditionally, hardware was selected first and then application software was built around it. Only the operating system and a software development kit came along with the hardware. The data resided on flat files and was coupled tightly to the programs. But the introduction of a database management system (DBMS) and a relational DBMS (RDBMS) to decouple the programs (software) from the organizational data added one more layer between application software and the operating system. Oracle was perhaps the first RDBMS that worked on multiple hardware platforms.

In time, hardware vendors started offering certain application software products along with the hardware that would work only on the supplied hardware. But the advent of the IBM PC in 1981 spurred development of software products that would work on any PC. By the end of the 1980s, PCs could process business data with a plethora of application software products and RDBMS. For low-load applications that can run on a PC, the selection of hardware became irrelevant as the software products available in the market would function in the same manner on any IBM PC clone.

The Internet adds one more layer between the user and the final hardware that would process business data. Presently, we have a minimum of five layers: a user (presentation) layer, a network to carry our data to the hardware, an RDBMS, and the final hardware that would process data. We also have the web server layer to interpret data from the Internet. The network and hardware layers are built with hardware while the user layer, RDBMS, and web server are software layers. We need to size all these layers to assess their suitability as part of the sizing IT components process. Commercial off-the-shelf (COTS) products are available for all software layers. For the web server and RDBMS layers, COTS products make sense because developing them in-house from scratch is very costly. Software for the presentation layer can either be developed in-house or a COTS product can be implemented.

There are multiple options for applications software, ranging from complete custom development to implementing a COTS product without any customization and everything in between. If we decide to custom develop all application software, we should select the hardware first. If we decide to implement a COTS product, with or without customization, select the software product first and then choose the hardware that supports the selected COTS product.

Selecting the hardware first limits your software options and vice versa. So, which should be selected first? I suggest that you choose the hardware first as it is the critical component of the system for delivering the needed performance and carrying the processing load efficiently and effectively.

Availability of the System

Before we move on to hardware and software sizing, we need to make some decisions: should the system and live data be available around the clock and should internal information be made available over the Internet?

There are situations where the system must be available 24/7 such as online ticket reservation systems and other e-commerce outlets. In these cases, not only should the system be available at all times, but so should the live data. There can be no variation between the organizational data and the live data.

In certain cases, the data are completely internal and no external agency needs to have access to it. For example, manufacturing organizations have operational production planning data, warehouse information, product stock, and so on, which is purely internal. These types of data can be made available only for the duration the organization is functioning during the work day. When the organization closes, the information can be closed too. Sometimes, it is not desirable to allow live data to be available on the Internet around the clock. The data may contain sensitive information or intellectual property that can be stolen. In these cases, the data center would work only during the working hours of the organization.

In some cases, there can be a lag between live data and organizational data, and it is acceptable for the public accessing the data to have slightly older information. The people accessing such information would not need it in real-time. Availability of real-time information has an impact on the components being selected for our IT project. Below is a summary of the influence of system availability on the selection of IT components:

1. Around-the-clock availability needs:
   a. A server that can run continuously without interruption or needing repairs
   b. A rugged infrastructure that can be *hot-maintained* (repairs/upgrades possible when the system is still running)
   c. A rugged operating system that doesn't hang/freeze when faced with the occurrence of unexpected events
   d. Hardware fault tolerance
   e. A backup infrastructure for server, power supply, and networking against possible failures
2. Availability over the Internet necessitates:
   a. A secure environment to protect against external attacks
   b. A secure environment to protect against information theft

c. Mechanisms to track intruders should that event occur

In addition to the IT components, to guarantee around-the-clock availability over the Internet, we need:

1. Processes to ensure that *all* operations are performed continuously
2. A rigorous system of audits (both conformance and investigative) to make certain that the defined processes are implemented
3. A defined system for continuous process improvement

Therefore, we need to define the desired system availability for our IT project before we embark on sizing other IT components. It can be:

1. Around-the-clock availability over the Internet for both the organization and the public
2. Around-the-clock availability for the organization and the public, but the systems are insulated from each other with the information for the public periodically updated from the organizational server (The organizational server shall never be accessible to the public.)
3. Around-the-clock availability for the organization only over the Internet
4. Around-the-clock availability for the organization over a private network (Access to the general public over the Internet to be explicitly excluded.)
5. Availability for the organization only during its working hours

Once this decision is made, we can move forward with the sizing of other IT components.

Sizing of the Server

A data center can have multiple servers (organizations like Microsoft, Yahoo, Google, and Skype have multiple servers at one location in their data centers). There needs to be a minimum of two servers: the web server and the database server. These can be on the same piece of hardware or on separate machines. We may also have an e-mail server, an application server, and a security server machine. All these can also be on the same machine or handled separately. Here's how to size each of these machines.

Web Server Machine

A web server receives the connection request from the Internet and establishes the connection between the end-user machine and the data center. All data transfer to the end user from the system flows through the web server machine. This machine would need the following software loaded on its random access memory (RAM):

1. Server operating system
2. Security software, if there is no separate security server
3. Web server software
4. Administrative tools to administer the website
5. Any other organization-specific software utilities

In the above list of software products, the server operating system and the web server occupy large amounts of RAM. In addition to these products, we need some amount of RAM for each connection attached to the server from the end-user machine.

Software vendors list the amount of RAM needed for their products. But normally they do not reveal, unless insisted upon, the amount of RAM their product needs for each connection. Find out this information. This chunk of RAM would hold session variables that include the beginning time of the session, IP address, login ID, password, authorizations/restrictions to access data/applications, class of user, and so on. Present-day COTS products are built using dynamic-link libraries (DLLs). A DLL is loaded into RAM only when it is needed and removed from RAM when it is closed inside the software. An operating system would have hundreds of DLLs and so do other large software products. So the utilization of RAM by these products would vary from time to time. Thus, each product would need two levels of RAM:

1. The minimum level which is the amount the product occupies when it is initially loaded and before any user starts using the product
2. The maximum level which is the amount when all the DLLs are loaded into the RAM

Which one should we consider when computing the amount of RAM required for our software? If the number of users is limited on our system and their usage is predictable, consider using an average of the minimum and maximum RAM required for each product. But if we do not know the number of users and what exactly would be used, consider using the maximum RAM needed for each product. Table 4.1 shows an example format for RAM computation. We need to understand what would happen to the system if the RAM is less than the amount we computed above.

Today's computers have Von Neumann or *stored program* architecture. That is, the program and data being executed are resident in the RAM. The

Table 4.1 Computation of RAM requirements in MB (megabytes)

Software product	**Minimum RAM**	**Maximum RAM**	**Data overhead**
Operating system			
Web server			
Number of concurrent connections (sessions) expected			
Security server			
Administrative tools			
Any other utilities			
Total			
Additional RAM for contingencies and adding software utilities later on @ 25%			
Total RAM required for the server (sum of the above two rows)			

architecture needs only the current set of data records from secondary storage, and the temporary variable data must be inside the RAM. Presently, most operating systems use a segmented, demand paged memory management system with virtual memory facility for the allocation of RAM to applications. In this method, the RAM is segmented and allocated to applications. Each segment of RAM is normally 64 KB with each page of memory being 1 KB, but these sizes could vary from system to system. When the entire RAM is allocated and used by applications, and an application demands more RAM, it is taken from the virtual memory (a dedicated area on the hard disk). The operating system removes a page (or pages) of application space from the RAM and moves it to virtual memory and loads a page (or pages) from virtual memory into the RAM to satisfy the new demands of the application. The operating system uses a least-recently-used page of memory or any other efficient algorithm in order to move a page from RAM to virtual memory.

Now, if the RAM is much less than the demanded RAM, the pages will be moving in and out of RAM continuously. This is a condition called "thrashing." When thrashing reaches a crescendo, the performance of the system degrades significantly. Thus, having RAM substantially less than what is demanded would degrade system performance. It may even hang/freeze the computer system. Therefore, we need to ensure that an adequate amount of RAM is available for applications. It is better to have some additional RAM than just enough for the system to perform predictably.

Once we have determined the RAM requirement, we have to determine the capacity of the CPU (central processing unit), which is specified in MIPS (millions of instructions per second). But MIPS ratings are not honestly disseminated by the vendors of computer hardware. There are standards for measuring MIPS, but they are more often flouted than conformed to in order to convince prospective customers that their hardware is as powerful or more powerful than competing hardware and to score points in competitive advantage. The important thing to note is that the CPU is never the bottleneck in information processing. The CPU is many times faster than the I/O (input/output) devices, which include RAM, monitors, disk drive, and printers. Printing is usually taken off-line in most applications except when a receipt type of printout is required. Therefore, the speed of throughput is decided more by RAM and the disk drive. The velocity of the RAM and the disk drive is specified by the access time and speed of data transfer. RAM is by far the faster of the two. That leaves the disk drive and the monitor as the bottleneck.

The next questions to ask are, "How do I assess throughput when all of these variables need to be assessed? Should optimization techniques like linear programming be used to determine server configuration?" Fortunately, these questions have answers already available.

Instead of assessing all these variables and coming up with a configuration, if we supply the number of transactions expected to be placed on the server per day to server vendors, they will come up with a proposal that best fits their offerings. All we need to do is run some independent benchmark tests on them. These tests are referred to as *transaction processing* (TP) tests. You can develop your own TP test software or obtain it from available TP test vendors. These tests will determine the throughput of the system, testing a combination of the CPU, RAM monitors, and hard disk. These tests include reading and writing from the disk, mathematical computations, and a combination of these two. Conduct some tests on vendor products and arrive at the best offering. The capacity to handle many concurrent connections on the server would be tested using a load test tool. Only after conducting the above two types of testing (TP and load) can we determine the optimal server for our IT project.

Now, let's look at which server to select: a PC (microcomputer) server, a mini/midrange server, or a mainframe server. Think of a mainframe as a coach bus, a mini/midrange as a van, and a microcomputer as a two-seater. Although using 25 two-seaters to carry 50 people from place to place is feasible, using a coach bus is a much better option. If we need to transport eight people, a van is the best choice. The differences between the three types of computers are as follows:

1. *Hardware components*. The CPU is built using multiple components in mainframe and minicomputers and a single component (very large

scale integrated circuit chip) in microcomputers (PCs). The capacity of a multicomponent CPU is much greater than a single component one. Therefore, the processing capacity of mainframe and minicomputers is much greater than that of a microcomputer. Similarly, the components that control data flow with I/O devices have special interfaces in mainframe and minicomputers with built-in buffers to handle the differences in the speed of the CPU and I/O devices. The main differentiator in favor of mainframe and minicomputers is the ability to control numerous I/O devices. For example, take a bank that has thousands of automatic teller machine terminals across the country. They all need to be controlled by a central computer. Only a mainframe can handle that load as it would have powerful I/O controllers to interface with the I/O devices without overloading the CPU. The microcomputer would have one or two processors to handle all processing functions. The mainframe computer would have multiple processors: one to process information (arithmetic and logic) and others to handle multiple I/O and direct memory access devices. All in all, mainframes would have higher capacity hardware components to handle more processing work, and more I/O devices to provide much higher throughput than any other category of computer. Microcomputers would have one or two CPUs that handle both processing and controlling of I/O devices. Mini/midrange computers would be in between the mainframe and microcomputers in terms of hardware components. Another aspect is the amount of RAM each can support. Mainframes would have many gigabytes (GB) of RAM whereas microcomputers usually have limited GB (say 4 or 6) of RAM. Disk space is another differentiator. Mainframes would support terabytes of disk space whereas microcomputers have it measured in GBs. Again, minicomputers would support less RAM and disk capacity than mainframes but more than microcomputers.

2. *Operating system*. The operating system of a mainframe is much larger in size than that of a microcomputer. It is built to enable adding hardware or software components dynamically, that is, without restarting the computer. Even the operating system itself can be updated without restarting the computer. With such flexibility, the mainframe computer can run without interruption for any length of time. Once the mainframe computer is switched on, it keeps running around the clock for months, if not years. The microcomputer needs to restart when the operating system is updated and if any special new hardware or software is added to the system. The mini is in between mainframe and the

microcomputers. Some minicomputers have mainframe features and others have microcomputer features but with different capabilities.

3. *Input/Output device handling.* Mainframes are built to handle multiple and diverse I/O devices efficiently, either locally or at remote locations. This is achieved by special hardware. Microcomputers lack this capacity. Performance degrades when a microcomputer drives an I/O device. When I/O devices are dumb (i.e., they do not possess any data processing power), mainframes are much more efficient than microcomputers.

The spend decision depends on the application and the load placed on the server. Table 4.2 summarizes the comparisons of these computers. Unfortunately, there are no benchmarks available to decide what a high, medium, or low transaction rate is.

The following guidelines will help determine which type of server is best suited to your organization:

1. If your server is likely to be accessed from all over the world, at all times, then select a mainframe server. It is much more reliable in continuous operation and handling high transaction rates.
2. If your server is accessed only by the staff of your organization and within the country, then consider either a mini- or microcomputer server depending on the transaction load.

Table 4.2 Comparison of the capabilities between the types of computers

Parameter	Mainframe	Microcomputer	Minicomputer
Ability to add peripherals dynamically	Possible	Not possible	Possible in some cases
Update OS dynamically	Possible	Not possible	Possible in some cases
Add software dynamically	Possible	Possible in some cases	Possible in some cases
Handling dumb peripherals	Does not degrade performance	Degrades performance	Degrades performance
Continuous operation	Can run continuously for years	Can run continuously for days	Can run continuously for months
Transaction processing capability	Highest	Lowest	Medium
Cost	Highest	Lowest	Medium
Cost per transaction	Lowest when the transaction load is highest	Lowest when transaction rate is lowest	Lowest when the transaction rate is medium

3. If your server provides only static information or derived information with simple processing, a mini- or microcomputer server would be best.
4. If your server provides derived data with a medium level of complexity and the transaction rate is average as well, purchase a minicomputer server.

Finally, think back to the bus, van, and two-seater analogy. A two-seater is excellent for carrying a couple of people over a short distance, say a hundred miles. If you need to carry 50 people 500 miles, a bus is the most appropriate. If you need to carry three to seven people, a van is much more appropriate than either a two-seater (you would need multiple vehicles) or a bus (wasting capacity) even though they could be used as well.

Another issue to consider is the web server software. Every hardware machine does not support every type of web server software. If you select the hardware first, selection of web server software is constrained by the hardware. If you select the software first, then the hardware selection is constrained by the software.

Database Server Machine

The choice of the RDBMS is constrained by the hardware for the database server and the application software (the reverse is also true). Select the RDBMS using the following guidelines:

1. It must be able to store the estimated data records and leave some spare capacity for future growth. We can use the data volumes established during the feasibility study for computing the estimated data records to be stored by the database. Extrapolate the load for the next five years so that the RDBMS would be able to support applications in the short term.
2. It must support standard SQL (structured query language) so that special training is not required for data manipulation. It also ensures porting of our application to another RDBMS should this become necessary in the future.
3. It must have a robust database engine so data integrity is ensured.
4. It must have a base of installations from which we can obtain feedback on field performance.
5. It must be compatible with the hardware and application software if already selected.

If we selected a mainframe or a high-end minicomputer for the web server, we can host the RDBMS on the web server machine itself. If we selected a low-end minicomputer or a microcomputer, then it may be a better idea to have a separate machine for the database server to host the RDBMS.

E-Mail Server

There are basically two types of servers for e-mail. One would hold all the e-mails on the server and the e-mail client can read and send e-mails from the server itself. The second type of server allows for downloading of e-mails onto the e-mail client machine. The logic behind keeping all e-mails on the e-mail server is that they can be backed up regularly to protect against corruption. Also, any important e-mails can be retrieved should it become necessary, even if the recipient deletes it. The flip side is that it takes an enormous amount of disk space to store all the organization's e-mails in one place. The logic behind allowing e-mails to be downloaded onto the user machines is to conserve disk space on the server. The flip side is that if the recipient deletes an important e-mail, it would not be possible to retrieve it.

Whether to store all e-mails on the e-mail server or on client machines is a decision for management. If the organization is a government department or deals with the public at large, it may be necessary to keep all e-mails for later retrieval. If the organization has no purpose to keep all e-mails for later retrieval, it may opt for allowing download of e-mails to user machines. If we decide to keep all e-mails on the server, it is better to have a separate e-mail server. If we decide not to keep e-mails on the server, we may not need a separate e-mail server.

An e-mail server can be a high-end microcomputer or a minicomputer. We do not need a mainframe computer to act as an e-mail server. Here, the basic activity is downloading and uploading e-mail. There is very little processing except for scanning each of the e-mails for viruses or sensitive information conforming to the organization's e-mail policy. In this case, the decisions are:

1. Choosing the software for the e-mail server and where to store the e-mails
2. Whether to have separate hardware to act as the e-mail server or utilize the web server machine itself (This is dependent on our decision about keeping e-mails on the server or on client machines. If we decide to keep e-mails on the server, it is better to have a separate e-mail server.)
3. Whether to use a high-end microcomputer or a minicomputer if it is decided to have a separate server (If the e-mail arrival rate, coming in

or going out, is high, get a minicomputer. Although there is no benchmark, we may obtain the speed, in messages transmitted per second, of the server from the respective vendors and compare it with our projected load. A mainframe is generally not used as an e-mail server.)

An e-mail server also needs to provide uninterrupted service 24/7. If a high-end microcomputer is chosen, fault tolerance features must be provided. These may be a standby server of similar capability or a single machine equipped with a redundant CPU, hot maintainability of hardware, and disk-mirroring capabilities so that a hardware failure will not hamper operations.

Security Server

When the application software is Internet-based and is being accessed from all over the globe, it is possible that various types of malware including viruses, worms, adware, and spyware can intrude our infrastructure and cause damage to our data/software or slow down the system. We need to protect our infrastructure against all of these by installing firewalls, antivirus and anti-spyware software, and anti-adware utilities on the servers and client machines. To make it more robust, many companies have a separate machine to handle all security threats, referred to as the *security server*. Viruses normally do not affect mainframes and minicomputers, but they can enter through web applications and cause damage to the data accessed by Internet-based software.

A security server is the machine that runs security software for the infrastructure. It may be a separate machine or it may reside on the web server. Whether to have a separate machine or use the web server itself is a decision based on the traffic and sensitivity of data being handled. This machine, as it intercepts all traffic to internal servers, must be very fast in order to maintain rapid response times. It does not need to have a large amount of RAM or disk space as it does not store data. The data would just be passing through it.

Application Server

An application server (often referred to as an app server) is not actually hardware itself but the middle layer of a software application. This software product provides some specialized services to the application software. It may be hosted on the web server or on a separate machine. Application software can access all the routines available inside the app server software using the application programming interface protocol. App servers are used more in Java-based application software to provide software services such as EJBs (Enterprise Java Beans), JSPs (Java Server Pages), Servlets, and so on. On

Microsoft platforms, an app server provides the DOT NET framework. App servers also provide a failover facility and switch to a redundant or standby server in the case of failure of the regular server. App servers provide load balancing when used in a cluster of computers so that the processing load is balanced between various server machines available in the infrastructure.

App server machines normally host the application software developed specifically for the organization (along with app server software). Therefore, the app server machine would have all the business logic necessary to process incoming data and provide the required outputs. Since an app server is basically a software product, it can be hosted on the same machine as the web server or separately.

The following aspects need to be considered while selecting the app server:

1. It must be compatible with the programming language selected for developing the application software or the COTS product chosen for implementation.
2. It must be compatible with the server hardware.
3. It must provide all the services expected from it efficiently and effectively.

Mainframe computers may not need a separate app server. Application software and the operating system itself may provide the services. Even if an app server is supported on a mainframe, it can be hosted on the same mainframe on which the web server is hosted. If we select a minicomputer that can host an app server too, we need to take the transaction processing load into consideration along with the capacity of the server and make a decision if a separate machine is required. If the web server machine has spare capacity after considering the transaction processing load, then we can host our app server on that same machine. Otherwise, there must be a separate machine.

Networking Hardware

Networking hardware consists of:

1. *Routers.* A router is a crucial Internet device that, simply put, directs Internet traffic to the desired location. A router is the interface between the organizational networks and the Internet. It will direct the incoming traffic to the appropriate organizational network and outgoing traffic to the appropriate external network. A router achieves this functionality using a combination of hardware and software that ensures the right network receives the message and that traffic is not directed to networks that are not intended to receive the traffic. This

action reduces clogging on the network. Routers come in different varieties, including edge routers, subscriber (customer) edge routers, inter-provider border routers, and core routers. It is important to know that one or more routers are essential for an organization to connect to the Internet and the size of the router is measured in the number of packets and types of data (textual/graphics/voice/video) it can handle per second. Once router size is determined, verify the offerings by vendors and select the one that best suits what is needed. Selection of the appropriate router is the most crucial decision for the organization to connect and transfer data over the Internet efficiently and effectively and to work with computers at a remote location. Routers also come with firewalls to detect and prevent intrusion by unauthorized connections. This would improve the protection of organizational data from external attacks. We should evaluate this firewall facility and include it when deciding the right router for our organization.

2. *Switches.* Switches provide a connection, either wired or wireless, between the Internet and the end-user machine. In most cases, the connection is through a router. Switches connect organizational routers to end-user computers and come in various sizes. The main determinants of a switch are the number of ports it provides and the speed it can handle. Unless we opt for a wireless network, we need to lay a cable from the switch to end-user computers. So, if we have a hundred computers, we need to have a hundred ports on the switches and lay a hundred cables from the switch bank to each of the end-user computers.
3. *Cables.* There are numerous cable alternatives available. They are either copper conductor cables or optical fiber cables. Slowly but steadily, optical fiber cables are replacing copper conductor cables in organizational networks because the speed of transmission is faster and there is better insulation from electrical noise. It is important that the cables are compatible with the selected switches and the connectors on end-user computers.

Power Requirements

Electrical power is required for running everything in the data center and the IT infrastructure. We have to estimate the requirements of electrical power for all the components of the proposed IT infrastructure. Once we do this, it will allow electrical designers to provide the appropriate type of sockets, switches, and cables to supply electrical power to all components of the proposed infrastructure. Estimate the power requirements in these categories:

Air-conditioning. Air-conditioning includes both temperature control (heating and cooling) and lessening dust and humidity. Normally, this is handled by the building designers to maintain the room temperature and working environment. Server rooms and computer banks are usually kept cooler than the rest of the office environment because of the heat the machines emit. It is key to give computer equipment details to building designers so the correct type of air conditioning is provided.

Lighting. Normally, room lighting is taken care of by the building designers as well. Lighting depends on the floor area it needs to cover. The floor area would also be computed by the building designers based on the equipment that needs to be housed inside the facility and the human resources that would work there.

Computer equipment. For computers, servers and other specialized equipment, it is crucial to understand the power these machines would consume. Desktops consume about 250 watts of power with laptops averaging about 60 watts. Monitors use about 80 watts if they are of the cathode ray tube variety and about 25 if they have a liquid crystal display. The power consumption of a server varies, but it can be upwards of 500 watts. Product specs will provide power information and these numbers should be totaled and provided to electrical designers.

Communication equipment. Gather the details of the power consumption and quantities of routers and switches for electrical designers. Each router consumes approximately 500 watts of power and each switch about 100 watts. However, make sure to review product specs carefully as the development of better components has reduced the necessary power consumption.

Backup power. Power failures, blackouts, and brownouts, although they may be rare events, are still a reality. You never know when they are going to happen or how long they will last. Sometimes, power may be there but at a much lower voltage. Because power breakdowns are unpredictable, backup power is a must for servers and communication equipment so the system remains online. The length of time that backup power is needed depends on your location. For countries like the United States, an hour of backup power may be adequate. For countries like India, two hours or more may be needed. An uninterruptible power supply (UPS) and standby generators should be used for providing backup power. A UPS, per se, would just convert direct current (DC) power to alternating current (AC), and the length of power backup depends on the number of batteries that supply the DC power. However, we cannot provide an unlimited number of batteries to extend the time of power backup. Normally, UPS backup is limited to about two hours. For longer backup power, use standby generators. Generators use fuel to generate AC power directly and can run for much longer periods depending on their design. Which one to use or both is a unique decision for each organization.

Software Sizing

Application software is necessary for the IT infrastructure. In fact, this software is the heart of the IT infrastructure. We may:

1. Implement a COTS product without customization
2. Implement a customized COTS product
3. Develop all the software from scratch
4. Develop software for some applications and implement COTS products for others

Sizing the required application software helps estimate its cost and aids the *make versus buy* decision (more on this below). To size anything, we need a unit of measure. Pounds measure the weight of an object. Feet and inches measure the length. There are multiple ways to find the size of a software product, but not one is universally accepted as the measurement standard. Some of the popular software size measures are:

1. Lines of code
2. Function points
3. Object points
4. Use case points
5. Software size units
6. Feature points
7. Internet points
8. Project size units

We have to select one of these units of measure and size the proposed application software using that unit of measure. The specifications required for measuring software size were covered in Chapter 3. (Measuring the size of software is a large subject requiring separate treatment. My book, *Software Estimation Best Practices, Tools & Techniques*, covers this topic in depth for those interested in learning more about it.)

Contracting

The objective of sizing all the components of IT infrastructure is to determine whether we should execute the work in-house or use a contractor. Obviously, we would not be able to execute all the work in-house. We need to outsource some of them. The decision on which to outsource is classically referred to as a "make vs. buy" decision.

Make vs. Buy?

Consider the following factors carefully before deciding to use an external agency:

1. If the component is available off-the-shelf, buy it.
2. If the component is not available off-the-shelf, is there a contractor that specializes in custom developing the type of component desired using the technology we want?
3. If there is a significant cost advantage (greater than 30%) then consider outsourcing the work. Ten percent of the proposed savings could be wiped out in the administrative costs of outsourcing the work to a company to build a component. Another 10 percent could be spent on overseeing the process and inward quality assurance activities. Yet, this would still result in a savings of at least 10 percent.
4. Do we already have the expertise and facilities necessary to execute the work in-house and if available, do we have the spare capacity?
5. Can the contractor deliver the component on time?
6. Is it desirable to outsource from the standpoint of protecting intellectual property rights?

Since setting up IT infrastructure is a one-time activity, outsourcing to specialized contractors is typical for the following assignments:

1. Facility design (including electrical)
2. Building the facility
3. Site preparation
4. Networking
5. Hardware supply, installation, and commissioning
6. Software development
7. Data entry for master data
8. Software implementation
9. Training

While detailed engineering is not part of project management, it is necessary to have a fair understanding of engineering activities, such as sizing the components of IT infrastructure, so that they can be managed efficiently. The intent of this chapter was to provide readers a working understanding of the subject.

5

Planning in IT Project Management

If I were given six hours to fell a tree, I would spend the first four hours sharpening the axe.

–Abraham Lincoln

He who fails to plan, plans to fail.

–Proverb

Introduction

All accounts about achieving success in any endeavor begin with the necessity to plan well. Success may be possible without planning occasionally, but it greatly increases the chances for success. Better still, planning coupled with control (from the point of view of project execution, including measuring progress and taking corrective actions) brings predictability to the probable outcome of the venture. Any human endeavor is riddled with the risk of failure. The only tool or technique that cuts that risk drastically is *planning*.

The thoroughness of planning is composed of the following:

1. *Thinking through the project.* This involves contemplating the project in terms of what (goal or objective to be accomplished), how (methodology, tools and techniques to utilize), who (resources needed), and

when (timeframe to execute each of the activities), and then firming up the alternative selection for each of these questions.
2. *Documenting the plan*. This involves capturing all the frozen (selected) alternatives in a structured manner. In fact, we need to spend more time on thinking through the project than on capturing the thinking. The document can be a hard or soft copy.
3. *Performing verification and validation quality control activities on the documented plan*. This involves carrying out peer, managerial, and expert reviews to ensure that our selection of alternatives is appropriate for the project.
4. *Organizational support for the planning activity such as a process to follow, a knowledge repository, expert assistance, and so on*. This demonstrates management's commitment to the planning and will be discussed in greater detail in later chapters.

Most managers agree on the importance of planning. But the question most often asked is, "Can I plan in my head or should planning be documented?"

Although planning is a necessity, it need not always be documented. For instance, for small short-duration endeavors, mental planning may be adequate. In fact, none of us fail to plan; we do plan. However, it is the degree of rigor of the planning (documenting it is an important part of the rigor) that is open for discussion. Documenting a plan has the following advantages:

1. The author *can review the plan* after a little time has passed to see if any important aspects were missed.
2. Humans are forgetful, especially concerning small details. Our memory becomes a little hazy after the passage of time. Documenting the plan *ensures that all details are captured* for reference by all stakeholders at a future date without having to rely on our fallible memory.
3. A documented plan acts as a *point of reference* for everyone concerned with or involved in the project.
4. *It facilitates control and performance evaluation* during execution.
5. *It facilitates validation* of the planning parameters by providing a baseline to compare the actual values generated during execution.

Except for very small projects, it is a good idea to document the plan. The next question that crops up, once you decide to document your plan, is the level of granularity. The granularity (required detail) of planning depends on:

1. The *duration* of the endeavor
2. The *number of resources* necessary

3. The *complexity* involved
4. The *relationship* between the above three aspects
5. The *geography* of the project

Now, consider the extensions to the above statements:

1. The longer the duration, the greater the necessity for increased rigor.
2. If you had all the time in the world to complete the project, the level of thoroughness and granularity would be reduced. However, in the real world, duration is often constrained and thereby increases the planning rigor.
3. Planning thoroughness increases as the number of resources deployed on a specific project increases. The higher the number of resources employed, the more thoroughness is required.
4. Complexity (of all varieties) above what is normal increases the need for planning rigor.
5. If the project is executed at one site, it would be less complex in terms of coordination. If the project is to be executed at multiple sites, the necessity for coordination increases. Clearly, multisite projects need more planning than a single-site project.
6. Different combinations of duration, number of resources employed, geography, and complexity require different levels of planning rigor.

The questions about project planning could keep coming but before proceeding further, let's first define what we mean by *planning*.

Definition of Planning

Planning is defined as the intelligent estimate of resources required to perform a predefined project successfully at a future date within a defined environment.

The key terms are:

1. *Estimate.* Estimation indicates anticipation using the best guess of the planner. It is likely to vary from the actual values. Estimation indicates that planning precedes performance. Estimation is carried out based on organizational norms (also known as organization baselines) or the best educated guess when such norms are not available. Estimation is basically a prediction of the future.
2. *Resources.* Cover the 5 Ms, "Men (people; the term *men* is only used for the sake of continuity), Materials, Methods, Money and Machines." Resources are always applied over a period of time (duration). Some resources deplete on utilization like money and materials. Other resources are recurring, like people, equipment, and methods.

3. *At a future date.* The dates for executing the project are in the future and are typically decided during the course of planning.
4. *In a defined environment.* This is the environment where the work is going to be performed. It is either known or is defined during the planning exercise. Any variation in the environment would have an effect on the plan. The environment refers to a wide variety of conditions including work logistics, workstation design, technical environment, tools, techniques, processes, methods of management, prevailing morale at the workplace, and corporate culture, to name a few.
5. *Project.* The specific scope of work defined as a *project.*

This definition gives us a framework to understand and assimilate the planning process.

Planning for IT projects is the same as planning other types of projects in many aspects but there are some unique attributes of an IT project that necessitate tailoring the planning process to fit the IT projects:

1. *Output not a product.* The deliverable is a working IT facility ready to serve end users. It is a combination of many interconnected components. The facility can include a data center, connected workstations for end users, and an open connection over the Internet to users outside the facility. It may or may not include the construction of a building. It is really bringing together a set of components from a diverse source of suppliers and putting them together to serve end users. The specialties required are heterogeneous; a multidisciplinary approach is necessary to successfully execute the project.
2. *Significant amount of preparatory work.* There is an unusually large amount of preparatory work in IT projects to determine the transaction processing loads, sizing of various components, make-buy decisions, finalizing the subcontractors, and so on.
3. *Multiple plans.* The IT project needs a number of plans and if application software for the proposed project is intended to be developed in-house, then even more plans need to be prepared for the many additional aspects of software development as this requires meticulous planning.
4. *Recent origin.* IT projects are relatively new phenomena. In the early days, it was just site preparation for the data center for a single-tier computing facility. Now, it is multitiered computing not limited to the data center alone and covering the end user too. Because of its recency, there is little documented experience or a body of knowledge available to guide the implementation.

5. *A program.* An IT project consists of multiple independent projects. They are facility construction/site preparation, electrical preparation, network cabling, and last but not least, software development. Each of these is a major project in and of itself, needing a different specialization. Therefore, an IT project is in fact a program comprising multiple projects, especially in large organizations.
6. *High amount of coordination.* It is very difficult to execute an entire IT project with in-house resources and even if the project is executed with in-house resources, there are going to be multiple specialties. Most likely, there will be multiple subcontractors so coordination becomes an important aspect of an IT project. If the IT project is not coordinated diligently, there will be many incongruent supplies waiting for their forward or backward activities to be started/completed. This will not only delay the project, but also escalate the costs.
7. The project has a *definite beginning and end* just as any other project.
8. The project *deliverable* is IT infrastructure ready for operation.
9. The *activities* in an IT project include sizing of components, determining the subcontractors, placing work orders with subcontractors, executing in-house tasks, coordinating the work of the subcontractors, receiving deliverables and carrying out inward quality control activities, deployment, integrating the infrastructure, quality control of the integrated facility, beta testing, and handover.

Due to the high amount of coordination demanded to obtain every component just-in-time, the rigor of planning assumes more significance than in other projects. In some engineering projects, a simple schedule based on a program evaluation and review technique/critical path method (PERT/CPM) would suffice, whereas IT projects (especially large ones) require increased control and more planning documents. The plans that are typically required are described in subsequent sections.

Types of Plans Prepared by Software Project Management

We need to prepare a number of plans for rolling out IT infrastructure in the organization. This section covers that subject with an exhaustive IT infrastructure in mind. You may scale down the planning depending on the size of your IT infrastructure. It is crucial to keep one thing in mind: Planning is not an exercise in document creation. Rather, it is an exercise in thinking through the project and of capturing that thinking in document form for reference by all the stakeholders of the project. Documentation is the result of planning but not *the* planning itself.

Here are the plans that are typically prepared in a large IT project:

1. Floor plan
2. Deployment plan
3. Application software development plan
4. Installation and commissioning plan
5. Data preparation plan for master data
6. Training plan
7. Quality assurance plan
8. Procurement plan
9. Networking plan
10. Risk management plan
11. Overall project schedule
12. Software maintenance plan
13. Infrastructure maintenance plan
14. Operations plan

Let's discuss each of them in greater detail.

Floor Plan

Floor plans are prepared when constructing a new facility or modifying an existing facility to suit the data center. Sometimes these are also referred to as "building construction drawings." Rolling out IT infrastructure involves placing components in the right place. If we are implementing a call center or software development center, almost every person in the organization would be equipped with a workstation. In such cases, we need to draw up the floor plan for the entire organization. In other cases, we need to prepare the floor plan for the data center and the places where computer workstations need to be deployed. This floor plan is an engineering drawing prepared by architects. The plans should be drawn to scale, dimensioned and helpful in planning network cabling. Floor plans are used for preparing the deployment plan (see next section). Floor plans include elevations, sectional views, and bills of material so that the construction contractor can build the facility using these drawings. If the building is already available, we do not have to prepare the floor plan anew.

Deployment Plan

The deployment plan shows where each component of the proposed IT infrastructure would be placed. It would also include details of the software that would be loaded on each of the servers and workstations. The deployment plan comprises three distinct items:

1. Deployment plan document
2. Deployment drawing
3. Deployment bill of material (BOM)

The deployment document contains details of the placement of IT components in the facility, earmarking the location of each of the components. The deployment document should include all details of the deployment plan. Figure 5.1 depicts the elements of a suggested template for the deployment plan document.

A basic equipment deployment plan drawing is depicted in Figure 5.2. It is a simplified drawing showing the placement of equipment in the server room. An actual drawing would contain the dimensions and references to BOM, cabling, etc.

Application Software Development Plan

Application software is a major component of an IT project. Hardware may be costlier than the software, but it is more or less available off-the-shelf. Application software, on the other hand, needs to be custom developed from

<*Title page*> **Deployment plan** **For <*Project ID*>** Revision history: <End of *Title page*>
Table of contents page
1. Introduction 2. References 3. Hardware deployment drawing 4. Bill of material 5. Schedule 6. Quality control activities 7. Handover plan 8. Waivers
Software deployment plan

Figure 5.1 Elements for the deployment plan document template (template exhibited in Appendix I)

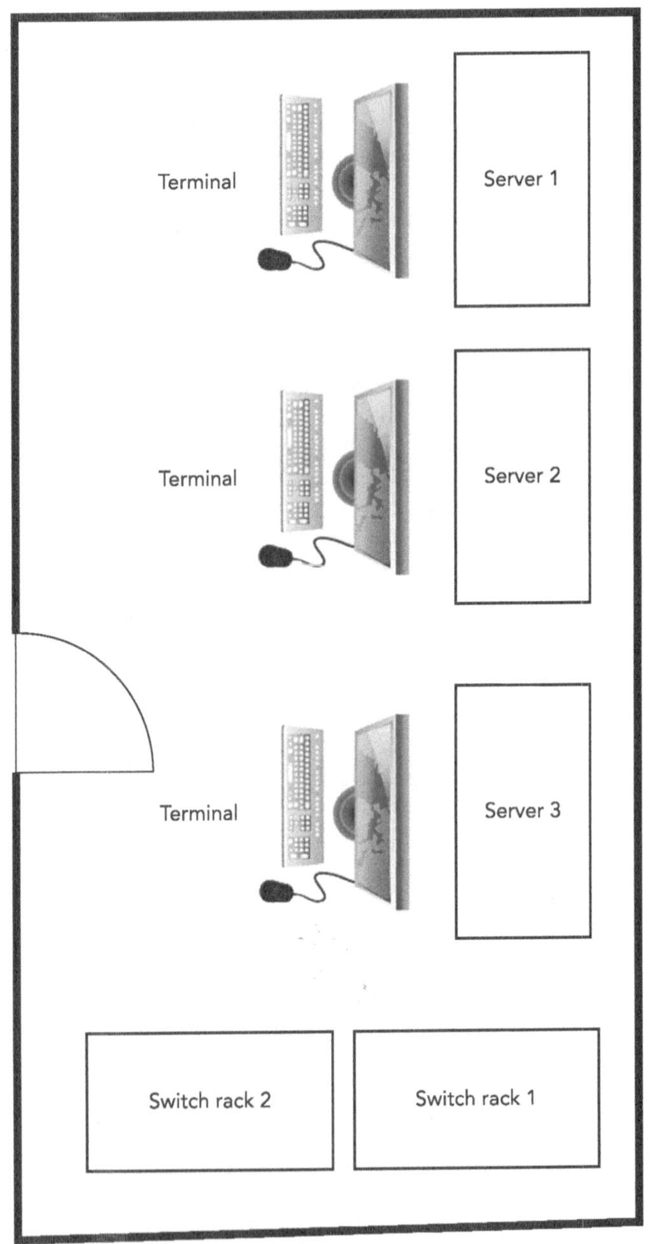

Figure 5.2 A sample equipment deployment plan

scratch. Even if we implement a commercial off-the-shelf (COTS) product, it still needs to be customized to suit the unique needs of the organization and then implemented. It takes more time to develop/implement than to procure the requisite hardware. Therefore, meticulous planning is required for software development activity. The following aspects of software development have to be thoroughly thought out to ensure success, and the final decisions made should be recorded in a software development plan for reference by all:

1. Strategy for acquiring the application software:
   a. Implementation of a COTS product with or without customization
   b. Development from scratch, either in-house or outsourced or a combination of both
   c. A combination of COTS product implementation and fresh development
2. Implementation strategy:
   a. In-house
   b. Outsourced
3. Software development life cycle
4. Quality assurance for the software
5. Software maintenance
6. Staffing
7. Change management
8. Delivery
9. Coding and other standards
10. Implementation

Documentation ensures that all stakeholders are on the same page and also acts as a point of reference. Figure 5.3 depicts the elements of a suggested template for developing a software development plan.

Installation and Commissioning Plan

The installation and commissioning plan includes the following activities: installing the hardware with its corresponding software, networking, testing the installation, and parallel run and cutover to the new system. It is possible to have multiple deliveries of application software, which means that we need to synchronize the deliveries of corresponding hardware to the delivery schedule of application software. This requires planning. Figure 5.4 depicts the elements of a suggested template for preparing the installation and commissioning plan.

<Title page>
Software development plan
For *<Project ID>*

Revision history:
<End of *Title page*>

Table of contents page

1. Introduction
2. References
3. Strategy for acquiring the application software
4. Implementation strategy
5. Software development life cycle
6. Quality assurance for the software
7. Standards
8. Software maintenance
9. Staffing
10. Change management
11. Delivery
12. Implementation
13. Roles and responsibilities
14. Managerial methods, tools and techniques
15. Communication
16. Issue resolution
17. Escalation
18. Risk management

Figure 5.3 Elements for the software development plan document template (template exhibited in Appendix I)

Data Preparation Plan for Master Data

Most application software, including COTS products, need master data to enable end users to start using the software. Unless we prepare the master data and load them in the appropriate files/tables, the entire IT infrastructure cannot be put to effective use. Master data would include information like employee data, vendor master, customer master, material master, account codes, prices, rates, discounts, routes, classes, categories, billing plans, and so on. Once the master data are in place, transactions can occur to accomplish business objectives and generate transaction data.

Similar to previous options, the preparation of master data can be done in-house or outsourced. Here is another make-or-buy decision. If we have spare resources and the software for capturing the master data is ready, then we

<*Title page*> **Installation and commissioning plan** **For <*Project ID*>** Revision history: <End of *Title page*>
Table of contents page
1. Introduction 2. References 3. Facilities 4. Hardware details 5. Software details 6. Installation team 7. Roles and responsibilities 8. Installation procedures 9. Quality control 10. User training 11. Piloting plan 12. Cutover plan 13. Handover plan 14. Schedule 15. Any other item

Figure 5.4 Elements for the installation and commissioning plan template (template exhibited in Appendix I)

can prepare the master data in-house. But this is a slim possibility. Normally, organizations outsource the work of preparing the master data because of the following advantages:

1. There is no need to release/spare resources (people, computers, software, and time) for preparing the master data.
2. There are plenty of organizations specializing in data preparation that would offer significant cost, schedule, and quality advantages.
3. We do not have to develop the software for capturing the data.

A detailed plan for this activity is not normally prepared. We capture this plan in the schedule to accomplish the activity, which includes the following:

1. Determining the course of action—in-house or outsourced
2. If the decision is for in-house preparation, the activities are:
   a. Create master data tables
   b. Develop software for capturing master data

   c. Allocate resources
   d. Train operators in data entry
   e. Enter data
   f. Verify data
3. If the decision is to outsource, the activities are:
   a. Identify agencies specialized in data preparation
   b. Obtain price quotes
   c. Select the agency and place the order
   d. Provide the selected agency with master data, perhaps in paper form
   e. Monitor progress
   f. Receive data and subject them to inward quality control activities
   g. Load data into master data tables
   h. Verify the master data files/tables for accuracy

Sometimes when we are migrating, porting, or converting an existing application, the master data would already be available, albeit in a different format. These data need conversion. The new system is most likely to need more data fields in the master data records than in the existing system. So, in addition to data conversion, the missing data may need to be entered. The following are the steps for data conversion/migration:

1. Study the existing and the new data formats.
2. Map the existing data fields with the new data fields.
3. Develop software to read from the existing master data files/tables and load data into new master data files/tables.
4. Perform quality control activities on the new master data files/tables to ensure integrity of converted/migrated data.
5. Carry out data entry for the new data fields added in the new master data files/tables. This may be carried out in-house or outsourced. The steps for data entry were enumerated in the preceding section.

This plan is normally embedded in the schedule of the IT project itself or a separate schedule can be prepared. What we need to ensure is that the master data files/tables should be ready by the time the application software is ready so that the software can utilize the master data files/tables to test the software effectively.

Training Plan

As part of an IT infrastructure project, the following training is necessary:

1. *End-user training*. Train end users to efficiently utilize the system for transaction processing and to perform their business functions. They will be trained on the functionality provided in the system to get their work done and will be taken through screen and report layouts to either capture or extract information as necessary.
2. *Systems administration training*. The designated individuals need to administer the system efficiently by learning how to take backups, restore data whenever necessary, perform user management (add/delete users, grant/modify user privileges), enforce security policies, produce exception reports, and so on.
3. *Network administration training*. The network is a major component in the IT infrastructure, especially when it comes to keeping users connected to servers and providing security from intruders, viruses, malware attacks, and data theft. We need to train the network administrators in the topology and architecture of the infrastructure, maintenance (both preventive and breakdown) of the network components, reporting incidents, incident tracking and resolution, etc.
4. *Management information system (MIS) training for managers*. Managers are one set of end users that have special requirements. They may not perform business transactions but they extract data through reports to make decisions and guide operations. We need to train them regarding special MIS reports and how to extract and interpret these reports.

For each of the training programs, we need to arrange for:

1. Training materials including presentation slides, reading handouts, exercises if necessary, and faculty notes
2. Faculty who can handle training sessions and impart training to the participants
3. Training equipment like PC projectors, classrooms, scribbling pads, etc.
4. Scheduling training programs in consultation with the concerned departments
5. Release of individuals for training
6. Preparation of materials for obtaining and evaluating feedback on the training

We can include these details in the schedule of the IT project itself or prepare a separate schedule using a software package like MS Project or an Excel spreadsheet.

Quality Assurance Plan

This is a very critical plan for the project. It is in this plan that we capture all the quality assurance activities for the deliverables as well as for the entire project itself. Quality control activities in IT infrastructure projects include:

1. Verification of artifacts:
    a. Peer review
    b. Managerial review
    c. Expert review
2. Validation:
    a. Inward quality control
        i. Testing of components/equipment as appropriate
        ii. Verification of code/information artifacts
        iii. Testing of source code artifacts as appropriate
    b. Software quality control:
        i. Verification of quality records
        ii. Acceptance testing
    c. IT infrastructure testing:
        i. Inspection of installation and deployment
        ii. Deployment testing
        iii. Network testing
        iv. Security testing
        v. Acceptance testing

We will discuss quality control in Chapter 9 as we are dealing with the planning aspects here. It is a good idea to document all the proposed quality assurance activities in a separate plan document. We need to make decisions about the processes, procedures, standards, guidelines, formats, templates, and checklists selected for use in the project as a means of preventing errors and defects. Then we need to determine the type of quality control activities to be performed against each of the proposed project activities. These are documented so that all the stakeholders can implement this plan in their activities to achieve the quality objectives of the project. Figure 5.5 depicts the elements of a suggested template to capture a quality assurance plan for an IT project.

Procurement Plan

Procurement is an activity that involves external organizations and legal contracting. Therefore, most organizations have a procurement process that has

<*Title page*> **Quality assurance plan** **For <*Project ID*>** Revision history: <End of *Title page*>
Table of contents page
1. Introduction 2. References 3. Quality objectives for the project 4. Quality control activities 5. Audits 6. Defect resolution 7. Metrics and measurement 8. Waivers

Figure 5.5 Elements for the quality assurance plan template (template exhibited in Appendix I)

been vetted and approved by their legal department. IT project managers do not usually define or improve the organizational procurement process, but still have to plan for carrying out procurement activities in conformance with the organization's approved purchase process. The following items need to be determined and documented for effective implementation by the execution team:

1. Items identified for procurement from outside the organization
2. Items that need to be manufactured to order
3. Services needed from specialized agencies including software development and networking
4. Timelines for each of the actions
5. The people/agencies responsible for taking various procurement actions

Procurement processes and subcontractor management are dealt with in greater detail in Chapter 6. The elements of a suggested template to capture the procurement plan can be found in Figure 5.6.

Networking Plan

Networking involves the following activities:

1. *Installing the router*. This involves putting the router in the designated place. Cables from the Internet and to the network switches are connected to it.

<*Title page*> **Procurement plan** **For <*Project ID*>** Revision history: <End of *Title page*>
Table of contents page
1. Introduction 2. References 3. List of items decided for procurement 4. Schedule 5. Waivers

Figure 5.6 Elements for the procurement plan template (template exhibited in Appendix I)

2. *Installing network switches*. This involves mounting the switches in the switch rack and providing power to them. Cables from the router and the workstations/servers are then connected to it.
3. *Laying cables*. This involves running the cables from each of the workstations/servers to the switch rack. Then terminate the cables at both ends with appropriate connectors so that they can be plugged into the concerned machine.
4. *Making connections to the equipment*. This involves plugging the cable terminations into the designated sockets on the machines, assigning IP addresses to each of the machines, and mapping them to the servers so they can connect with each other.
5. *Establishing connectivity to the Internet*. Once all equipment is installed and the cables have been laid out, connect the router to the Internet by activating our account with the selected Internet service provider.
6. *Testing and handover*. Test the connectivity from each of the workstations to the server and the Internet to ensure connectivity is properly available. Also, test the connectivity from the servers to the Internet and to some sample workstations. Examine the connection from an external computer to connect to the web server over the Internet to make certain connections are operational. Similarly, send a test e-mail to check the availability of our e-mail server. We should also perform cursory testing of the application software. Detailed application software testing is part of the acceptance of the application software from the development team.

Of all the above activities, laying out the cables is the most time consuming one. A plan document for this activity is usually included in the project schedule, although we can create a separate schedule and link it to the project schedule if necessary.

Risk Management Plan

An IT project, being very large and comprising many sub-projects, is much more prone to risk than many other types of projects. These risks could stem from equipment issues (servers, workstations, networking equipment, cabling, system software, application software, etc.) and people issues (organizational management and human resources). Risk management planning is vital if we wish to successfully implement IT infrastructure in an organization. The following activities form part of this process:

1. *Risk identification.* This is primarily a planning activity. Identify all sources of risk. These may arise from equipment selection (bad equipment may not hinder the implementation of the infrastructure but would affect the operations, but a delay in the selection of equipment would hamper project execution), selection of bad suppliers and contractors (especially for laying cables), software development, facility design and facility preparation, project human resources, and timely availability of funds. We need to identify all such risks so that mitigation activities can be planned for each.
2. *Risk quantification.* For each of the identified risks, estimate the probability of its occurrence as well as the damage it can cause in dollar terms. Obtain the probable damage by multiplying the risk damage (in $) by the probability of its occurrence. This computation should be completed for each of the identified risks. The summation of all the individual risk values equals the risk value of the entire project. This will give us an idea of what is at stake so that we can plan accordingly.
3. *Risk prioritization.* For each of the risks identified and quantified, assign a priority based on its risk value and probability of occurrence. Assign the highest priority to the risk whose value is the highest. If two risks have equal risk value, allocate a higher priority to the one with higher probability. Ensure that all the identified risks are assigned an appropriate priority.
4. *Identification of risk mitigation activities.* For each of the identified risks, determine appropriate mitigation activities. These may include risk prevention where possible, risk impact reduction activities, or

corrective actions if the risk cannot be prevented. These activities would depend on each of the types of risks.

5. *Implementation of risk mitigation activities.* During the execution of the project, implement and manage appropriate risk mitigation actions identified in the risk plan.

Figure 5.7 depicts the elements of a suggested risk management plan. It is normal practice to utilize an Excel spreadsheet or a specialized project management tool for this activity.

Overall Project Schedule

We need to prepare a schedule for the entire IT project. Normally, this is done in a software tool like MS Project or Primavera, both of which are based on PERT/CPM. Project managers should have a working knowledge of PERT/CPM or be trained on this subject (Appendix D provides an introduction). In preparing a schedule using a software tool, carry out the following activities:

1. Prepare a work breakdown structure comprising all the activities that need to be completed in order to execute the project successfully. The work breakdown structure would be embedded between two events, namely, the *Start* event and the *End* event.
2. Define the precedence relationships between the activities enumerated in the work breakdown structure. That is, ensure that every activity has at least one predecessor and one successor, excluding the *Start* event and *End* event which would not have a predecessor or successor respectively.
3. Allocate resources to each of the enumerated activities in the work breakdown structure. Resources would include people, time, money, and equipment.
4. Level the resource allocation such that no resource is overallocated in any time period.
5. View the network diagram and ensure that there is no dangling node in the network. A dangling node is an activity that is not connected to

Risk ID	Risk description	Risk probability	Risk damage ($)	Risk value ($)	Risk priority	Mitigation actions

Figure 5.7 Elements for the risk management plan template (template exhibited in Appendix I)

another activity either by a predecessor or a successor. Of course, the exceptions are the *Start* and *End* events.

Now the schedule is ready. The end date for the project is automatically computed by the software tool. Verify that the computed end date is acceptable. If not, we may need to pump in extra resources to reduce the project duration. This is also dealt with in Appendix D.

Software Maintenance Plan

Although software maintenance begins at the end of the IT project, we need to plan and be ready to take over the maintenance from the development team. Adopt one of the following strategies for software maintenance:

1. If the development of the application software is in-house, we may:
   a. Retain a few of the members from the development team to carry out software maintenance.
   b. Allocate a separate set of individuals for software maintenance work. In this case, the maintenance team must be trained in the design of the software and code maintenance methodology.
2. If the application software development was outsourced, we may:
   a. Outsource the software maintenance to the same organization that developed the application software.
   b. Outsource the software maintenance to an organization that specializes in software maintenance. In this case, the new organization would need to be trained in the application software functionality, design, and maintenance methodology.
   c. Take up software maintenance in-house. In this case, too, train the new team in the application software functionality, design, and maintenance methodology.
3. In either case, assign a project manager to coordinate the software maintenance work either with an in-house or outsourced team.

Now, to ensure that software maintenance work starts off smoothly, plan the following activities:

1. Determine the strategy for software maintenance, either in-house or outsourced.
2. Training the maintenance team to:
   a. Prepare the course/training material
   b. Determine the schedule of classroom training and hands-on training

   c. Conduct classroom training
   d. Conduct hands-on training
3. Determine the handover/takeover procedures.
4. Effect handover to the maintenance team.
5. Handhold the maintenance team for an initial period as necessary.

Figure 5.8 depicts the elements of a suggested template for preparing the software maintenance plan.

Infrastructure Maintenance Plan

All infrastructure needs maintenance. We normally carry out two kinds of maintenance: preventive and breakdown. Preventive maintenance, as the name suggests, is carried out to prevent equipment breakdown. Breakdown maintenance is undertaken to restore equipment to its working condition.

There are three types of preventive maintenance:

1. *Duration-based preventive maintenance*. Carry out preventive maintenance periodically (weekly, monthly, quarterly, etc.). This is done primarily where there are moving parts. Ensure electrical terminations are tight and free from dust and clean electronic equipment periodically. Dust is one of the major causes of electronic equipment (including computers) breakdown.

<*Title page*> **Software maintenance plan** **For <*Project ID*>** Revision history: <End of *Title page*>
Table of contents page
1. Introduction 2. References 3. Strategy for software maintenance 4. Software maintenance team 5. Initial training plan 6. Induction training plan 7. Metrics to be collected and analyzed

Figure 5.8 Elements for the software maintenance plan template (template exhibited in Appendix I)

2. *Condition-based preventive maintenance.* Monitor the condition of the equipment and carry out preventive maintenance whenever the equipment is on the brink of a breakdown. For some equipment, condition monitoring tools are available to alert us if maintenance is needed. In some cases, we can use the number of hours worked as the indicator of required maintenance while at other times a visual inspection will do the trick.
3. *Recommendation-based preventive maintenance.* For some equipment, preventive maintenance would be performed based on the manufacturer's recommendations in cases where those exist.

Breakdown maintenance is carried out whenever a breakdown of equipment is reported. This type of maintenance is usually managed through service-level agreements.

It is important to record all these activities in the infrastructure maintenance plan. However, infrastructure maintenance is part of operations. Therefore, this is a periodic plan prepared by the operations team and not really part of an IT project. It would start only after the IT project is completed and handed over to the operations team.

Operations Plan

This plan sets out how the IT infrastructure would be used. Unless the objectives to be achieved by setting up the IT infrastructure are defined and documented, the project itself would not be approved. The feasibility study would also document the objectives and the proposed utilizations at least in a rudimentary manner. A more detailed plan would be prepared by the operations team, which should be updated periodically after the IT project is completed and handed over to operations.

Quality Control of Planning

All the plans prepared ought to be subjected to quality control activities. Therefore, have them peer reviewed first and implement the feedback received. Then, before these are approved for use, a managerial review is carried out by the approving authority. Only after these two reviews are successfully completed would they be approved and used for executing the project.

Scaling of Planning in IT Project Management

Are all these plans required for every project? Not necessarily. All of these plans in the templates depicted in this chapter are required for large IT projects. In small IT projects, only a schedule may be adequate. In a medium-sized IT project perhaps some of these plans would be prepared. How many and what plans are required for a specific project depends primarily on the size of the infrastructure proposed and the confidence of the project manager and management that the organization can implement the infrastructure. Mature organizations that specialize in setting up IT infrastructure for other organizations usually use only the schedule as their plan, and standard operating procedures would enable project execution at peak efficiency. Organizations setting up IT infrastructure for the first time should make exhaustive plans. The required number of plans and their thoroughness are relative to the maturity level of the organization implementing the infrastructure.

Funds Flow Planning

Is the management of project finances a responsibility of the project manager (PM)? Does it not belong to the finance department? Good questions. Generally management of finances is the responsibility of senior management and the finance department. But it is the PM who projects the requirement of funds to execute the project as well as the receipts from project execution.

IT projects spend a significant amount of funds for the payment of procured items and to subcontractors for services rendered. IT projects are both revenue-earning (in the form of professional fee receipts from external IT projects executed for clients) and costly. The IT project manager plays a critical role in making payments as well as obtaining funds. Different aspects of funds flow management can be found in Chapter 8 and the topic of planning will be covered there.

This book has free material available for download from the Web Added Value™ resource center at *www.jrosspub.com*

6

Project Execution

Introduction

Project execution is that phase of the project in which the real work gets done. It is an action phase. Any human endeavor including IT projects, however well planned and initiated, can fail if the execution phase is not managed well. In fact, most of the planning done on projects in general is to ensure that this critical phase goes smoothly without any problems and is executed effectively and efficiently. IT projects are no exception. Results need to be delivered effectively (on time, without defects, and fulfill all promised functionality) and efficiently (conserve resources, produce a profit, and minimize waste).

During IT project execution, we perform the following activities:

1. Procure hardware
2. Procure system software including DBMS (Database Management System), configuration management tools, development and testing tools
3. Prepare specifications and acquisition of application software
4. Finalize subcontractors
5. Receive and deploy servers
6. Receive networking hardware and build communication network
7. Receive and deploy system software
8. Prepare master data tables/files
9. Receive and deploy application software
10. Define systems and procedures for running the operations
11. Recruit and train personnel for operations

12. Procure consumables for operation
13. Contract/contractor management
14. Set up configuration management process
15. Train end users in operating the system
16. Conduct trial runs
17. Change over to new system
18. Initiate maintenance

Let us discuss each of these in more detail in the following sections.

Procurement of Hardware

The first step in setting up IT infrastructure involves installing hardware. Therefore, we would procure the required hardware, unless the organization happened to be manufacturing computer hardware. Details of the hardware needed for the project would become known after completion of the hardware sizing exercise. Using these specifications and quantities, we would carry out the following steps to procure the needed hardware:

1. *Procurement initiation.* Most organizations have a dedicated purchasing/procurement department. Therefore, the IT project manager would need to raise a procurement requisition on the department to arrange for the procurement of the required hardware. The procurement requisition should contain the following information:
   a. *The project ID.* This is required for booking the expenditure.
   b. *Description of the item to be procured.* This should be in general terms so that price quotes can be obtained from multiple manufacturers/vendors.
   c. *Quantity of the item.* This should include the quantity actually required as well as spares, if any might be required. Spares should not be added for higher-end equipment such as servers and computers, only for low-cost hardware items like connectors, networking cables, and so on. Spares are added because some of the materials may be damaged during installation. If work stops for want of a low-cost item, the impact of the stoppage on costs may be much higher than the cost of the additional items (spares). We do not want the situation described in the adage "for want of a nail the battle was lost!"
   d. *Date the item is required.* This is the date the item needs to be delivered by the vendor. It is important to build in and ensure adequate time for inward quality control, including replacement

of any incorrect or defective items received and perhaps delivery to the installation site, as the vendor may not have been instructed to deliver the items directly to the installation site. The point to be noted is that vendor delivery date is not the same as the date the items are required at the installation site. It is slightly earlier.

2. *Procurement.* Once the procurement requisition is received by the purchasing department, the procurement action begins. The steps taken by the purchasing department are typically as follows:
   a. The first step is obtaining price quotes from probable vendors. These can be obtained in a variety of ways or forms including written paper quotes, verbal telephone quotes, or via vendor websites or price lists. Some purchasing departments may have price contracts from a few vendors for the required equipment in which case, orders can be placed immediately. In other words, these purchasing departments previously researched and evaluated pricing and terms offered by various vendors for their potential parts and equipment needs and have already negotiated and contracted agreed prices and terms. This would obviously make the process of obtaining price quotes unnecessary.
   b. If quotes are required and obtained, they are usually tabulated to show the comparative item specifications along with their price and terms. This information is sent to the originator of the procurement requisition. The originator considers the pricing, delivery schedules, and item specifications offered by the vendors researched and selects a vendor based on pricing, delivery dates, and terms. The originator then forwards the recommendation to the purchasing department.
   c. The purchasing department refers the recommendation to the finance department for allocation of funds. True, the budget for the project is approved and the requirement of funds is projected. But firm provision of funds is made before the purchase order is placed with the vendor. Once the purchase order is placed, the organization is legally bound to effect payment against the supplies. Therefore, we refer the recommendation to the finance department so they can consolidate the requirement of funds from various agencies in the organization and make those funds available at the right time. Sometimes the finance department may not be able to make funds available at the time requested due to heavy demand on outflows from various agencies. In such cases,

the delivery may need to be advanced or postponed. Or extended payment terms may need to be negotiated with the vendor. This step in the procurement action is the commitment of funds for the purchase.

d. Upon commitment of funds and receiving concurrence from finance, the purchasing department would place the purchase order with the recommended vendor for supply of the item. One purchase order may contain multiple items. The actual form of a purchase order varies depending on the practice prevalent with the organization. It may be a paper- or web-based order, an e-mail, or even be placed over the phone. Normally, each purchase order is sent with the organization's terms and conditions of the purchase. This may also be communicated by a reference to their standard terms and conditions. (Note: A purchase order is a legal document and can be produced in a court of law on demand of the concerned parties.)
e. The vendor needs to communicate the acceptance of the order formally either through an acceptance letter on paper or e-mail or on their web-based procurement system. Unless formal acceptance is received from the vendor, the purchase order cannot be deemed to be in effect.

3. *Supply*. The vendor delivers the supply of the ordered items. The supply can be delivered to the installation site directly or to a central warehouse if the consignment includes items for multiple projects. In such a case, the organization ships the required quantity to each of the project sites.
4. *Quality control*. The received item is processed through the firm's inward quality control to ensure that the right item was supplied in good condition and is working. These quality control activities normally include inspection and cursory testing. Once the item passes through quality control it will be passed on for the next stage, that is, usage in the project and for effecting payment to the vendor. If any individual item fails, a rejection report would be sent to the purchasing department to obtain replacements from the vendor.
5. *Payment*. Once the item passes the inward quality control and replacements for the defective items are received, the purchasing department passes on the vendor's invoice to the finance department with a recommendation for effecting payment. The finance department would then make payment either through a check or direct deposit to the vendor's bank account. Sometimes the finance department withholds a part of the amount against a performance guarantee, or shortfall in

supply quantity, or defective items. Once payment is made and accepted by the vendor, the purchase transaction is completed.

The foregoing is a very simplified and abridged purchase process. The actual process would be much more elaborate and cover many more alternatives and contingencies. This short narration is included to give readers an insight to the purchase process. For those interested in gaining a comprehensive understanding of purchasing and materials management, I recommend a visit to either the American Purchasing Society or Institute of Supply Management on-line bookstores.

Procurement of System Software

Procurement of system software such as the operating system for servers and workstations is ordered along with the hardware itself. The operating system is not separated from the computer hardware, but there is other system software that needs to be procured separately. This software is as follows:

1. RDBMS (Relational Database Management System), which supports data of the system
2. E-mail server to handle the e-mail communication system of the organization
3. Middle-tier applications such as application servers or frameworks that facilitate functioning of the application software
4. Configuration management tools that manage changes to the application software in production systems as well as protect their integrity
5. Data backup tools (Normally the RDBMS comes with its own backup and restore tools but there are other artifacts to be backed up. These include application software, information artifacts, e-mail files, audit trails, and so on. For these, specialized backup and restore tools are needed.)
6. Application software development kit and maintenance for it thereafter
7. Security tools such as antivirus software, firewalls, intruder prevention, detection, and tracking tools
8. Network monitoring tools
9. Administrative utilities for efficiently managing the data center
10. Any other software tools specific to the organization

Currently, most software is marketed and sold over the Internet, but some software is still marketed and sold in the traditional manner in the form of CDs against check payment. The specifications are usually available in the feasibility report. Using these specifications, the project manager needs to raise a procurement request on the purchasing department to procure these items conforming to the organizational purchase process described briefly in the preceding section.

Preparation of Specifications and Acquisition of Application Software

As previously stated, the feasibility report should contain specifications for application software at least in a rudimentary manner. The strategy for acquiring application software should also be included in the feasibility report. Our next steps would be to finalize the specifications for the application software and move forward with its acquisition conforming to the strategy decided during the feasibility study. It might be necessary to revisit the users to determine and finalize the detailed specifications required. Next we will discuss the possible strategies and the corresponding activities or steps that need to be performed for each course of action.

Commercial Off-the-Shelf Product Implementation

If the strategy is to implement a commercial off-the-shelf (COTS) product, we need to acquire the product first. Usually, some amount of customization is necessary for any COTS product implementation.

If a decision was made to customize the product in-house, the following steps should be performed:

1. Train in-house business analysts on product functionality.
2. Have business analysts carry out a gap analysis between the functionality available in the COTS product and organizational requirements.
3. Train in-house programmers on the customization programming language provided with the COTS product.
4. Initiate the project for developing the customized software layer for the product.
5. Accept delivery of the customization software layer and integrate it with the COTS product.
6. Roll out the software.

If a decision was made to outsource customization, the following steps should be performed:

1. Identify the subcontractor for outsourcing the work of customization.
2. Place a purchase order conforming to the purchase process of the organization for building the customized software layer.

3. Identify an in-house coordinator for the customization project.
4. Monitor project progress.
5. Conduct an acceptance test of the customized software layer on completion and accept it.
6. Integrate the layer with the product and roll out.

Fresh Development of Software

If a decision was made to develop the software afresh, the alternatives of developing it in-house or outsourcing it need to be considered.

If our decision was to develop the software in-house, the steps or activities to be performed are as follows:

1. Identify the software project manager.
2. Initiate the project.
3. Plan the project.
4. Allocate business analysts and software designers.
5. Conduct a detailed requirements' study and finalize the project requirements.
6. Carry out the software design.
7. Allocate programmers.
8. Develop the software in conformance with organizational processes and approved software design.
9. Carry out the required testing to ensure the software is defect free.
10. Deliver the software for implementation.
11. Close the project and release allocated resources.

Development of application software is an independent project that we would initiate, plan, and execute. However, the management of a software development project is by itself a large topic and therefore beyond the scope of this book. Anyone interested in gaining a comprehensive understanding of this topic should read *Mastering Software Project Management: Best Practices, Tools and Techniques*, by Murali Chemuturi and Thomas M. Cagley Jr., published by J. Ross Publishing.

If our decision was to outsource the software development, the steps or activities to be performed are as follows:

1. Prepare an RFP (request for proposal) and forward it to probable software development organizations.
2. Receive proposals for software development.
3. Finalize the vendor to whom the work of software development is to be awarded and place the purchase order in conformance with the organizational purchase process.

4. Monitor project progress.
5. Finalize acceptance testing plans.
6. Once the software development is completed, verify the quality records of the development team to ascertain due diligence shown during software development to ensure a defect free software product.
7. Carry out acceptance testing and resolve all issues.
8. Accept delivery of the software for implementation.
9. Make payment to the vendor for services rendered in conformance with the purchase order and the purchase process of the organization.

Gaining an understanding of the possible strategies that have been covered here, as well as the importance of preparing thorough and accurate specifications, cannot be overemphasized. While we would implement whatever strategy was decided upon during the project feasibility study, it is imperative that we acquire the application software necessary for the IT project. Application software is the backbone of an IT infrastructure. All necessary precautions and care must be taken to ensure the software is developed to our requirements and without defects. Its success defines the success of the IT infrastructure.

Finalize Subcontractors

Most IT infrastructure implementation projects need to subcontract some portion of the work. Apart from application software development, the following would be considered for subcontracting:

1. Facility design
2. Facility construction
3. Networking
4. Master data preparation

Facility Design

If no preexisting space is available for our proposed data center, we may have to design the facility including the construction portion.

If a facility already exists with spare space for extension and is available for use, we might not have to design the construction portion of the facility, but merely modify it to suit our data center requirements.

Sometimes building space may be made available which can be converted to a data center. In this case, the layout needs to be designed for the conversion to be carried out. So we would hire an architect to either design a new facility or the conversion of existing building space into a data center that meets our requirements, as well as a building contractor to construct/convert our facility. The architect would normally be expected to deliver the engineering drawings, bills of material enumerating those materials required for constructing the facility, and a cost estimate for the proposed facility. Architects usually charge 1–3% of the estimated cost of the facility as their professional fee.

Assuming our decision was to subcontract this work, we would need to provide details about the following to the architect:

1. Equipment to be installed inside the data center
2. Overall outside dimensions of each piece of equipment for determining space requirements
3. Electrical power required by each piece of equipment for designing the electrical wiring needed inside the data center
4. Rate of heat produced by equipment installed for planning air-conditioning requirements (This is usually expressed in British thermal units per hour of operation and would normally be available in equipment catalogs.)
5. Equipment anchoring specifications, if any required, for planning the anchoring facilities
6. Equipment vibration dampening requirements, if any, for designing a vibration dampening facility (Some equipment such as heavy-duty printers can cause vibrations that need to be dampened.)
7. Network cables to be routed to installed equipment including sizes and numbers for designing the cable layout plan
8. Type of lighting required inside the data center
9. Other special facilities required, if any, inside the data center

With these details, the architect would be able to design the data center facility. If aesthetics are important or desired for the data center, we might need to hire an interior designer. If an existing facility is being extended, we might want to consider designing it ourselves instead of hiring an architect and from there all we may need to do is procure the required furniture and house the new equipment. All in all, we need to consider these potential options and determine our subcontractor needs, if any, for facility design and construction.

Facility Construction

As discussed in the previous section, if the facility does not exist or an existing one is inadequate, engineering drawings and bills of material need to be prepared either in-house or by an external architect, and we would hire a contractor to build the required facility. Price quotes can be obtained from reputable building contractors by giving them the engineering drawings and bills of material. Price quotes provided by building contractors should be in Construction Specifications Institute format, so that the quotes are comparable. We need to consider reputation, track record, and price and make a decision that is most appropriate for our situation.

In reaching a decision, it is important to keep in mind that most building contractors will require payment of some advance toward mobilization of equipment, tools, and building materials required for facility construction. If the construction can be completed in a short duration, a contractor will typically bill for the balance owed upon completion. But if the construction duration is long the contractor may wish to bill at regular intervals ranging from weekly to monthly to quarterly. Sometimes milestone-based billing is possible. Whether the duration is short or long, we need to remember to include the payment of advance and the timing and amount of any required periodic payments in our cash flow plan for the construction portion of the project.

Another aspect to keep in mind regarding construction work is that once the project is completed, it is typically too late to uncover and address much in the way of potential quality issues. Therefore, we would need to carry out an inspection of the quality of work as it progresses and effect improvements; before the construction stage in which the defect is uncovered has been completed or the work has progressed to the next stage. Obviously the quality and price of building materials can vary, so we also need to ensure, as early as possible, that the contractor is using materials specified by our designer and that they are of the expected/desired quality.

Assuming the decision is to subcontract this work, we need to finalize the building contractor conforming to the purchase process of the organization.

Receive and Deploy Servers

This is perhaps the first step in project execution. Servers are needed to complete networking, test Internet connectivity, application software, and so on. However, we need not deploy servers until the network cables are laid out. Upon receipt from the vendor, we need to ensure that the right machines were supplied against our order through visual inspection and that no components were damaged in transit. Then, power on the machines to check their working condition and that the correct operating system was loaded.

Normally, the following servers are included:

1. *Web Server.* This server interacts with the Internet and provides the connectivity for the infrastructure to the Internet. It houses web server software. Optionally it may house the database server, e-mail server, and application servers too. Its deployment would include mounting or housing the server machine on a firm footing either inside a server cabinet or on specialized furniture, installing web server software and security software, and testing it cursorily to ensure the

server is functioning normally without any conflict between the various software packages that have been installed.

2. *Database Server.* This machine would house the RDBMS and provide data services to users on the network. In low-load networks, this server can be combined with the web server machine. Deploying this server would include mounting or housing the hardware in a server cabinet or on specialized furniture, installing RDBMS software, loading any other software utilities, and testing the machine to determine if it is working normally after all required software packages have been installed.
3. *E-Mail Server.* This machine would house the e-mail server software. It is normal practice to dedicate a separate machine for an e-mail server because the e-mail traffic is significantly high in any organization. Deploying this server would include mounting or housing the hardware in a server cabinet or on specialized furniture, loading the e-mail server software, creating mailboxes for the users, loading security software for preventing viruses and other malware from entering our network, and testing the server for normal functioning.
4. *Application Server.* An application server houses the middle tier such as the app server or the framework so the application software can perform as designed. Deploying this machine would include mounting or housing the hardware in a server cabinet or on specialized furniture, installing the app server or framework software and any other specialized software tools, and testing it to ensure the machine is working normally.

If any other servers are required for the data center, they need to be deployed as well. The activities again would include mounting or housing the machines in a server cabinet or on specialized furniture, installing the necessary software, and testing it in addition to any specific activities needed to make them work as designed. This completes the deployment of servers for the data center.

Receive Networking Hardware and Build the Communication Network

The next activity in construction of the facility is networking. The first activity of networking is laying out networking cables. While laying cables, care should be taken as follows:

1. If pulling cables through conduits, take care not to apply excessive force because the conductor inside the cable may be broken leading to a misconnection or no connection.

2. Cut the length of the cable carefully leaving a little extra at both ends for future needs.
3. Harness the cables into neat bunches to avoid tangling them with each other.
4. Place cable ID tags at both ends to easily identify the cable destination.
5. Anchor the cables to some type of support, so the cable harness does not sag, placing a burden on the conductors inside the cables.
6. If cables are going to be underground, run them inside a cement or steel pipe to avoid accidental damage from digging.

The work of laying cables is usually subcontracted to a specialized agency. The subcontractor should be evaluated and selected based on track record, schedule, and pricing. Upon reaching our decision, we would finalize the networking contractor conforming to the purchase process of the organization.

Once the order is placed, we need to obtain entry passes for the subcontractor's staff and hand over the site to them. The subcontractor's staff should be closely monitored for security and workmanship. Again, once the work is completed, corrections or quality issues can be very difficult to address. Therefore, in-process inspections need to be carried out to ensure defect free layout of cables.

Once the cables are laid out, the remaining activities include connecting servers and workstations to switches and switches to the router. We need to arrange it in such a way that the networking switches and router are received by the time cable laying is completed. Once these are received, our next step is to mount the switches in the switch racks and then plug the networking cables into the network sockets on the workstations. Then each switch needs to be connected to the router.

Now that the network is physically ready, we would assign IP (Internet Protocol) addresses to each workstation and server. IP addresses are not discussed in this book. However, there are plenty of articles on the subject of IP addresses available on the web for anyone lacking knowledge of the topic or for any reader interested in learning more about it. After IP addresses are assigned, we would map the workstations on the servers. How to do this depends on the operating system loaded on the server. The server operating system will provide the tools to map and connect the workstations. Our next step is to load the firewalls, network monitoring tools, antivirus utilities, and security software, as designed on the servers and workstations.

Now that the network is fully ready, our next step is to conduct the following tests:

1. *Connectivity*. Test the connectivity between servers and workstations. We do this by accessing all workstations, one by one, from the server.

The workstations must be accessible and the sharable folders/directories available for viewing and modifying based on the access rights granted to the user carrying out the testing. Similarly, we would access the servers and other workstations from all workstations. Of course, a sample of workstations could be selected while conducting the connectivity from the workstation end since the connectivity from the server to the workstation is already tested. Next we would test all (100%) of the workstations and servers because if there is no access, it might be that some of the required cable was not laid at all. It can be very difficult to lay an extra cable or two after the rest of the cables have already been laid out, run through a protective pipe, and buried.

2. *Data transfer*. Our next step would be to test the capacity of the network to handle large amounts of data. This can be done by trying to send large files over the network to and from a few workstations/the server. It is also wise to check the real speed of the network. There is a common misunderstanding that the baud rate (network speed) expressed as MBPS is "megabytes per second." This is not the case. MBPS expands to "megabits per second." Within networks data are transferred in packets. The packet size is usually 1024 bits. The actual data transferred per packet is typically only 4 to 8 bytes. Speed can be curtailed if network traffic is very high because the networks use Carrier Sense Multiple Access with Collision Detection protocol. With very high traffic, many collisions during peak-load times occur leading to retransfer of data packets, slowing down the transfer. This test is performed to ensure the network components are well designed to handle large amounts of data.
3. *Internet connectivity*. We conduct this test by trying to access the Internet from a few workstations and servers to ensure the software that connects the machines to the Internet is working well. We also need to test the speed of the Internet connection to ensure it is the speed ordered.
4. *Security testing*. We conduct this test by trying to invade our own network with known viruses, worms, spyware, and adware to ensure firewalls, security software, and antivirus and anti-adware utilities are functioning and blocking all types of malware from entering our network.

Once these tests have been successfully completed the network is ready for handover to operations. From a project management point of view, we need to ensure that all these operations take place in conformance with the project schedule and within the budgeted expenditure.

Receive and Deploy the System Software

As noted earlier, the operating system for the servers and workstations is bundled along with the machine itself, and there is nothing to do in that respect as part of IT project execution. It is taken care of during procurement of those machines. But other system software is procured separately, as noted earlier in the section on *Procurement of System Software*. These are COTS products, and once procured and received, we would install them on designated machines and configure each software package as follows:

1. *RDBMS*. We would configure the number of concurrent users, file size options, and create users and access rights for various users and backup devices, and so on.
2. *E-mail server*. We would next need to create mailboxes for the users, define e-mail policies, restrict e-mail sizes, scanners for e-mail based viruses/worms, action alternatives for e-mails violating e-mail policies and so on.
3. *Middle tier*. Our next step would be to configure the middle tier (app server or framework) to suit the application software. This configuration would depend on the specific software package.
4. *Configuration management tool*. This tool needs configuration of the production directories, user creation, user access rights' definition, changeover schedule definition, directories/folders for configuration management, and so on.
5. *Backup/restore*. This tool needs configuration of user creation, user access rights' definition, backup schedule, and backup process definition (full/incremental backups, testing of backup files and so on).
6. *Software development kit*. This software is provided for application software development and maintenance. It is deployed on the servers and workstations of the software developers and the web server for the development installation as well as the software maintenance personnel who also need to be provided with the development environment of the database separate from the production database. Personal web servers for each of the developers and testing environment need to be set up.
7. *Security*. Security tools need configuration. They should be set up with IP addresses to be blocked, websites for which access is to be restricted, protection against phishing, and so on.
8. *Network monitoring*. Network monitoring software utilities require configuration. The purpose of this software is to ensure that no undesirable activity is taking place on the network. When network-hogging

viruses infiltrate the network, they greatly increase the load on the traffic causing official communication to be hindered. Network monitoring detects such hogging in the early stages. We would need to define threshold levels for suspicious activity, action alternatives when suspicious activity is detected, alarms to be raised and so on.

9. *Administrative utilities*. These utilities also require configuration. Administrative utilities monitor usage of the IT infrastructure by end users and apportion the expenditure to departments based on their utilization. These utilities also assist in keeping track of administrative expenses, such as stationary, consumables, issue capture, tracking and resolution, preventive and breakdown maintenance and so on. Administrative utilities also assist us in keeping track of hardware and software assets of the infrastructure and their history. Hardware and software assets are often moved from one location to another and from one user to the next as required by the organization. IT assets allocated to employees need to be repossessed when they leave the organization and be reallocated to other existing employees or the new ones coming in.
10. *Additional software*. If any other software is installed, it too needs appropriate configuration.

Installing the system software on the appropriate machines and configuring them completes the activity of deploying the system software.

Prepare Master Data

Another activity to be performed is the preparation of the master data using the approach decided upon during project planning.

If the outsourced approach was adopted, we would perform the following activities:

1. Finalize the vendor specialized in providing data preparation services in conformance with the organizational purchase process.
2. Provide the vendor with master data and formats. One alternative would be to provide paper records, and another would be to scan the records and provide an electronic version of the master data to the vendor keeping the originals safely in our custody.
3. Receive the prepared data from the vendor.
4. Perform quality control activities on data, which would include sample verification.
5. Load the data into master data tables/files.

6. Test the data with application software on a sample basis to ensure compatibility between data and software. Testing 10% of the records for accuracy is the norm. Yet, in critical cases we would test 100% of the records, even though the vendor performs 100% verification of all data.
7. Ensure repossession of data records provided to the vendor for data preparation.
8. Receive invoice from the vendor for services rendered and arrange for releasing payment.

If the in-house data preparation approach was adopted, we would perform the following activities:

1. Develop software for data entry.
2. Develop software for data verification. This software is similar to data entry software except the data entered is compared with the stored data and differences between the two, if any, would be displayed. The operator would have the option of accepting the stored data, or either the new data or enter afresh, replacing the stored data. This approach is common practice in data preparation. Another less common approach is to perform data entry just once, produce a printout, subject it to manual verification and correct any mistakes found. Either way, the objective is to eliminate data entry mistakes and make data as correct as possible. Keep in mind that getting data 100% error-free is not really possible! Even when 100% data verification is carried out, the maximum error would be 0.1%, meaning 0.1% of the characters entered could be in error—not 0.1% of the records! Such errors need to be corrected when detected.
3. Allocate resources; that is, data entry operators and machines.
4. Set up data entry environment:
   a. Set up the server to receive entered data.
   b. Load data entry/verification software on workstations.
   c. Set up connectivity between workstations and server.
5. Train operators in data entry and verification.
6. Carry out data entry and verification.
7. Resolve any issues that arise.
8. Release resources.
9. Load prepared data into master data tables/files.
10. Test the data with application software on a sample basis for compatibility.

Two more data preparation approaches are being adopted by organizations that are variations of those previously discussed:

1. Carry out the data entry in-house but with contract resources working on the premises to make employing data entry operators for the peak load unnecessary.
2. Outsource the data entry work but retain the server for receiving the entered data inside the organization. Outsourcing can be either onshore or offshore. Records are scanned and electronic versions of the documents are made available to the vendors. Data entry is performed over the Internet. This approach allows utilization of freelance data entry operators that would be required to use the same software as that residing on the organization server.

These approaches are used by a significant number of organizations.

Data from the existing applications may need to be migrated to the new system. Oftentimes migration of application software is performed for one or more of the following reasons:

1. Major technological advances that necessitate upgrading of the application software
2. Increase in the workload on the system due to increased transaction volumes
3. Changes in statutes that necessitate major changes in the application software
4. Competition forces upgrade of the system by offering better services at cheaper rates using technological advances
5. Events such as Y2K or Euro introduction that necessitate upgrading software

In such cases, data from the existing applications would likely be migrated to the new system. When building new application software, the database is typically freshly built as well to enable handling of more data with better efficiency. The new database may have more or less tables, but the number of data fields in the tables would usually be greater than the earlier database.

Normally, most modern RDBMS packages come with utilities that facilitate data import from other RDBMS packages including the previous version of the same package. While the data can be migrated using this facility, there are some issues to consider as follows:

1. The data types can vary from one RDBMS to another. Examples are date formats (long/short format), numeric data (currency, integer, long integer, single/double precision), and character data (character,

byte, bit, string) whose definition can vary from one package to another. If the data are being migrated from an earlier version of the same RDBMS, we can use the migration facility provided in the new RDBMS without hesitation, but it may be better to migrate the data programmatically. Why?

2. Sometimes an auto-increment field is included in the table to use as a primary key if there is no single data field that can be utilized as one. A primary key needs to be unique and cannot have duplicates in the table. If the built-in data import utilities of the RDBMS are used, migration of the auto-increment field could cause some issues. The migration may fail, the auto-increment field may not be filled, or its definition may be modified.
3. If the field names are the same in both tables, the import is very simple. If not, it may be necessary to script the data migration with Structured Query Language to map the fields between the source and destination tables.

So our best course of action would be to utilize the data export-import facility provided by the new RDBMS for all data that can be imported without any issues. For the remaining data, we would perform the following steps:

1. Develop software for importing data from an earlier database table/ data file.
2. Test the software on sample data and ensure no defects are present.
3. Run the software and import the data.
4. Test a sample of the data for accurate import.

At this stage, data entry may be needed for missing information in the new database for fields that have been added to the new system. We would prepare the data in the same manner discussed earlier in this section. Since the data must be entered against the specifications of the new database, we would utilize the data export-import utility built in the new RDBMS and load it into the corresponding tables. If for any reason this was not feasible, an alternative is to develop a small software utility to load the data into their corresponding tables.

Preparation of master data is a vital activity of setting up IT infrastructure that needs to be performed diligently. Master data must be ready by the time the application software is ready and delivered or it would become difficult to test the application software effectively.

Receive and Deploy Application Software

Whether the development of application software is outsourced or in-house, its delivery is accepted from the development team. Acceptance of delivery consists of the following activities:

1. *Verify the quality records.* This will give us valuable information about the quality of the developed software. The quality records verified are the review and test logs. Verification of review logs will indicate the types of reviews (peer, managerial, and expert) used in the development and coverage of the artifacts subjected to review. Review coverage of 100% is ideal but most organizations are not performing the review on all artifacts. However, 100% review coverage for at least the code artifacts is necessary because it is nearly impossible to carry out 100% testing of the code. Verifying test logs would indicate the code coverage in testing. It will also show if unit testing was carried out by an independent peer or not. In software development, unit testing is the only type in which white box testing (stepping through every line of code) is possible. If it is not carried out by an independent peer, the best opportunity to uncover lurking defects is lost and as a result, some defects will likely remain in the code. Another aspect disclosed by the verification of testing logs is the types of tests conducted on the software. We would also know if the testing was thorough or just cursory. Verification of quality records can tell us a lot about the diligence of the development team on the quality of the code being produced and enable us to form an idea about the reliability of the software being delivered. On this basis, the acceptance test plan can be tailored to ensure that critical aspects of the application software are covered in acceptance testing as well as increase the rigor. Another artifact to verify is the requirements' traceability matrix, which will indicate if all stated user requirements are met by the software.
2. *Prepare the test plan and test cases for acceptance testing.* Sometimes the acceptance test plan is prepared by the development team. If so, the customer (end-user representative) would need to either be associated with the preparation or approve the plan and test cases. Sometimes the customer prepares the acceptance test plan and test cases. In most instances the IT project team is the customer. Therefore, diligence is needed in preparing/approving the acceptance test plan and test cases in order to cover all stated end-user requirements.
3. *Conduct the acceptance test.* We need to ensure that the acceptance testing is conducted diligently. Acceptance testing is positive

functional testing; that is, we test the software positively using it as software designers intended. We would not perform any actions that are not meant to be performed on the software or attempt to enter incorrect data in any field or specify any wrong parameters in our enquiries or reports. Then, test the functionality to ensure that it is as specified by the end user. We would use real-life data in acceptance testing rather than test data prepared by the development team. It may be essential to use actual master and transaction data to test the software. If any defects are uncovered in the acceptance testing, we need to track them through to resolution.

4. *Accept delivery*. Upon delivery, we would ensure receipt of the following artifacts:
   a. Source code
   b. Executable code
   c. Object libraries, if any
   d. Table scripts
   e. Any other scripts used for configuring the middle tiers
   f. Graphics
   g. Web pages
   h. Configuration files
   i. Installation manual
   j. User manuals
   k. Operations manuals
   l. Troubleshooting manuals
   m. Quality records
   n. Requirements' traceability matrix
   o. Configuration register
   p. Project records (e.g., project plans, training materials, and quality records)
   q. Any other relevant records

The next step is to ensure the correct versions of all the foregoing artifacts were received. We would do this by comparing the version of the artifact with the entry in the configuration register and ensuring agreement with one another.

Once received, we would deploy the software artifacts on their corresponding machines, subject all code artifacts to configuration management, and bring them under the rigor of configuration management. From this point forward, changes to any artifact would be carried out conforming to the process of configuration management with proper authorizations.

Once the application software is deployed, we would conduct trial runs testing the system using a limited amount of transactions and ensure the results are as expected and desired. If defects are uncovered during the trial runs, we would get them resolved by the team responsible for correcting defects under the warranty of the application software. Once the application software successfully passes the trial runs the system is ready for rollout.

Define Systems and Procedures for Running the Operations

Running an IT infrastructure is complicated because of the various agencies involved and a number of activities to be performed. The department that runs the IT infrastructure is normally the IS (information systems) department. It may be referred to by another name in different organizations. Let us use the name of "IS department" for the purpose of taking over the responsibility for the organizational IT infrastructure. IT infrastructure is used by other organizational entities to accomplish their business objectives. It is a cost center. The objectives of the IS department are:

1. Make the IT infrastructure available to the organization during working hours, which may be 24 hours a day!
2. Keep the costs of running the IT infrastructure as low as possible.
3. Provide operations support as required conforming to a service-level agreement (SLA).
4. Produce bulk reports on schedule.
5. Provide consumables, as required, conforming to an SLA.
6. Provide a safe and secure operating environment.
7. Protect the integrity of data and programs so all operations produce desired results accurately.
8. Investigate and resolve any undesirable incident as and when it occurs.

The most important objectives obviously are keeping costs low, maximizing system availability, protecting integrity of data assets, and ensuring security and safety. To accomplish these objectives, we need to develop the systems and procedures by the time the IT infrastructure is ready to be handed over to operations. Perhaps the manager and the team that oversaw setting up the IT infrastructure may operate it too. It is essential to set up systems and procedures for the following activities:

1. SLAs for various support activities:
   a. Hardware troubleshooting
   b. Software troubleshooting
   c. Installation of new software
   d. User management (add/modify/delete)
   e. Restore data from backups
   f. Handholding support
2. Support procedures for all the support provided to users
3. Software maintenance procedure for defect fixing, functional expansion, or software modification
4. Data processing procedures
5. Operations procedures
6. Hardware maintenance support procedures
7. Procurement of consumables
8. Procurement of new hardware/software
9. Backup and restore procedures
10. Disaster management procedures
11. Periodic data processing
12. Safety and security procedures
13. Incident management procedures
14. Systems audit procedures for conformance as well as investigative audits

These procedures could be defined in-house or an external consultant specializing in process definition and improvement could be hired.

Whichever the case, a process or standard operating procedures (SOPs) for all these activities need to be defined and be available for use by the time the infrastructure is ready. We would next train all concerned staff in the process and procedures to ensure smooth and efficient takeover and running of the operations.

Recruiting and Training Personnel for Operations

An IT project typically takes a minimum of three months from conception to completion. Therefore, it might not be necessary to recruit the required personnel at the beginning. Of course, the end users would already be there if the organization is an ongoing one. If the project is for setting up infrastructure for a software development or business process management organization (BPM), there would definitely be little point in recruiting the required personnel before the infrastructure is ready. Ideally, personnel should be recruited in such a manner that they are ready (just-in-time) upon project completion. Recruitment includes getting people into the organization and trained. End-user recruitment is the responsibility of the functional departments, but recruitment of personnel needed to operate the IT infrastructure is the responsibility of the IS department. In this section, we will cover the recruitment and training of personnel for running IT operations. The type of personnel needed to perform and manage the various functions of IT operations are as follows:

1. *Data processing function.* The people responsible for this function handle the bulk-data processing activities such as payroll, statutory reports, exception reports, weekly/monthly/quarterly/half yearly/yearly processing, and so on:
   a. A manager to take ownership of the function and guide all other resources working in the function
   b. Data processing staff to perform data processing activities
2. *Operations function.* The people responsible for this function ensure that the infrastructure is properly utilized and expenses are apportioned to user departments. They also enforce system security, user management, and take ownership of the organization's IT assets, configuration management, backups, restore, and so on:
   a. A manager to take ownership of the function and guide all other resources working in the function
   b. Operations staff to run the operations
3. *Hardware and network support function.* There is an option to outsource this activity and a significant number of organizations are already doing so. Even if this function is outsourced, at least one person is needed to coordinate the function from within the organization. If handled in-house, hardware support engineers would be needed to troubleshoot the machines and network when they break down.
4. *Software support function.* The people responsible for this function are software support engineer specialists. They provide hand-hold support to users for ensuring the organizational software assets are effectively utilized. These specialists provide clarifications on how to achieve a function, clear up any confusion about usage, and ensure that the reported malfunctions are indeed software defects and so on. They are experts in using the software including the COTS product, application software or any other utility. Nowadays when multiple utilities are loaded on machines, many requests are typically received for clarification/troubleshooting software malfunctions or configuring the utilities,

operating system, or development kit. These specialists support the software maintenance teams as well as handle periodic updates/patches to the operating systems, middle tiers, RDBMS, web server, and so on.

5. *Application software maintenance function.* The application software needs to be maintained. There is an option to outsource this function and a significant number of organizations are already doing so. Even if this activity is outsourced, at least one person is needed to coordinate this function between the end users and vendor providing software maintenance support. If handled in-house, a software project manager and software engineers are needed for carrying out the software maintenance.
6. *Help desk function.* When an individual user has an issue, he/she needs a one-point center to take the call and track it to resolution. Typically several persons per shift are needed to handle the help desk. They receive calls, log the complaint, forward it to the appropriate function, log resolution details, and apportion the cost to the department that utilized the service. Normally, people with good communication and phone skills are recruited for this position.
7. *Administration function.* As the IS department would be staffed with a number of people, administrative support would be needed to handle purchasing consumables, billing the user department for utilizing the infrastructure, maintaining software and manuals libraries, and so on.

Normally, recruitment and training are handled by the human resources department (HR), but they need to be supported in these activities in the following manner:

1. Provide the details of the personnel required:
   a. Educational qualifications and experience necessary for each position
   b. Number of personnel for each position
   c. Date personnel required to report for duty: duration required for training must be considered when indicating this date.
2. Scrutinize applications received and short-list applicants for personal interviews.
3. Assist the HR department in the technical interview of candidates.
4. Assist the HR department in short-listing candidates for making a job offer.

Sometimes, in an existing on-going organization internal candidates may exist, and HR may move people from other departments to the IS department.

In this case, the IS department would still need to evaluate suitability of candidates for the positions they are recommended to fill.

Thus, in coordination with the HR department, the required personnel are brought onboard. The new personnel would need training on the following topics:

1. Introduction to the organization
2. Introduction to the department
3. Training on infrastructure
4. Training on systems and procedures defined for running the IS department
5. Training on individual functions
6. Explanation of the SLAs

Some training is best delivered in a classroom and the other on the job. Once training is finished, and upon completion of the IT project, these resources should be ready to take over the infrastructure and run operations effectively.

Procure Consumables for the Initial Operation

Consumables are required for testing the infrastructure and running the operations during the initial period. Therefore, we would procure the following:

1. Printing paper for the data center's high-speed printers and personal printers spread across the organization
2. Backup media (e.g., tapes, CDs, pen drives, and so on)
3. Printer ribbons and cartridges
4. Mouse and keyboards
5. Networking spares such as connectors
6. Electrical spares such as power cables

These are low cost consumables capable of causing a major nuisance. It is common knowledge that most equipment failures occur during the initial operation. Once the equipment stabilizes, failures drop to predictable levels. Therefore, it is better to procure and keep these consumables ready so equipment issues and breakdowns can be quickly attended to.

Contract/Contractor Management

As noted earlier, a diverse group of specialized capabilities are required for setting up an IT infrastructure. Consequently, it would be quite rare for this type of project to be executed without using multiple subcontractors.

Therefore, the topic of contract/contractor management is significant to IT project managers.

So what needs to be considered when entering a contract? Our first step would be to ensure that the person we are signing the contract with is competent and eligible to do so. As such we would consider the following:

1. The person is authorized by the organization to sign contracts. This is specific to each organization. Authority to sign includes:
    a. Persons authorized by the Board of Directors
    b. Persons to whom authority to sign is delegated by a person authorized by the Board of Directors
    c. Implicit authorization; that is, a person deemed to be authorized by virtue of his/her official title (For example, a purchasing manager/officer is authorized to sign purchase orders, and a contracts manager/officer is authorized to sign contracts.)
    d. The person who signed the proposal often is authorized to sign contracts as well
2. The person must have attained the age of majority chronologically and not be considered a minor, which is normally 18 years of age. However, this may differ from country to country.
3. The person is legally competent and does not have some mental disorder. Temporary insanity is accepted in courts of law!
4. The person is not under suspension from employment at the time of signing the contract, and therefore not authorized.
5. The person has not been barred by an executive order of that organization, government or by a court of law from signing contracts.
6. The signature should not have been obtained under duress.

Before signing a contract, we need to realize it is a legal document; that is, it can be produced in a court of law. Therefore, ensure the language is such that it would be interpreted in the same manner by all stakeholders including lawyers and judges. The best way to achieve that is to route the draft contract through the legal department or a lawyer specializing in contract/corporate law.

Signing a contract is part of the organizational purchase process and the beginning of the relationship between contractor and client. Once the contract is signed, it is essential to manage the contractor to ensure execution of the entrusted assignment on time and within the approved budget. Supply of off-the-shelf items can be governed by fixed price, but work contracts (to execute specified work at a client site against supplied specifications) differ.

Normally the schedule of work with itemized rates and expected quantities are agreed upon. Actual quantities may differ from purchase order quantities due to unforeseen occurrences. In such cases most contractors will likely overlook minor differences, but bill extra if the deviations are significant. Therefore, execution needs to be monitored closely to keep the scope in check.

Some contracts include a price escalation clause, which needs to be carefully reviewed. Normally, this clause provides for escalation due to conditions beyond the contractor's control, which may include an increase of applicable levies by the government, unforeseen material price increases, union-negotiated pay increases across the industry, and so on. Another thing to look for is clauses pertaining to penalties from both sides. For example: If a contractor delays execution beyond a specified date, they become liable for penalties. Similarly, if the client is late on payments or causes execution to fall behind schedule due to delays in approvals, handing over the site, or in providing contractor workers entry passes to the site and so on, the principal becomes liable for penalties.

These types of clauses are not unusual, but they bring focus to the fact that these activities must be managed carefully, as part of contractor management, to enable the contractor to complete the assignment on time and within the approved budget for the sake of the project and to avoid penalties. As such we need to do the following:

1. Carefully scrutinize the contract before signing and ensure it is legal and protects the interests of the organization.
2. Hand over the work site on time so the contractor can begin work on time.
3. Provide entry passes to the contractor's staff in a timely manner to enable them to enter the required premises and carry out the assignment.
4. Process contractor bills expeditiously and arrange payments on time. Delay in payments can cause cash flow problems for the contractor possibly causing delay in execution. Delay in payments is a justifiable reason in the eyes of the law for delay in execution of the assignment.
5. When approached by the contractor for approvals, review and accord them on time.
6. Issues are common in any assignment. When the contractor raises an issue following the process defined in the contract, attend to and resolve it quickly within the time defined in the relevant SLA. This facilitates the contractor to move ahead with the assignment.
7. Quality is paramount for any assignment and although the contractor is responsible for quality, we need to ensure that all quality control activities pertinent to the assignment are being performed diligently.

In many cases of contract work, per our earlier discussion, quality cannot be ensured after the event. Therefore, we need to carry out in-process (while the process is being carried out) inspections and provide inspectors as required by the contractor so the work is not delayed for contract purposes as well as the reasons previously cited. Of course, there will be an SLA for providing the inspectors and we need to adhere to it.

8. Assess the progress of work periodically, independent of the contractor, and conduct progress monitoring meetings regularly to discuss issues and resolve or remove any impediments.
9. Ensure that a healthy relationship exists between both parties' staff, so the assignment is executed smoothly and in an amicable atmosphere.

Another important aspect of contract/contractor management is the need to maintain meticulous records of correspondence and minutes of meetings with the contractor's representatives. We need to recognize the possibility of issues at the staff level and instances of legal wrangles between the principal and contractor and be ready for it. Should the relationship sour and the case is presented in a court of law, we must be ready with all relevant records to support our case. A contractor/contract dossier should be maintained with all relevant records from the RFP, proposal, order, and all correspondence, minutes of meetings, bills submitted and payments released, issues raised and resolved, and approvals requested and accorded. This is another important aspect of contract/contractor management.

It is essential that we clearly understand what everything contained within a contract means in relation to the project and the organization and how it would likely be interpreted in a court of law. While having legal counsel review them is a wise idea, he/she is not the party signing the contract or an expert in IT project management.

Setup Configuration Management Process

When we are setting up the application software; creating the database tables and loading the master data, we also need to set up the configuration management system. Normally, this tool is used to manage configuration of the production system. The configuration of system cannot be changed without proper authorizations. This is the final step in setting up the IT infrastructure before it can be handed over to the operations. This covers setting up configuration management for the entire system. Changes to any component must happen through this system. It safeguards the entire IT infrastructure. The configuration management tool performs the following activities:

1. Forms another security layer over the operating system to protect IT assets
2. Allows access to IT assets based on the rights granted to users
3. Manages changes to IT assets conforming to a defined change management policy
4. Maintains a record of changes made to IT assets to facilitate investigation should an undesirable event occur

For the configuration tool to function properly, a configuration management system process needs to be defined, which should consist of the following:

1. *Formation of a CCB (Configuration Control Board)*. This CCB would consider all change requests and approve or reject them. If the change request is approved for implementation, a copy of the artifact is checked out (i.e., copied) and provided for effecting the changes. Once the changes to the artifact are completed and tested, they would be approved by the concerned executives. Then the artifact would be submitted to the CCB for promoting it to the production system. The CCB would verify the approvals and approve the artifact for promotion to the production system. The CCB would designate a configuration controller responsible for actually carrying out the decisions of the CCB. The configuration controller would be an operations executive in the IS department.
2. *A change management system*. The change management system would consist of:
   a. *The approvals necessary before a changed or new artifact can be promoted to the production system*. The project manager of the software maintenance team, the IS department, and the concerned end-user department head need to approve the artifact before it would be considered by the CCB. Normally an artifact is not promoted unless it is approved by the CCB.
   b. *The approvals necessary for requesting an artifact from the production system to be checked out*.
   c. *The day and time of the changeover*. Unless the need is very urgent, artifacts would be changed only once a week. Normally, midnight on Friday is when the existing artifact would be replaced by the new one, thereby not causing hindrance to normal work. The timing might change depending on the week end-day (if not a Friday) followed by the organization.
   d. *The configuration audit*. We need to define the types of audits, their periodicity, and procedures, and the probable auditors qualified to

audit the implementation of the defined configuration management system.

3. *The directories for the configuration within the configuration management tool*:
   a. Software directories in the production system depending on the software design
   b. A directory for submitting changed/new artifacts to the configuration management tool: the tool would look for artifacts in this directory when the change is triggered at the appointed time.
   c. A directory for checking out artifacts: when an artifact is checked out from the production system for any purpose, it would be copied into this directory and transmitted to the person who requested it.
   d. Any other directory necessary for the organization
4. *The changeover process*. Normally, the tool manages the change of an artifact into and out of the production system. However, in some cases, the change may be effected manually; that is, a person replaces the artifact in the production system. For this event, we need to define the changeover process.
5. *Policy about retention of old artifacts*. When an artifact is replaced, typically the old artifact is not immediately discarded but retained for investigative purposes. The period of time an artifact shall be retained needs to be defined.
6. *Users*. Identify the set of users who will be granted access to the configuration management tool, manage the production system configuration setup needs and define user rights.

Upon performing these activities, the configuration management system setup is complete, and the production system is ready for use by the end users.

Train End Users in Operating the System

End users are of three classes: the staff that performs business transactions, managers who supervise and take ownership of business functions, and senior management who takes ownership for results of the departments under their charge. In addition to end users, there are system administrators who manage the production system and perform various other duties so end users can utilize it in performing business transactions. We would need to train all these people so the system can be utilized effectively.

Staff training should consist of the facilities provided by the system to perform business transactions. Staff would be taken through each of the screens, reports, and inquiries that assist them in their function. Any clarification required by these users on how to achieve their desired functions utilizing the system must be provided and all questions and concerns addressed. It is essential that we clearly explain the set of inputs these users need to provide the system so it functions properly. They should be shown how to extract the desired information using reports and enquiries and also when approvals from managers become necessary and how to obtain them. Training consists of classroom training, demonstrations, and hands-on system trials. In addition, they should be trained to obtain help when in doubt about any functionality. Training provided to these end users should be very detailed about the functionality and usage of the system, so that upon completion the end users are ready to operate the system.

Manager training should consist mainly of according (granting) approvals digitally, the functionality of the system, extracting necessary information from the system that can aid them in decision making, as well as the contents of the training conducted for their end user staff, albeit in brief. They need to be shown how to accord approvals, the alerts received for pending approvals, and how to extract information necessary to approve or reject. We need to explain to them the system (process) defined for requesting changes to the system based on the changing business scenario as well as approving the changed artifacts. To be effective, classroom training, demonstrations, and hands-on exercises are required. Manager training can be limited on the system's functionality and staff usage, but it must be detailed on extracting information, according approvals, and requesting changes to the system, so that upon completion they are ready to manage their functions effectively using the system.

Senior management training should consist of an overview of the functionality provided by the system and how to extract necessary information that can assist them in their decision making. We need to show them how to intervene in special cases in business transactions. It is essential that we clearly explain the security and integrity features built into the system, and any clarification required by these users must be provided. We would need to explain the configuration management system, as well as the system (process) for requesting changes to the system and approving changed artifacts. To be effective, classroom training, demonstrations and hands-on sessions are required. The training can be cursory about the usage of business transaction processing, but must be detailed on extracting information, intervention, and security of the system, so that upon completion senior management are ready to use the system effectively for running the organization.

System administrator training should consist of managing the production system effectively, enforcing system security, user management (add, delete, or modify user privileges), backup management, and handling support requests, troubleshooting the system, and management of the system configuration. System administration personnel are normally part of the IS department. To be effective, classroom training, demonstrations, and hands-on exercises are required.

To conduct a training program we need to prepare training materials (training slides, faculty notes, and exercises for hands-on training), course materials for handouts, and self-study materials for future reference. A demonstration system for hands-on exercises is needed, and faculty for handling classroom sessions, demonstrations, and hands-on sessions would need to be arranged or hired.

Conduct Trial Runs

When hardware or software is received, it must be subjected to inward quality control activities. When the network is installed, and software is deployed, they both must be tested. When the infrastructure is ready, we must ensure that all subsystems work as designed. What remains is testing the system together to ensure all subsystems work smoothly together and produce the desired results. This is achieved through trial runs.

Upon completion of all the foregoing activities and processes, and when the users are ready for utilizing the system, we would begin operating the production system on a trial basis. In trial runs, the system is made available to all, but the organization does not depend on the system for business transactions. However, one or two business functions may be included to utilize the production system for business transactions. That is, a department is selected to use the system on a pilot basis while others are just trying out the system. During trial runs, initial problems are likely to emerge. These might include:

1. Network and connectivity problems relating to hardware (switches or router not functioning as expected), cables (damaged connectors, wrong routing of cables, or damaged cables), and workstation (damaged network interface card) issues
2. Communication software issues (incorrect IP addresses, mapping of IP addresses, not joining a workstation with a server), failure to install the required protocol, or incorrectly configuring it

3. Application software defects which could be anything related to the accuracy of results, unexpected failures, system freeze, or any other issue
4. Processing speeds or response times for user commands being poor and unacceptable due to a variety of reasons
5. Usage issues such as innocently or intentionally wrong usage of the system (to uncover defects), not understanding the system, and so on

Many other issues could arise during trial runs. The warranty team would be standing by to handle all such problems and immediately rectify the system. The intention of the trial run is to uncover issues not detected in normal testing. A trial run can be considered as the alpha (testing by the users on-site)/beta (testing by the users off-site) testing. The duration of a trial run depends on the size of the system. It may range from a week to a month.

The main objective besides uncovering lurking defects is to stabilize the system. Once it stabilizes, we can change the system over to production.

Changeover to New System

There are two approaches to changeover to the new system. One is the big-bang approach and the other is the phased approach.

In the big-bang approach, we would do the following:

1. Conduct the trial runs.
2. Take a day or two to clean out the production system of all trial data.
3. Disconnect the existing system on a weekend.
4. Change all operations on the first working day after a holiday or a weekend.

The advantages of the big-bang approach are:

1. All departments/business functions would be working either on the existing/new system. This would make it easy to support the operations.
2. All data would be either the existing or new system making it easier to extract required information by senior management.
3. The load on administrators would be a onetime occurrence and of short duration.
4. Data migration and testing would only need to occur once.

The disadvantages of this approach are:

1. In the initial period of operation, the need for handholding of users may be very high, stretching support resources to a breakdown point.

2. For some unforeseen reason, the system may break down and cause serious disruption to business operations.

In the phased approach, we would:

1. Conduct the trial run and switch one department/business function to the new system.
2. Stabilize the first department/business function that was switched over to the new system.
3. Then another department/business function would be switched over to the new system while others would be continuing trial runs.
4. After stabilizing the second department/business function, we would switchover the third department/business function and so on.
5. In this manner, one or a few departments at a time are switched over to the new system.

The advantages of the phased approach are:

1. The load on the administrators is distributed uniformly over a period, making it easier to change over to a large system.
2. System breakdowns, if any, would not disrupt the entire business operations.
3. In the implementation of large-scale systems, this is a safe approach.

The problems with the phased approach are:

1. The changeover is of much longer duration. During this transitional period, getting exception reports to senior management may not be possible as the data are on two disparate systems.
2. Both systems need to operate concurrently, which places an extra load on system administration staff.
3. Since the changeover occurs department by department, data migration has to be performed multiple times. Each time data are migrated, they need to be tested. There is also the risk of data migration defects.

Which is the right approach? *It depends*. Although I hate to use the phrase so popular among IT staff and hated by users, I have to use it in this instance. Here are the reasons:

1. If the organization is small, a big-bang approach is the right one.
2. If the organization is large and covers a large number of department/business functions, a phased approach would be advantageous.
3. If the organization is large but consists of highly experienced human resources, a big-bang approach would succeed.

4. If the organization is a software development/BPM organization, a big-bang approach is the right one.
5. If the organization has sensitive data where security is paramount, or operates in a highly competitive environment, a phased approach may deprive senior management of vital exception reports. Therefore, a big-bang approach is preferred.

In summation, we need to evaluate case by case and select the approach appropriate to the organization for changeover from the existing to the new system.

Initiate Maintenance

Once all the business functions have been changed over to the new system, we need to initiate maintenance of the hardware and software of the IT infrastructure. The main activity involved is handover of the infrastructure. The prerequisite for handing over the infrastructure is the finalization of the strategy for maintenance. We would finalize strategy for the following assets:

1. Hardware maintenance:
   a. In-house
   b. Outsourced
2. Networking:
   a. In-house
   b. Outsourced
3. Application software maintenance:
   a. In-house
   b. Outsourced

After finalizing the strategy for maintenance of each of the three classes of assets, we need to determine the policies for preventive maintenance. This would include the trigger for preventive maintenance (duration- or condition-based), stocking of spares, if we decided on in-house maintenance for hardware and networking, SLAs for various categories of support requests, and procedures for carrying out maintenance. We would document all these maintenance policies either as an organizational process or as SOPs and then release them.

If the decision was to outsource maintenance for any infrastructure category, we would finalize the subcontractor conforming to the organizational purchase process. At this stage we are ready to hand over the infrastructure to the agency designated for maintenance.

IT Infrastructure handover format
Date of handover:
Handed over by:
Taken over by:
Assets:
All the above enumerated assets are verified by me and are in working condition.
Signed:
Name of the person taking over the assets:
Date:

Figure 6.1 Elements for the handover/takeover format template (template exhibited in Appendix I)

We now need to make a list of all the assets being handed over, sign it, and hand it over to the maintenance team. They should verify the existence of all assets enumerated in the list, sign it if satisfied, and take over the assets. Figure 6.1 depicts elements of a suggested format for handover/takeover of the IT infrastructure. The same format can be used for hardware, software, or networking assets.

The maintenance team would need some guidance and training in IT asset maintenance. For hardware and networking assets, we would hand over the user and troubleshooting manuals and show them the location of all assets. Normally, the maintenance team is adept at carrying out maintenance and able to take it over with these few aids. How to maintain hardware and networking assets does not require training by the implementation team.

When it comes to maintenance of application software, we need to ensure that knowledge transfer takes place from the development team to the maintenance team. This can be done both in the classroom and with hands-on sessions. In the classroom, the development team needs to explain the architecture and design of the software. In hands-on sessions, they need to demonstrate the functioning of the software. The development team should hand over the software design documentation, test plans, cases, and logs to the maintenance team for reference when in doubt. Some amount of hand-holding is usually required in maintaining application software. This hand-holding period would range from a calendar month upward, depending on the size and complexity of the software and maturity (experience level) of the maintenance team.

When the processes are defined for maintenance, all assets are handed over, and the maintenance team is appropriately trained, they are ready to take over the maintenance.

This completes the execution of an IT infrastructure implementation project.

When Would All These Actions Be Taken?

You might have noticed that although I discussed various activities to be performed, I have not discussed their timing. We need to perform all the above activities conforming to the project schedule prepared during the project planning phase. The schedule would have specified the date for each of the activities to be performed during project execution.

What if some activities are delayed due to unforeseen circumstances? Should we rework the schedule? We do not have to. But we need to monitor progress regularly and fill in the actual start and end dates for all the activities that have either begun or are completed. When we do this the scheduling tool will automatically rework the schedule and present us with new dates.

Now, if some activities are delayed and this affects project completion date—what then? This is indeed a common occurrence. What we need to do in such a condition is complete some of the immediate activities ahead of their scheduled end date so the schedule comes back on track and the project completion date is back to an acceptable date. The duration of an activity can be shortened by pumping in more resources, if possible, or using better tools and methods, or subcontracting some portion of the work so project completion is not affected.

Therefore, we need to continuously monitor progress and update our schedule with actual data, namely, the start date, end date, and the consumption of resources, in the scheduling tool. We will discuss more about project control in the next chapter.

How about Quality Control?

Quality is vital in setting up the IT infrastructure in an organization. How is quality controlled during project execution? This aspect will also be discussed in detail within Chapter 7 on project control.

Coordination

In IT project execution, we have to deal with multiple agencies either within the organization or subcontractors. Coordination assumes greater importance when the agencies do not administratively report to the project manager. We cannot use authority; we can only coordinate. Although the relationship is principal-contractor, it is not direct reporting. The relationship between the project manager and other agencies is that of partners engaged in a common endeavor with the project manager having the final say in the matter. We need to use consensus and persuasion rather than authority when dealing with agencies that are administratively independent. True, the project manager has the authority to hold up payments and cause trouble for subcontractors, but it could boomerang on the project causing delays or quality issues. Therefore, we cannot use this authority as a weapon to get agencies to toe the line.

Coordination is like a thread in a garland. People can see the flowers but not the thread. But without the thread the flowers will not form a garland. The IT project manager should coordinate the project like the thread in the garland, so that stakeholders see the results, but not the coordination.

The main task of a project manager in an IT infrastructure project is that of coordination to see that everything happens on time and within the estimated cost during project execution.

This book has free material available for download from the Web Added Value™ resource center at *www.jrosspub.com*

7

Project Control in IT Project Management

Introduction

The word "control" has a sinister connotation associated with it in the general public. The epithet "control freak" is hated and if it is attached to a manager, few subordinates may wish to work with that manager! However, in some environments and disciplines such as project management, the word "control" has a very positive connotation. In fact, control is an essential part of efficient and effective project management. For a project to be completed on time and within the approved budget, close control of project execution must be exercised. In the parlance of project management, the word "control" involves the following activities:

1. Planning activities based on approved organizational norms/baselines
2. Measuring progress (schedule, quality, productivity, and cost) of the project periodically
3. Comparing the actual progress with the planned progress and finding the variances
4. Taking corrective actions for undesirable variances, if any
5. Taking preventive actions to keep the actual progress aligned with planned progress in the future

This is what I mean by the phrase "project control."

As part of project control, we control the project's success parameters, namely:

1. *Schedule.* This indicates the planned duration for each of the activities and consequently, the project completion date. We control project execution to align it with the planned dates for each of the activities so that the project can be completed on time.
2. *Cost.* A budget is established upon project approval. Although the budget is not set in stone, we need to maintain control of the expenditures within the approved budget. It is possible that some activities may cost more and some less than the budgeted expenditure. Overall, we need to contain the project expenses within the budgeted expenditure.
3. *Quality.* Quality is of paramount importance in an IT project. The design and material specification defines project quality. What remains is workmanship, which is guided by the organizational standards. There are many activities that we will need to perform to ensure the actual quality achieved in the project is as designed.
4. *Productivity.* In an IT project some of the activities are performed by us and our resources and some by subcontractors and their resources. Subcontractor performance is governed by the contract, but the performance of our resources is guided by the organizational baselines for productivity. We need to continuously measure the actual productivity achieved in the project and ensure it is maintained within the organizational baselines.

To control these four project parameters, we need to take several measurements, analyze them, and perform numerous activities to keep the project under control. Each of these will be discussed in greater detail in the following sections.

Schedule Control

Control of the project schedule is the most important aspect of IT project execution. Uniformly bad quality is totally unacceptable, but we can put up with a few quality issues that are amenable to rectification later on. We can also tolerate a little cost overrun, which may be less than the cost of delay in the completion of the project. Productivity and schedule are interrelated. If planned productivity is not achieved, the schedule will not be met.

Delaying the schedule would have the consequences of delaying the planned business operations. That means we would not only have to bear the cost of project delay, but also lost revenue that would have accrued from the planned business operations using the IT infrastructure set up by the project. All activities in the forward chain of linkages of the project would consequently be delayed.

How do we control the project schedule? Well, it begins with the scheduling itself. Appendix G within this book is dedicated to scheduling the project. While working on the schedule, we need to identify the activities that are to be performed sequentially (one after the other), the activities that can be performed in parallel (at the same time, concurrently). When we enter the activities into the scheduling tool, such as Microsoft Project or Primavera, and define the precedence relationships between the activities, the tool will prepare a network diagram. The scheduling tool utilizes this network diagram to identify the critical activities of the project. Critical activities are those that cannot be delayed at all. Any delay in completion of a critical activity would delay the entire project by the same amount of duration. The path on the network diagram from the start event connecting all critical activities to the end event is referred to as the critical path. We need to ensure that all critical activities are completed on time by providing the resources necessary and closely monitoring their performance. The activities that are not critical can be delayed, within limits, without adversely affecting the project completion date. The scheduling tool will also provide information about how much duration a noncritical activity can be delayed without delaying project completion, as well as the earliest and latest completion dates for every activity. The difference between the earliest and latest dates is referred to as the "slack" or "float" of the activity. Critical activities will have zero slack; in other words, the earliest and latest dates will be the same for a critical activity. The noncritical activities can be completed between the earliest and latest completion dates and the project will not be adversely affected in terms of schedule. The method of computing the earliest and latest dates in a schedule is discussed in Appendix D on PERT/CPM.

In summation, to control the project schedule, we need to ensure that:

1. All critical activities are closely monitored and all required resources are provided on time.
2. All critical activities are completed on time conforming to the schedule.
3. The noncritical activities are completed before their latest completion dates.

Now, it is possible that in spite of our diligent effort a critical activity is delayed. This would have the following consequences:

1. The project could be delayed.

2. The critical path would change and a new set of critical activities and critical path could emerge.
3. There would be negative slack for some of the activities, if the project completion date was not postponed. This means the activities with negative slack would need to be completed before their latest completion dates.

Obviously, the focus would change. One easy solution would be to postpone project completion by the amount of the delay in the critical activity. However, more often than not, this is undesirable and not agreed to by management. Therefore, if the project completion date was not postponed, our other option would be to bring the schedule back on track by completing the activities next to the delayed critical activity sooner than their earliest completion dates. We could do this by:

1. Using overtime. Work overtime until the project is back on track. This may increase effort, but duration would be reduced. We do tomorrow's work today to make up the lost duration.
2. Pumping in more resources to the critical activities so they are completed ahead of their schedule. We do this until the schedule is back on track.
3. Using alternatives. Sometimes pumping in more resources is not feasible due to the technical nature of the work. For example, a house may be built in 100 days using two carpenters. But can we complete it in two days using 100 carpenters? It may be possible in arithmetic, but not in real life. When faced with such a situation, we have the following alternatives:
    a. Use better tools that improve the speed of performance, if such tool usage is feasible.
    b. Use more expert resources that are faster than normal resources and can complete the work earlier.
    c. Use better methods. There are usually better methods and if the best are already being utilized, we could perhaps innovate or invite an expert such as a consultant to help us improve the speed of performance.
4. Subcontracting some of the work to an expert organization specializing in the proposed work. This can significantly reduce the project completion time.

To utilize any of these suggested methods, scan the remaining activities on the schedule and locate those that are amenable to increasing the pace of execution. It is essential to select any critical activities that are yet to be completed for reducing the duration. Once these activities are located, select and implement an effective alternative method for each to reduce their completion time. We can change the durations on the scheduling tool, and it will automatically re-compute the schedule, to aid us in this effort. It is necessary to perform this exercise activity by activity until the schedule is back on track. Upon completing this objective, we would use the new schedule to guide our project execution and meet the project completion date. The steps to implement should a critical activity get delayed during project execution are as follows:

1. Assess the remaining critical activities and locate those whose duration can be reduced by working overtime, pumping in additional or higher-skilled resources, using better tools/methods, or subcontracting.
2. Take the first feasible activity (chronologically) and reduce its duration by the maximum amount possible and rework the schedule using the scheduling tool.
3. If the new schedule is not acceptable, take the chronologically next activity and reduce its duration to the maximum amount possible and rework the schedule.
4. If the schedule is acceptable, finalize it. If the schedule is still unacceptable, continue to iterate steps 2 and 3 until it is acceptable. Then finalize the schedule and implement it.

There is a section on "crashing" in Appendix D on PERT/CPM that deals with reducing the project duration, which gives more information on this topic.

It is better, of course, to ensure that no critical activity is delayed in the first place. Should it occur, we need to reduce the duration of the subsequent activities and bring the schedule back on track. We also need to communicate the new schedule to all stakeholders so they are aware of what is happening on the project.

There is one important aspect to take note of when applying any of the methods enumerated here to reduce the duration of an activity. Although every effort must be made to minimize the amount spent on this additional effort, the cost of the project is going to increase. We need to obtain approvals for increased costs. If the delay is caused by uncontrollable issues and the increased cost is within reason, approvals are normally given.

Cost Control

Before the project is submitted for approval, we need to estimate the costs to be incurred to execute the project. Upon approval, this estimate would be set as the project budget. When the project execution begins, we draw money from this budget for meeting the project expenses. And as mentioned previously, it is essential to keep close tabs on costs to complete the project within the approved budget.

Before we look at how to control costs, we need to gain a reasonable understanding of the subject of costing. There are two types of costs: fixed costs and variable costs.

Fixed costs are those costs that are not tied specifically to project execution or any deliverable, but instead to the duration of project whether we accomplish anything or not. These include salaries for staff working on the project, office expenses, interest on borrowed money, loss of interest on money allocated for the project but not utilized, interest on any advances paid to subcontractors, and so on. Fixed costs increase or are reduced proportionately with the duration of the project. If we wish to control the fixed costs of the project, the only way is to complete the project as early as possible.

Variable costs are those expenses that are tied to payments made for the execution of the project. These include payment for materials procured, contractor payments against completed work, and expenses on utilities such as power, communications, and so on.

So how do we contain or save fixed costs? The most obvious way is to complete the project on schedule or sooner than planned. Another way is to set these costs low in the first place. The major expenses of fixed costs stem from overhead, salaries, and office expenses. If we fully staff our project from the beginning, this fixed expense will be high. If we instead allocate just a few essential staff at the start and ramp up the allocation only when additional resources become essential, we contain this fixed cost. Another way to contain this fixed cost involves the de-allocation of staff no longer required. Many project managers fail to de-allocate staff immediately upon completion of their assignment on a project, overlooking the fact that they would realize a fixed cost savings. De-allocating staff as soon as their assignment is completed saves the fixed cost component of the project. We need to carefully plan the project and schedule the ramp-up and ramp-down of resources in order to contain our fixed costs.

Another source of fixed cost is the cost of capital. If we borrow, interest is paid, and if we use our own money, interest is lost, as is the opportunity to use the money for something else. In either case, an expense is incurred. The best way to minimize the cost of capital employed is to carefully plan ahead and meticulously schedule the requirement of funds. When these dates are accurately predicted, funds are not unnecessarily locked up waiting to be spent. Accurate projection of the funds requirement and ensuring the project adheres to the schedule during execution would reduce wasteful expenditure on the cost of capital employed.

Variable costs often get escalated by using more resources than estimated, procuring more material than actually required, or by increasing the quantities of the work given to subcontractors beyond what was planned.

Allocation of more resources than absolutely essential is another source of cost escalation. Schedule slippage on an activity and efforts to complete the next activity faster to bring the schedule back on track by pumping in more resources are often the culprits as alluded to previously. Every schedule slippage causes escalation of costs. So to control costs on resources we obviously need to prevent schedule slippages. Another way is to execute the project with less costly resources so there is a buffer when schedule slippage occurs. Subcontracting can enable us to save on resource costs, and as mentioned previously their performance is governed by contract.

Splurging on materials is another source of cost escalation. Some project managers, in their eagerness to ensure supply of material for project execution, order more spares than estimated/recommended, which increases material costs. We need to adhere to the estimated/recommended quantities while ordering the materials to keep their costs under control and thereby the project cost within the approved budget.

When subcontractors are employed, we assign some amount of work. The actual quantities of work executed by subcontractors can be less or more than the quantities specified in the contract. While estimating quantities, some assumptions have to be made and the actual conditions on the site could differ. For example, let us assume that a subcontractor was employed to build our facility. To avoid interferences, cables might need to be rerouted, or different materials may have to be used while building the facility. Sometimes the materials specified in the bills of material are not available, and alternative materials may have to be procured at a higher cost. All of these issues escalate project cost. It is essential to carefully control the scope of work assigned to subcontractors as a means of keeping project costs under control.

An IT project has many avenues leading to escalated project costs. Unless we keep close control of all our costs, they can easily spiral out of control. Therefore, all means described previously need to be utilized to keep the project cost within the approved budget.

Quality Control

Quality is a very important part of any human endeavor. Human effort is the critical component of an IT project, putting together all the equipment, connecting it, and configuring software to make it all work, and that human effort injects errors and gives rise to quality issues.

Ensuring quality begins in the planning stage of a project wherein standards are selected to which the project must adhere to. Selecting and communicating the appropriate standards to all concerned with project execution is our first step. If an order is placed with a subcontractor, we need to communicate the standards their assignment must adhere to as well.

Ensuring the standards are adhered to is our next and crucial step. Quality control of the materials used in the project is a good place to start. All equipment, such as servers, workstations, networking hardware, cables, and so forth, must be subjected to inward testing.

For testing each piece of equipment, we need to prepare a test plan, define test cases, and execute them. If the vendors selected are known to produce equipment that conforms to recognized national or international standards, testing can be limited to ensuring the correct equipment was received and in good working condition. If suppliers are not reputed to conform to national or international standards, their supplies need to be subjected to rigorous testing to ensure quality is indeed built into the equipment. For low-cost consumables such as network connectors, hardware items, paint, and so forth, we need to subject them to visual inspection on a sample basis to ensure the correct items were received. All in all, for the equipment and materials used in the project, reasonable effort should be spent to ensure utilization of the correct quality equipment and materials.

For equipment and materials used by subcontractors, we need to insist they perform reasonable, inward quality control activities to ensure the correct quality equipment and materials are used. This has to be specified in the contract as well as by verification of their inward quality control records.

For the portion of project work executed in-house, we need to define the stages for quality control activities and perform those activities scrupulously. The main quality control activity during project execution is "in-process inspection." This method is implemented while the work is in progress. Assessments and quality control should be carried out as appropriate for each activity.

In some cases, it is necessary to hold up execution to perform an inspection or test. This would be the case for site preparation and construction of the data center. Just prior to the concrete being poured, we need to inspect and clear the quality of the mix and the site for correct preparation, which should only hold up execution for a few minutes. Similarly, just before powering on equipment, we need to inspect for proper equipment mounting, ensure everything is in order and the right type of power and voltage are readied, and then clear the power on. Here too, work would be held up for the duration of the inspection, which again takes only a few minutes.

In other cases, we would not hold up work, as it is necessary to perform inspections while the activity is being carried out. For example, when laying cables, we inspect the harnessing of cables, application of force while pulling the cables through conduits, and the crimping of end connectors.

Testing has limited applicability in the execution of an IT project. Equipment testing is performed when it is received from suppliers. Similarly, all material is tested to the extent applicable and possible when received from respective suppliers to ensure it is the right equipment and in good working condition.

Acceptance testing of the software is conducted when the development team offers it, to ensure all our requirements are met and it is working as desired. During project execution we need to test the continuity between the various equipment of the network before switching on the power. When all equipment is installed and the network is connected, we conduct system testing cursorily before beginning the trial runs. Trial runs test the system thoroughly.

One important aspect of quality control to note is that we have the authority to hold up work even to the extent of affecting the schedule. Sometimes it may genuinely be necessary to delay the work even at the risk of affecting the schedule. Yet a judicious decision must be made when faced with the necessity to hold up work to the extent that the schedule may slip. Quality control should act as the brake on an automobile, but not as a jam on the engine itself!

Productivity Control

Productivity has multiple definitions. The one we will use in this context is a simplified version. Productivity is the amount of effort expressed in person-hours/minutes for accomplishing a unit of work by an averagely skilled person putting in an average level of effort.

We make use of productivity while estimating the human effort required in accomplishing the work earmarked for in-house execution. If productivity is poor, it takes more effort per unit of work than estimated. The ramifications of poor productivity are an increase in project effort and related costs and schedule slippages.

Although we considered a person with an average level of skill, putting in an average level of effort for our definition of productivity, the following scenarios may occur in real life:

1. Some of the actual resources allocated to the project may have a less than average level of skill. In this case, more effort is likely to be needed to accomplish a unit of work, but these resources are, usually, less costly than average skilled persons.
2. Some of the actual resources may have an average level of skill in which case they meet the estimated scenario.
3. Some of the actual resources may possess a higher level of skill than average. In this case, resources would be spending less effort to accomplish a unit of work, but would, usually, cost more than average skilled persons.

Therefore, it is essential to ensure that the allocated number of resources equals the estimated number when normalizing the skill levels of allocated team members to the average level of skill. If the number is not equal, there will be a variance between the estimated effort and actual effort, leading to possible slippage/advancement of the schedule and a cost variance (CV).

Now that we have covered the impact differences in skill levels can have, let us discuss the differences in levels of effort individuals may expend. Every employee is expected to put in an average level of effort and it is assumed that they will. However, if employees are negatively motivated, they may not exert themselves resulting in less-than-average level of effort. If highly motivated in a positive way, they may put forth better-than-average levels of effort.

When a person joins a project, his/her skill level is fixed. We cannot increase their skill level in a short time during project execution. Yet a person can be motivated to put in a better-than-average level of effort.

Now you are sure to ask, "How do we define average level of skill and average level of effort?" Without accounting for variances in individual aptitudes, a person is deemed to have an average level of skill when:

1. The person is not a trainee or someone that recently entered employment.
2. The person completed on the job training and has been working independently for at least one year.
3. The person joined the organization at least six months ago and is well versed in the required methods, process, tools, and techniques.

A trainee is deemed to be of poor or low skill and requires close supervision and guidance. A full-time employee with up to two years of experience is assumed to be of fair skill and does not require close supervision, but needs some amount of guidance. A person with two to four years of experience is deemed to possess average skill, can be trusted to work independently, and only requires guidance occasionally. A person having four to six years of experience is considered to be of very good skill and does not need supervision or guidance. This person is fully capable of achieving results independently with minimum instruction and is able to guide others. A person with more than six years of experience is deemed to be a superior-skilled person, fully independent, and capable of guiding others. This individual is often used to mentor trainees in the organization and is capable of innovation and development of better methods too.

Similarly, a person not taking any breaks and using additional time for official work is said to be contributing superior effort. A person taking a few of the allowed breaks and not using additional time for official work is said to be putting forth very good effort. A person taking all the allowed breaks but no other breaks and not using additional time is said to be expending an average level of effort, adhering to the organizational expectation of the amount of time spent on official work. A person taking all the allowed breaks and wasting some additional time is said to be contributing a fair level of effort. A person taking all the allowed breaks, a few more breaks, and wasting a significant amount of time is said to be putting forth a poor level of effort.

We have now defined our skill levels which are fixed for the project duration. We have also defined our effort levels which are not fixed and can be influenced, but how? Generally speaking, employees can be motivated to maintain or increase their levels of effort by:

1. *Assigning them a fair workload comparable to other colleagues.* Employees often become less motivated if they perceive their assigned workload to be unfairly higher or lower than their peers. For many people, work is their greatest motivation. They come to the workplace and like to feel they contributed to the organization in a significant way when leaving work for the day. Therefore, they should be assigned a workload that they can feel pride in accomplishing. The workload on all resources should be as uniform and commensurate with the position and skill level as possible.
2. *Giving recognition for individual accomplishment commensurate with the results produced.* Recognition or rewards should never be based on subjective criteria. It should be based on objective and verifiable data collected and analyzed for making this decision. As project managers, we need to spend time and effort collecting and analyzing data for this purpose diligently. If recognition and rewards are given based on subjective decisions, the resources are likely to become demotivated.
3. *Giving positive and negative rewards (punishments) without fear or favor.* Many managers tend to overlook giving minor negative rewards, when it often improves results. Douglas McGregor's "hot stove"

analogy provides valuable insight into why and how to implement this corrective action as follows:

a. A hot stove causes burns to anyone touching it. It will not excuse anyone based on designation or rank; it causes burns to all who touch it.
b. The burn is commensurate with the amount of touch. If you touch it for just a fraction of a second, the burn will be less severe than when you hold it for a minute.
c. The burn is immediate. If you touch it now, it will burn now but not after several days. So, the negative reward should be administered as soon as the infraction occurs and not six months later.

4. *Applying the philosophy behind the hot stove analogy for recognition of positive performance.* Except for periodic awards, this is a good practice.

Since we can motivate people to expend better-than-average or at least average levels of effort, it is essential to monitor the productivity achieved on the project and take corrective action in a timely manner. One common corrective action required on IT projects is to motivate employees whose productivity is below the organizational baselines. Naturally, the big question is: "How do we motivate employees when we can't promise any financial rewards or threaten the stability of their employment? True, more often than not, the IT project manager would be unable to grant any financial reward immediately, much less to underperforming employees. Terminating these employees in an ongoing project would cause further delays in the form of time lost replacing the resources and training new individuals to pick up speed. Effective techniques for motivating underperforming employees are as follows:

1. *Counsel the individuals on the necessity to perform better.* This can start with comparing the employees' performance with others doing similar work. When done carefully with objective data, there will usually be marked improvement because no employee wants to be seen in a poor light on the performance front.
2. *Coach the individuals.* Sometimes their performance can be lower due to a lack of certain skills. We can bridge this by coaching them using more skilled seniors or providing specialist assistance when needed. Sometimes there may be hurdles causing their under-performance and we can help remove them.
3. *Encourage the individuals.* Sometimes a bit of encouragement as to your belief in their ability to perform produces significant improvement.
4. *Appraise the individuals.* Measure the individuals' performance periodically and see if the trend is one of improvement. If it is, wonderful. If not or it is deteriorating, implement the above three steps again.

Controlling productivity would automatically control the schedule and the project cost. Therefore, we need to keep a close watch on the productivity being achieved on the project and control it.

Tools and Techniques for Project Control

Tools and techniques are used in controlling IT projects. We utilize a scheduling tool such as MS-Project or Primavera as the main tool for IT project management and control. We use the scheduling tool along with a progress report and periodic progress review meetings in project control. We monitor the schedule and resource usage during progress review meetings and compare the actual achievements with those planned as recorded in the scheduling tool. If there are any variances, we need to analyze them and take corrective actions, as discussed previously. Let us now discuss techniques for project control.

Progress Reports

Project progress should normally be reported once a week. Each of the subcontractors and other agencies working on the project should send their progress report to the project manager, who reviews each report and sends a consolidated progress report to the organizational management and other stakeholders. Figure 7.1 depicts the elements of a suggested progress report

Progress report for sub-project

Sub-project ID: Date:

Project manager for the sub-project:

Overall progress:

Activities completed this week:

Ongoing activities:

Activities proposed for next week:

Issues raised:

Special events:

Process improvement suggestions:

Any other relevant information:

Figure 7.1 Elements of the progress report for a sub-project (template exhibited in Appendix I)

template for subcontractors or agencies handling sub-projects. All persons holding charge of sub-projects would fill in this template and send it to the IT project manager, who would review the sub-project progress with the individuals concerned, note any issues, and provide guidance for the next period. The review would be recorded in MOM (minutes of meeting) format. Figure 7.2 depicts the elements of a suggested progress report template for the project.

Progress Monitoring Meetings

Progress monitoring meetings are conducted as an adjunct to project progress reports. Monitoring meetings can occur either in a face-to-face manner or as teleconferences or videoconferences in which all stakeholders meet and analyze the project progress using project plans and progress reports as the base. During the meeting stakeholders agree upon any corrective actions to be implemented. These meetings are conducted one or two days after the progress report is communicated to all stakeholders. Stakeholders discuss the progress as well as issues necessitating resolution and assign action points to the concerned persons participating in the meeting. These action points are recorded

Progress report for project

Project ID: Date:

Project start date:

Project scheduled completion date:

Project manager:

Executive summary:

Overall progress:

Progress of the sub-projects

Earned value analysis:

Issues needing management attention:

Project metrics:

Special events:

Process improvement suggestions:

Any other relevant information:

Figure 7.2 Elements for an IT project progress report (template exhibited in Appendix I)

Minutes of meeting

Meeting conducted on:

Chaired by:

List of participants:

Highlights of the meeting:

Action points:

Any other items discussed:

MOM prepared by:

Date:

Figure 7.3 Elements of the format for recording meeting minutes for progress review meetings (template exhibited in Appendix I)

as the minutes of the meeting (MOM) and distributed to all stakeholders. This record would be used as a reference for monitoring further progress.

Multiple progress monitoring meetings may be conducted such as the following:

1. Project manager (PM) and project team
2. PM, project team, and organizational management
3. PM with managers of sub-projects and subcontractors
4. PM with organizational management

Figure 7.3 shows the elements of a suggested format for recording MOM for progress monitoring meetings.

Metrics

Metrics also assist in quantitatively assessing project health and facilitate close control of the project. Five classes of metrics are typically collated, computed, and distributed to project stakeholders. The project progress report is a good tool to distribute metrics. Another method is to publish the metrics in a big chart (dashboard). The five classes are:

1. *Quality metrics* such as the defect injection rate of various activities and the defect removal efficiency of each quality assurance activity
2. *Schedule metrics* such as schedule variance (SV), percentage of activities that met the schedule, were delayed, and were completed ahead of schedule

3. *Productivity metrics* showing the productivity of each project activity executed with in-house resources and variances from the plan
4. *Cost metrics* such as actual vis-à-vis the budgeted expenditure (Variance analysis would also be included.)
5. *Effort metrics* showing actual effort expended vis-à-vis planned effort and variance analysis

Computation and compilation of these metrics and analysis of variances give an objective view of the project execution efficiency. The metrics also facilitate the corrective action necessary to bring the project back on track to synchronize with the project schedule.

Earned Value Analysis

Earned value analysis (EVA) is an important method for measuring project performance. In its simplest terms, EVA indicates what portion of the budget should have been spent compared to the amount of work currently completed. Earned value is also referred to as budgeted cost of work performed.

EVA measures project performance using financial terms. It is difficult to measure the progress of a large project by simply tracking a sizable number of activities that are in various stages of completion. It is far easier to keep track of the money spent on the project. Contrasting the value of money actually spent with the budgeted expenditure allows us to express the project progress with a single figure. It is as simple as saying, "We should have spent $5,000 by this date but we actually completed $4,000 of work, therefore we have completed only about 80% of the planned work." EVA is extensively used in large construction and defense projects in the United States as well as in IT projects.

EVA uses three primary values for the project or each activity:

1. *The budgeted cost of work scheduled* (BCWS) is the portion of the cost that is planned to be spent on an activity (or project) between the start and status date. For example, the total planned budget for a four-day activity is $100 and it starts on a Monday. If the status date is set for Wednesday (day three), the BCWS is $75.
2. *The actual cost of work performed* (ACWP) is the total actual cost incurred while performing work on an activity (or project) during a given period. For example, if the four-day activity actually incurs a total cost of $70 by Wednesday, the ACWP for this period is $70.
3. *The budgeted cost of work performed* (BCWP) is the percentage of the budget that should have been spent for a given percentage of work performed on an activity (or project). For example, if by Wednesday,

60% of the work has been completed, you might expect to have spent 60% of the total activity budget; that is, $60 in the above example.

Several other key values are derived from these three primary values. The most common and useful ones follow. To understand the values below, let us use the above example of a four-day activity, with a BCWS of $100, ACWP as $70, and BCWP as $60.

CV is the difference between an activity's estimated cost and its actual cost:

CV = BCWP – ACWP
CV = 60 – 70
CV = (–) 10

As seen here, we budgeted $60 but already spent $70; that is, we overspent $10! It may be necessary to cut back in the future or allocate more funds for the completion of the activity/project.

SV is the difference between the current and scheduled progress of an activity in terms of cost:

SV = BCWP – BCWS
SV = 60 – 75
SV = (–) 15

This indicates that we are behind schedule, since only $60 was spent of the budgeted expenditure of $75. One might conclude that we saved on the budget, which is possible, but this would be revealed in the next two indices. If the cost performance index (CPI) and schedule performance index (SPI) are more than 1, it can be inferred that we saved on the budget.

The CPI is the ratio of budgeted costs to actual costs:

CPI = BCWP/ACWP
CPI= 60/70
CPI = 0.86

The CPI is 0.86, which means that we overspent on the activity/project. A CPI of less than 1 indicates overspending and a CPI of more than 1 indicates that we are saving on budget.

The SPI is the ratio of work performed to work scheduled:

SPI = BCWP/BCWS
SPI = 60/75
SPI = 0.8

The SPI is 0.80; that is, 80% of the work is completed. An SPI of less than 1 indicates the project is behind schedule and more than 1 indicates it is ahead of schedule.

Benefits of Earned Value Analysis

The following are the benefits of performing EVA:

1. It results in reliable answers to key questions such as:
   i. Is there enough money left in the budget to complete the project?
   ii. Is there enough time remaining in the schedule to finish the project on time?
2. Earned value indicators express project progress in terms of cost and schedule. An EVA is an excellent and easy way to determine whether you'll run out of money before work on the project is completed or have a surplus after it's over.

Interpretation of Earned Value Analysis

EVA figures are interpreted as follows:

1. Earned value indicators that are variances, such as CV, can be either positive or negative. A positive variance indicates the project is ahead of schedule or under budget. Positive variances might enable the reallocation of money and resources from activities or projects with positive variances to those with negative variances.
2. A negative variance indicates the project is behind schedule or over budget and action must be taken. If an activity or project has a negative CV, it may be necessary to increase the budget or accept reduced profit margins.
3. Earned value indicators that are ratios, such as the CPI and SPI, can be greater than 1 or less than 1. As stated previously, a value greater than 1 indicates that the project is ahead of schedule or under budget. A value less than 1 indicates the project is behind schedule or over budget. For example, an SPI of 1.5 indicates only 67% of the planned time has been taken to complete a portion of an activity in a given time period, and a CPI of 0.8 means 25% more has been spent on an activity in a given time period.

Earned value analysis is a very useful tool for IT projects, especially for large projects of longer duration.

Audits

Audits are dealt with in greater detail in Chapter 9. We use audits to ensure project execution is in conformance with the process and on schedule.

A phase-end audit is utilized to ensure a project has successfully completed a phase and is ready for the next one. Phase-end audits are performed after the project initiation phase, then planning, execution, and closure. A mid-project audit is conducted during project execution since this phase takes the longest duration. Both of these are conformance audits. An investigative audit is performed when the project is either behind schedule or significantly overshooting the approved budget. Audits are used by management to ensure project execution conforms to organizational processes and to assist in project control.

8

Cash Management

Introduction

IT infrastructure projects involve spending significant amounts of money toward equipment purchase and infrastructure deployment, as well as system software procurement and application software acquisition. Although cost control is very important on IT projects, cash management is equally important. Anyone can spend money, but few know how to do it wisely on a consistent basis. IT project managers need not be great finance managers, but they must be equipped with at least some rudimentary knowledge about cash management to be successful. This chapter aims to provide just that.

Elements of Cash Management

What is cash? Cash is money that can be accessed very easily. It is typically on our premises or in an account at a bank. Gold, property, bonds, and bills to be collected are assets that may appreciate in value over a period of time, but they are not cash. Cash does not appreciate and if the rate of inflation is high enough, it may deteriorate in value over a period of time by losing its purchasing power.

What is cash flow? It is the flow of cash into a business as income and out as expenses. Certain outflows aid income generation. These outflows are expenses toward purchase of materials, wages, utilities, and so on, which are utilized to produce products or services that can be sold to bring cash into the business. Some outflows do not aid income generation, such as expenses toward taxes, interest on borrowed money, investments, and so on. These are often referred to as the "cost of doing business."

It is important to note that money spent on IT infrastructure in an organization is not for generating income. It is a business expense that aids employees to improve the efficiency of doing business. Of course, now that computers are used for doing business in most organizations, some might argue that money spent on IT infrastructure indirectly aids income generation. For example, software development or business process management organizations are completely dependent on computers, and IT infrastructure is an essential part of their business transactions. Yet in truth, it is still an investment.

Where does the money to fund our IT infrastructure project come from? The organization may choose to borrow or use its own money. The organization's own money comes from two sources: share capital/equity or retained earnings/reserves (surplus of profits that were set aside for investment). Each source has an associated cost. For share capital, the organization may choose to pay dividends from profits earned. If money is taken out of organizational reserves, there is loss of interest or such other income arising out of investing those reserves. When an infrastructure is implemented, it is normally capitalized to be treated as an asset and subjected to depreciation. The manner in which the source of funding is selected is referred to as project appraisal and project financing. Methods such as return on investment, discounted cash flow, and duration analysis are used to evaluate competing alternatives. The source of funding is decided based on availability, cost, and the relative advantages of funding from the source. This decision is made prior to project execution. So we need to focus on spending the allocated funds wisely.

Budgeting

Budgeting is an exercise carried out by organizational management with assistance from the finance department to plan the requirements of funds needed to run business operations and the means of acquiring those funds. A budget shows both cash inflows and outflows. The budgeting exercise within an organization is usually performed at the beginning of a financial year and implemented during the year. Unless a cash outflow (expenditure) has been budgeted, it will not typically be allowed except in extraordinary circumstances and only with special approval. Large organizations maintain rolling forecasts and review and modify their budget on a quarterly or semi-annual basis to align it with the changing business scenario.

As mentioned previously, a budget will show cash inflows and outflows. Outflows must be equal to inflows to have a balanced budget. When an item is shown in the outflows of an approved budget, it means the expending of funds is sanctioned on that item. Normally, we refer to inclusion of expenditure in the budget as "allocation of funds" for that item. However, that does not mean the required funds are set aside and can be drawn as and when required. Budget allocation implies permission to spend funds subject to the condition they are available. Organizational management would juggle the inflows to provide funding to the approved items.

Suppose the budget is allocated but funds are not available to meet an expense. What would happen? If funds are not available from internal sources, but the item was included in the approved budget, and the expense cannot be postponed, the organization would typically borrow funds. When funds become available, the loan would be paid off but the fact remains that more money was spent than budgeted because of interest paid on the borrowed funds. The important aspect to remember is that approval of the project budget does not necessarily mean funds are set aside for project expenditure.

With this clearly understood, we need to let the finance department know when to set aside the funds for the project. This is accomplished through a cash flow statement which only shows the outflows.

Cash Flow Statement

In the cash flow statement, we project the amount of funds the project needs along with the date the funds will likely be required. We do not give a deterministic single date on which funds are required. Of course, salaries must be paid on a specific date and can be projected accurately, yet the actual requirement for other funds can certainly be different from the projected date for a variety of reasons. The supplier may delay supplies or the subcontractor may not submit the bill for progress payment. Therefore, two dates are projected: the earliest and latest by which funds would be required. The earliest date is when payment is likely to fall due by all indications. The latest date is the one which, if payment is not made, we may be liable for penalties.

A second aspect to consider is the amount of money to be paid. Suppose the organization is unable to raise the required amount of funds within the indicated duration. Payment can be delayed and penalties accepted, or some amount of money can be paid with a promise the remaining amount will be paid by a specified future date. The second alternative would avoid penalties. Business partners do not like to levy penalties for fear of losing the reputation of cooperating partners. So, we need to indicate both the full and minimum amounts required during a period. Of course, paying the minimum amount only avoids penalties and the liability for the full payment still remains. Figure 8.1 depicts the elements of a suggested template for a cash flow statement.

Cash flow statement for IT project	
Project ID:	Date:
Project manager:	
Funds requirement:	
Notes:	

Figure 8.1 Elements for the cash flow statement template (template exhibited in Appendix I)

To prepare this statement, we need data, which are available in the schedule prepared during the planning stage. If we diligently prepared it using a tool such as MS-Project or Primavera, the information will be very easy to extract.

MS Project and Primavera both contain a feature referred to as Resources Management, which facilitates the following:

1. Multiple resources are defined.
2. Resources could be individuals, materials, equipment, or tools.
3. Each resource has a cost per unit time associated with it, such as $100 per hour.
4. Resources are of two types:
   a. Depleting resources, such as material consumed/spent with usage
   b. Recurring resources, such as equipment available every day for use and not consumed/spent with usage
5. There is a maximum time limit for resource availability.
6. Each task/activity can utilize multiple resources.
7. Resources can be overallocated. For example, although the working day might be eight hours, we could allocate the resource for nine hours. This would be akin to planned overtime.
8. If we did not wish to overallocate resources, the tool would automatically recompute the schedule. This is referred to as "resource constrained scheduling."

When the resource feature of the scheduling tool is used, it would indicate both the task cost and the cost of each resource. There are built-in reports from which these costs can be extracted. Once the data are available, we can easily prepare the cash flow statement.

The cash flow statement would be the reference used by the finance department and organizational management to make funds available on the dates mentioned in the statement. However, we would be responsible for managing the project using the funds made available and ensuring the project is not delayed due to nonavailability of funds.

Cash Management

If everything were to go as planned, there would be no need for management or a project manager to become involved in cash management. Yet, things go wrong and execution deviates from the plan. Even when we meet the final project completion date, plenty of activities can be delayed or completed earlier.

Just as project activities can be delayed, they may also be advanced and completed earlier, leading to earlier payment release demands. In this situation we would need to persuade the vendor/subcontractor to wait. This requires cordial relations with the vendor/subcontractor.

Sometimes an activity may be completed on time but payment is not ready or funds are unavailable. Again, we would need to persuade the vendor/subcontractor to wait using good relations built up earlier.

Sometimes funds may be ready but the activities for which they were earmarked are not completed. What do we do in this situation? Keeping funds idle does not earn any interest. In such eventualities, we would alert the finance department of the new dates of funds' requirements. This would provide them the opportunity to utilize the funds for alternative purposes or investment in short-term interest-earning deposits, to realize some extra money for the organization.

Although withdrawal of funds and remitting payments are activities performed by the accounting function upon direction and approval of the project manager and others in a finance function, a project manager must have a good understanding of when to direct the accountants to draw funds. So when should we have money drawn to meet obligations during project execution? The first alternative is to draw funds as or when they fall due. Obviously, any need for funds is elastic in terms of the payment date. There is always an earliest and a latest date. If we draw it at the earliest, the organization loses interest and if we draw it at the latest date, the goodwill of the vendor/subcontractor may be lost. So, we must balance both aspects when deciding to draw funds and make payments. If at all possible we should not draw funds at the earliest requirement date or wait until the latest date. Based on the elasticity available for releasing payments, funds should be drawn somewhere between the earliest and latest due dates. If we do not manage cash intelligently, we may incur cost/loss of interest on the funds allocated to the project. Even if the project cost is maintained within the approved budget in absolute terms, we may be losing money for the organization.

The objective of this chapter, as stated previously, was to provide readers an introduction to the basics of cash management and an understanding of why it is so important. This is not, nor was it intended to be a comprehensive treatment of the topic. To be successful, IT project managers must be equipped with the basic knowledge articulated here, but they really ought to be adept in cash management to ensure project cost is controlled and that the organization realizes whatever benefits can be derived from cash spent on the IT project.

9

Quality Assurance in IT Project Management

Introduction

Quality assurance refers to all the activities that are performed to ensure quality in project deliveries. Quality assurance is a large topic on which many books are written. As such, this chapter simply represents an overview of the activities relevant to IT project management.

Quality is generally defined as *fitness for use* with the critical words *fitness* and *use* to be elaborated separately for each scenario. *Fitness* refers to the robustness of the product and the limits of what it can handle. *Use* defines how the product will be utilized. These two terms need to be interpreted in deliverable specifications in the project scenario. Simply put, these are the objectives and they influence the infrastructure design.

We define quality management in a project scenario as the need to ensure quality in the following:

1. Specifications (or objectives)
2. Infrastructure design
3. Project execution

Figure 9.1 illustrates these inputs to quality assurance.

Environment Conducive to Quality

First, it is essential to prevent defects from creeping in. Note that quality control activities cannot add quality to the infrastructure; they can only detect

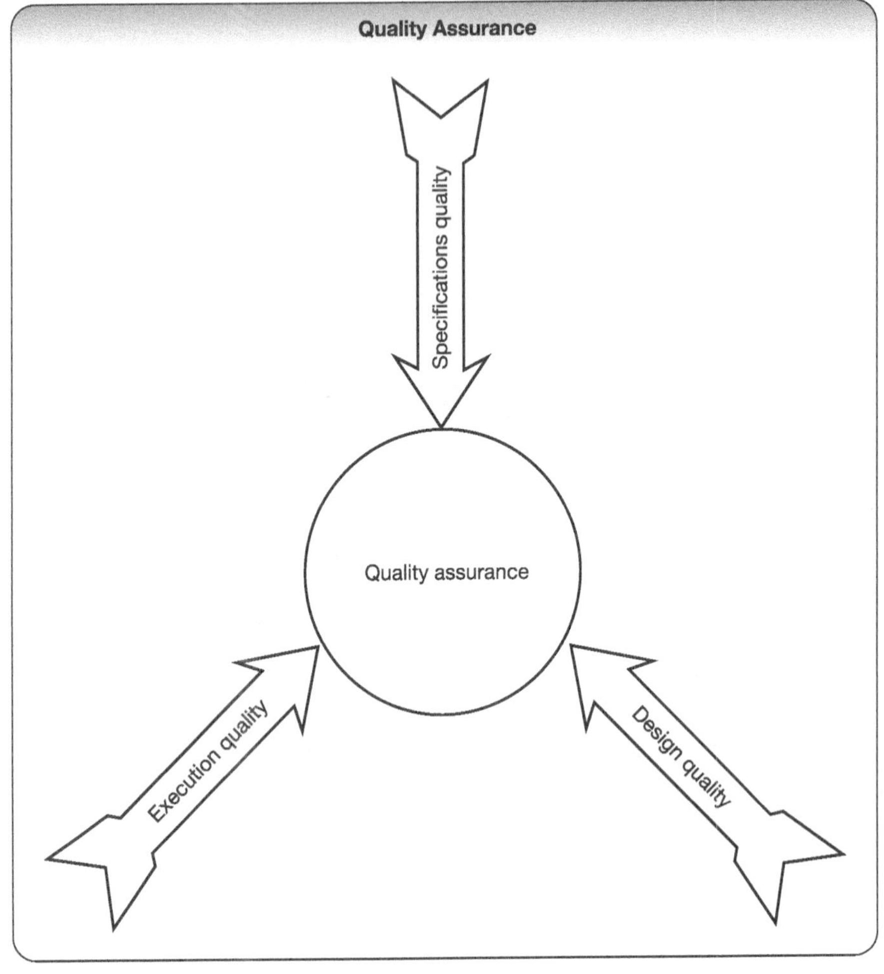

Figure 9.1 Quality assurance inputs

defects present in it. Therefore, it is imperative to create an environment that ensures quality is built into all deliverables. The following are the prerequisites to ensure this quality:

1. Organizational process
2. Standards and guidelines
3. Measurement and metrics

Let us discuss each of these in the following sections.

Organizational Process

Organizational process includes: procedures, standards, guidelines, formats, templates, and checklists that guide the organization in carrying out various activities.

Procedures contain step-by-step instructions on how to carry out an activity including applicable quality control activities, approvals, standards, guidelines, formats, templates, and checklists. Everyone in the organization must internalize the procedures applicable to their line of activity.

Standards and *guidelines* provide technical details regarding how to execute the work including tools to be used, pressure to be applied, measurements, limits of use, and so on. Most organizations have standards for the activities they perform. Quality control activities are carried out by comparing the work with the standards to uncover discrepancies.

Formats and *templates* assist in capturing information in a uniform manner across the organization. They are used for preparing plans, reports, logs, and various other documents. The difference between formats and templates is that a format is generally limited to one page and does not contain any explanation for entries to guide the user, whereas templates span multiple pages and include explanations to guide the user where necessary.

Checklists contain a list of items to be checked off when carrying out an activity or review/inspection of an artifact. Checklists facilitate verification of every aspect of work, as well as inspections and reviews to ensure completeness and that everything has been attended to.

The organization should have a defined process and internalize it in their human resources for uniformity in the deliverables irrespective of the person carrying out an activity. A defined process also facilitates periodic evaluations and improvements to align it with changing conditions. The organizational process normalizes the experience of the resources and brings uniformity to the deliverable.

Standards and Guidelines

Standards and guidelines are part of the organizational process but deserve a separate section because of their importance in determining the quality of deliverables. Standards and guidelines define the technical and material specifications for all deliverables and activities carried out in the organization. Standards also contain details about how to make connections, the voltages to be applied to equipment, force to be applied while tightening nuts and bolts, the insulation resistance of the cables, earthing (connecting the metal body of the equipment to earth) of equipment, and so on. Specific details are contained in the standards. It is the standards and guidelines that set the platform for quality and ensure that minimum quality is achieved and maintained. Design guidelines help to ensure that the design is complete and take into consideration all applicable aspects to achieve a robust infrastructure. Workmanship standards and guidelines facilitate robust workmanship and project execution. Testing guidelines facilitate efficient testing. All in all, standards and guidelines are the backbone for achieving quality in all aspects including project design and execution.

Measurement and Metrics

Measurement and metrics are of significant importance to organizations involved in setting up IT infrastructure for other organizations. For organizations that are going to be end users of the infrastructure, only a few metrics would make sense since they are not going to repeat the process in the near future. For organizations specializing in setting up IT infrastructure for other organizations, a bigger set of metrics is necessary to continuously improve their process. Measurements are taken to derive metrics and assess project performance. We would take the following measurements:

1. Quality
2. Schedule conformance
3. Effort
4. Cost
5. Productivity

Quality Metrics

Quality in a product or service is measured by the presence or absence of defects. In setting up IT infrastructure, we would know the number of defects uncovered by quality control activities. The defects left undetected would be known only during the actual operation of the infrastructure.

The defects, if detected in the procured equipment or material, really do not belong to us. They are injected by the manufacturer. But we do need to measure the defects in setting up the infrastructure. The main data are the number of defects uncovered during quality control activities and trial runs and both should be considered. Therefore we would compute various metrics as follows:

Network defect injection rate = total number of network connections ÷ number of defects uncovered. This is expressed as the number of connections per defect. (Note: one cable with connectors at both ends is considered one connection, not two.) Currently, it is well accepted in the quality management field that it is not possible to uncover all the injected defects. The efficiency of uncovering them (defect removal efficiency) is at most 90%. This metric shows how many defects remain in the infrastructure. Assume that we have 100 connections and uncovered 20 defects. The defect injection rate in networking is 5 connections per defect. These 20 defects are 90% of the total assuming the efficiency of detecting errors is 90%. The remaining 10%, or 2 defects, are left undetected and will surface later during actual usage.

Application software defects metric = size of software ÷ number of defects uncovered in all quality control activities. Software size may be measured in function points, lines of code, software size units, or any other unit of software size measure. This metric is expressed as one defect per unit of software size. Here too, using the defect removal efficiency we can estimate the defects remaining in the software when it is put into production.

Infrastructure defect injection rate = total cost of infrastructure ÷ number of defects uncovered in all quality control activities. This is expressed as one defect per so many dollars. Using the defect removal efficiency, we can calculate the remaining defects to be uncovered during operation.

Schedule Metrics

Data for calculating schedule variance metrics come from the project schedule and progress reports, which we need to compute on the day of project review.

Schedule variance for the project for the completed work = number of days actually taken ÷ number of scheduled days. If the metric is greater than 1, the project is behind schedule. If less than 1, it is ahead.

Percentage of activities meeting schedule = (number of activities meeting the schedule ÷ total number of completed activities) × 100.

Percentage of activities ahead of schedule = (number of activities ahead of schedule ÷ total number of completed activities) × 100.

Percentage of activities behind schedule = (number of activities behind schedule ÷ total number of completed activities) × 100. This is an important metric because management need not be concerned with activities that are either completed ahead of or on schedule. Management needs to focus attention on tardy activities, and this metric reveals the focus area.

Cost Metrics

Data for computing cost variance metrics come from the project schedule and progress reports as well, assuming the project manager maintained the cost data in the progress reports. If not, the finance department is likely to have the accurate cost data. So, in some cases, the cost actually incurred would have to be computed by the concerned agency and be made available for derivation of the metrics. We calculate and interpret these results as follows:

Cost variance for the project for completed work = amount of money actually spent ÷ estimated cost. If the metric is greater than 1, money has been overspent. If less than 1, money has been saved.

It may be necessary to determine the actual cost for completed activities, which should be done using the following formulas on the day of project review:

Percentage of activities meeting budgeted cost = (number of activities meeting cost ÷ total number of completed activities) × 100.

Percentage of activities that saved on budgeted cost = (number of activities that spent less than the budgeted cost ÷ total number of completed activities) × 100.

Percentage of activities that overspent budget = (number of activities that overspent the budget ÷ total number of completed activities) × 100. This is an important metric because management need not worry about activities that met or saved on budgeted cost. Management needs to focus attention on activities that overshot the budget and analyze the reasons.

Effort Metrics

Data for developing effort metrics also come from the project schedule and progress reports and should be calculated on the day of project review.

Effort variance for the project for completed work = number of person days actually taken ÷ number of estimated person days. If the metric is greater than 1, estimated effort has been exceeded. If less than 1, effort has been saved.

Percentage of activities meeting effort = (number of activities meeting effort ÷ total number of activities completed) × 100.

Percentage of activities that saved on the estimated effort = (number of activities that consumed less than the estimated effort ÷ total number of completed activities) × 100. We compute these metrics in addition to performing the earned value analysis described in Chapter 7.

Percentage of activities overshot estimated effort = (number of activities that consumed more than the estimated effort ÷ total number of completed activities) × 100. This is an important metric because management need not concern itself with the activities that are either completed within or saved on the estimated effort. Management needs to focus attention on the activities that consumed more than the estimated effort to analyze the reasons and take corrective action to bring the schedule back on track.

Productivity Metrics

Productivity metrics are computed for the activities carried out by in-house resources, but not those performed by subcontractors.

Productivity metric = the number of person-hours consumed in completing that work ÷ the quantity of work completed. This is expressed as person-hours per unit of work.

There is no point in calculating the productivity metric for activities such as purchasing and other administrative chores. This metric can be determined for testing (person-hours per test case), reviews (person-hours per page), and any other technical activity.

Once measurements are taken and metrics derived, it is essential to analyze them to detect trends and patterns, if any, that emerge. Based on the trend and pattern detected for each metric, corrective action can be taken to fix the present situation and preventive action to avert future recurrence. The organizational process, standards and guidelines, metrics and measurement, coupled with analysis and dovetailing the analysis findings back into the process, create an environment that fosters quality in all aspects of organizational functioning and thereby the execution of IT infrastructure projects.

Quality Control

Quality control refers to the set of activities performed to ensure that quality is built into the deliverables. These activities are performed during project execution. There are four sets of tools and techniques for ensuring conformance to quality:

1. Verification, which includes peer review and managerial review
2. Inspections
3. Validation, which includes testing and expert reviews
4. Audits

Each of these subcategories is explained below.

Verification

Verification is an activity carried out to confirm that something conforms to its documented specifications, standards, regulations, and so on. It is confirmation that "the right thing is done" and that all required components are present in the right quantity. Verification doesn't involve confirming the functionality by testing the artifact/object under consideration. It is carried out by visual means and at most by touch and feel, but not by running or powering up the artifact. Verification uses the techniques of peer review and managerial review to ensure quality. Inspections can also be included in verification but certain types of inspections in the engineering field also include testing. Therefore, inspections may belong to both verification as well as validation. For this reason a separate section is dedicated to it in this chapter. In the context of IT projects, verification is used for ensuring quality in information artifacts (documents, engineering drawings, and bills of material). Peer reviews and managerial reviews are discussed in greater detail as follows.

Peer Reviews

A peer review is a process in which one or more peers (with similar experience and knowledge as the author of the artifact) walk through every sentence of the artifact assessing its usefulness, necessity, accuracy, and compliance to standards. A peer review may be assisted or unassisted. In unassisted peer reviews, the artifact is given to a peer who reviews each line and makes a report of any defects uncovered. In assisted peer reviews, the author of the artifact presents the artifact to one or more peers and notes down the improvement suggestions. Typical peer review objectives are:

1. Ensuring completeness of information
2. Ensuring accuracy of information
3. Ensuring conformance to organizational guidelines and standards in all aspects of efficiency, effectiveness, safety, and security in the information provided
4. Encouraging teams conform to guidelines of efficiency, defect prevention, and naming conventions
5. Ensuring no defects in the information provided by the artifact

There are three types of peer reviews:

1. Independent
2. Guided
3. Group

Independent Peer Reviews This type of verification is also referred to as an *unassisted review.* Independent peer reviews are carried out in the following manner:

1. The author of the artifact completes the work and informs the project manager to arrange for the review.
2. The project manager allocates the work of reviewing the artifact to a peer of the author.
3. The artifact to be reviewed is made available to the reviewer. This may be achieved by pointing to the location of the artifact or by physically transferring the artifact to the reviewer. When the location is pointed out, access rights are limited to "read only."
4. The reviewer examines the artifact to identify defects/issues and any opportunity for improvement, prepares the review report, and hands it over to the project manager.
5. The project manager scrutinizes the review report and arranges for defects pointed out in the report to be fixed.
6. The project manager requests the reviewer to verify the veracity of the fixed defects.
7. The reviewer verifies the rectifications.
8. If all defects are properly fixed, the reviewer records the details in the review report and closes it.
9. If defects remain in the artifact, Steps 5, 6, 7, and 8 are reiterated until all defects are fixed.
10. When all defects are closed, the review activity for the artifact is completed.

The notable aspect of this review is that the author of the artifact need not be present while it is being carried out. If the reviewer needs any clarification, he/she needs to contact the author and obtain the required clarifications. Thus, the author is free to devote time to another activity while the artifact is being reviewed. However, if the artifact is poorly developed or ambiguous, the reviewer may not understand and, as a result, may not be able to unearth all defects effectively. The process of an independent peer review is depicted in Figure 9.2.

Guided Peer Reviews Guided peer reviews are also referred to as *assisted peer reviews.* They are carried out in the presence of the author of the artifact being reviewed. In this method, the author of the artifact guides the reviewer through the artifact. This type of verification is conducted in the following manner:

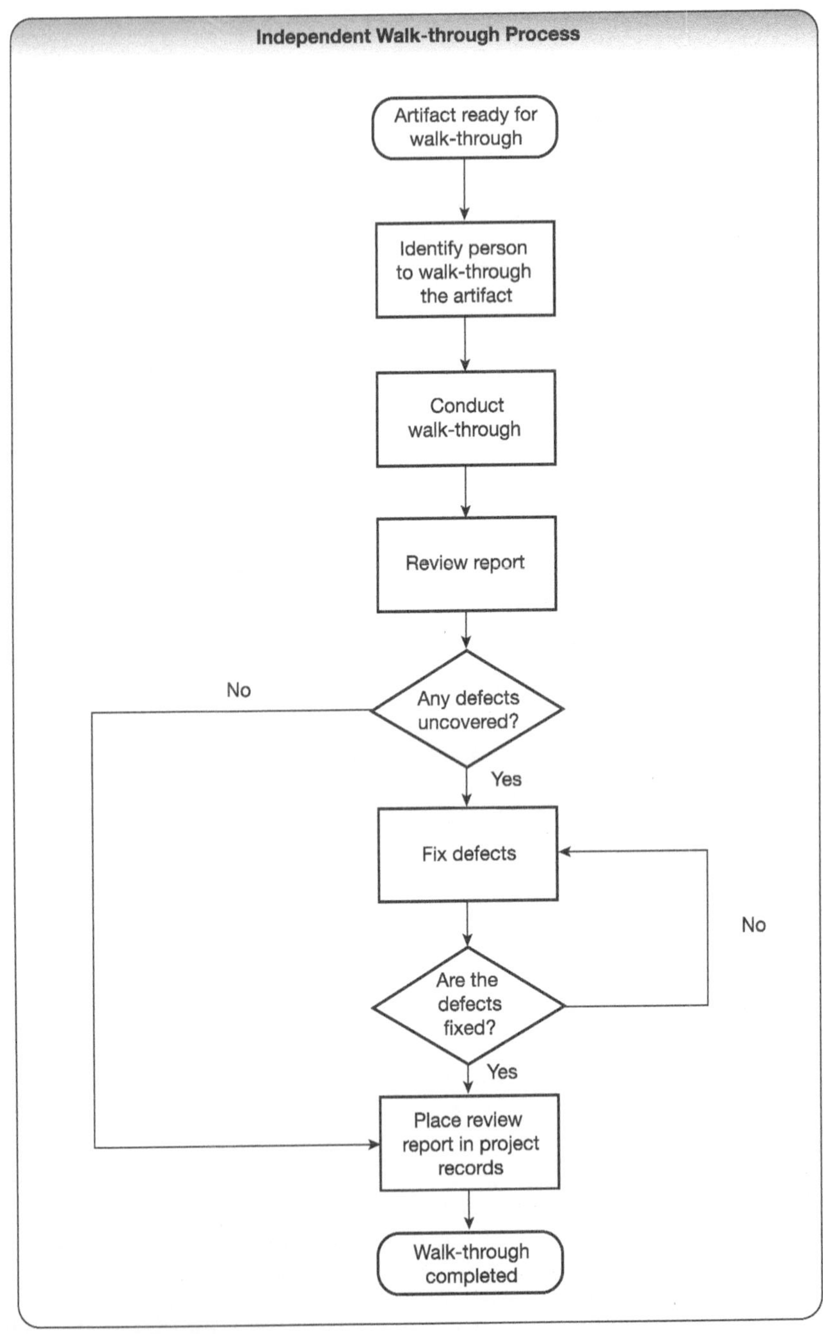

Figure 9.2 Independent peer review process

1. The author of the artifact completes the work and informs the project manager to arrange for the review.
2. The project manager allocates the work of reviewing the artifact to a peer of the author.
3. The author interacts with the reviewer and arranges a time for the review.
4. The author then walks the reviewer through the artifact, explaining its contents.
5. The reviewer seeks additional explanation when necessary.
6. Wherever the reviewer finds an opportunity for improvement, the author and reviewer discuss it, and if a consensus is reached, the author makes a note of the correction to be carried out.
7. By the end of the peer review, the author will have noted all opportunities for improvement and the accepted manner in which they are to be carried out.
8. Optionally, the author may implement the corrections at the time of the review, closing each defect as it is uncovered.
9. The author implements the accepted corrections and closes the defects in concurrence with the reviewer.
10. The reviewer informs the project manager the artifact passed the review.
11. Optionally, the reviewer might prepare a formal review report.

The advantage of the guided peer review is that the review duration is much shorter compared to an independent peer review. The total turnaround time for review completion is also shorter. One disadvantage, however, is the possibility that the author and reviewer will disagree vehemently over an improvement opportunity, which may end up in arguments that need resolution at a higher level. Another disadvantage is that the author might convince the reviewer that a defect is in fact not a defect!

Group Peer Reviews Group peer reviews are also referred to as *group reviews*. These are used when it is felt the knowledge of more than one person is necessary while reviewing the artifact, especially in strategic artifacts such as product specification documents, design documents, and test strategy plans. Group peer reviews are conducted in one of the following three modes:

Postal reviews: In this method, the project manager takes the responsibility for coordinating the review. The advantage is that reviewers can conduct the review at their convenience and location rather than try to find time all at once to conduct it in a meeting, which could delay the review altogether.

Also, with each member of the reviewing group focusing on the artifact, knowledge from different areas can often shed light on a greater number of possible improvements than when only one person reviews the artifact. The disadvantage, however, is that it may take longer to complete, having to wait for the slowest reviewer to finish. The following steps are carried out in this type of review:

1. When an artifact is constructed and ready for review, the project manager selects a review team consisting of members slightly more experienced than the author.
2. A review coordinator is nominated either by the review team itself or by the project manager. Sometimes the project manager acts as the review coordinator.
3. The artifact is handed over to each member of the review team.
4. The review team reviews the artifact and each member hands over their individual report to the review coordinator.
5. The review coordinator consolidates the reports, eliminating duplicates, and prepares a final review report.
6. Alternatively, the review coordinator might organize a meeting to collate the findings and prepare the review report.
7. The review report is handed over to the author.
8. The author interfaces with the review coordinator, obtains clarifications if any are required, and implements the corrections based on all report findings.
9. The author interfaces with the review coordinator and closes all report findings.

Meeting reviews: Meeting reviews are used to reduce the turnaround time of the reviews. One disadvantage, however, may be that, except for the review coordinator, others might not focus adequate attention on the artifact to contribute to its improvement. The following steps are carried out in this type of review:

1. When an artifact is constructed and is ready for review, the project manager selects a review team consisting of members slightly more experienced than the author.
2. A review coordinator is nominated either by the project manager or the review team.
3. The artifact is handed over to each member of the review team in advance of the meeting.
4. The review coordinator arranges for the review meeting in consultation with all the review team members.

5. All review team members come to the meeting prepared with their review comments.
6. The review coordinator collates the review comments from each member, and they are discussed in the meeting.
7. The meeting finalizes the review report, which is documented by the review coordinator.
8. Review team members are released, and the review coordinator continues the remaining steps in the process.
9. The review coordinator submits the report to the project manager, who has the defects rectified by the author of the artifact.
10. The author interfaces with the review coordinator until all defects are fixed and closed by the review coordinator.

Guided meeting reviews: This review is conducted in the same manner as the *Meeting Review* just described, except the team members need not come to the meeting prepared with comments. The artifact is presented by its author, and the review team members discuss each topic, giving comments. The review coordinator collates the comments and prepares the review report. The advantages to this method are that the turnaround time is reduced to the least possible amount; the review team members need not spend time reading and forming comments prior to the meeting. One disadvantage, however, is that review team members might not focus adequate attention to add value to the artifact. Figure 9.3 provides a depiction of this process.

Managerial Reviews

The managerial review is the approval step and is performed by the person designated as the approving authority in the project plan. This manager typically uses his/her experience and judgment as to the level of review required based on their knowledge of the environment and circumstances. Generally, this does not entail a review of minute details, and reflects an overall perspective of the artifact contents. The approving manager also ensures that a peer review has been conducted on the artifact and all defects uncovered were fixed to the extent necessary. Their objective is to confirm that the artifact can be implemented in the project without any concerns.

All reviews except the managerial review result in a review report. Figure 9.4 depicts the elements of a suggested template for this report.

Inspections

Formal inspections are structured processes used to find defects in deliverables and entail checking or testing some object with the purpose of ensuring

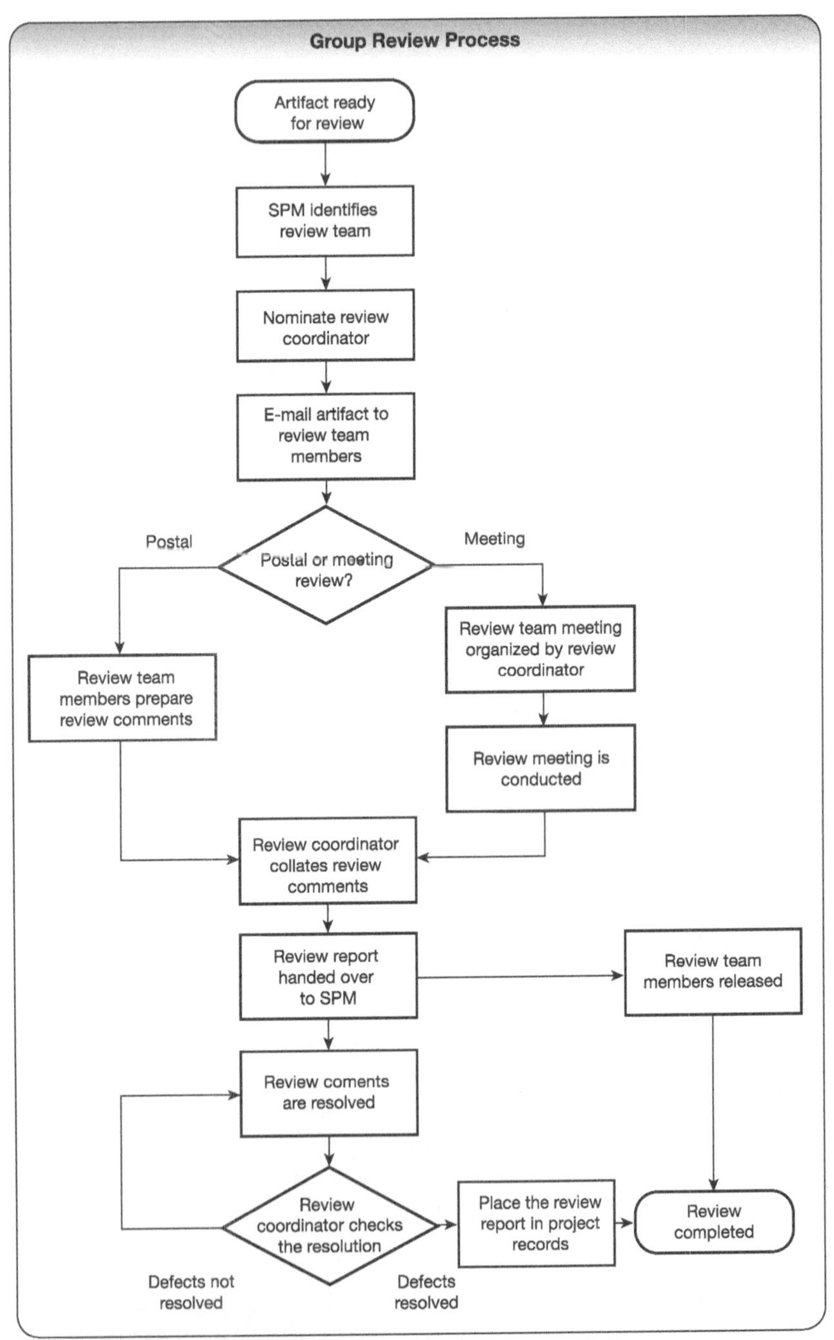

Figure 9.3 Group peer review process

Review/Inspection Report

Project name:

Name of the artifact/work being reviewed/inspected:

Name of the lead reviewer/inspector:

Date on which the review is conducted:

Type of review/inspection:

Defects uncovered during the review/inspection (use an additional sheet if required):

Signature of the lead reviewer/inspector:

Date:

Closure action by the author:

Corrective actions implemented:

Preventive actions implemented:

Signature of the person resolving defects:

Date:

Defect closure actions (to be filled in by the lead reviewer/inspector):

I have verified and found that all the defects described above are closed satisfactorily, except the following defects, which are retracted or pending:

Signature of the lead reviewer/inspector:

Date:

Figure 9.4 Elements for the review/inspection report template (template exhibited in Appendix I)

it conforms to specifications or organizational/national/industry/international standards. Inspections have played a prime role in ensuring quality in construction projects and to some extent in manufacturing projects. They are carried out at the end of a phase in a project. Normally, the team leader submits the project for inspection and the work is held up until inspection clears it to move on to the next stage. But there are some activities that cannot be held up, such as pouring concrete without damaging the concrete mix. Sometimes it is not possible to either inspect or test after the event. Examples are heat treatment in manufacturing, vacuum in a light bulb, or the strength of a chalk piece. Therefore, in-process inspections are carried out.

Inspections are a valuable tool for ensuring quality in IT projects. In this context, they are used in the field to ensure project execution is carried out conforming to the specifications and standards. Both phase-end and in-process inspections are utilized.

Phase-end inspections are carried out after the following phases:

1. Deployment of servers
2. Deployment of workstations
3. Deployment of networking hardware routers and switches
4. After the network is ready but just before testing of the network
5. After the infrastructure is ready and just before testing the infrastructure

During these inspections, we ensure the following:

1. The work is complete in all respects.
2. All required materials/components are mounted as required.
3. The quality of work is verified visually to ensure it is without defects.
4. The work is ready to begin the next phase.

Phase-end inspections result in an inspection report. Exhibit 9.4 in Appendix I depicts a suggested template for an inspection report.

In-process inspections are performed while the work is being carried out without interruption. During the in-process inspection we observe the manner in which the work is being carried out. The basis would be the organizational standards and guidelines for workmanship and other aspects. If any aberrations are uncovered, the persons carrying out the work are suitably advised. If they do not heed the advice, the issue is escalated on the spot and pursued until it is resolved. In-process inspections are for immediate resolution of aberrations, not for giving a report and hoping the issue will be corrected later. In-process inspections can hold up the work if necessary, but poor work process is not permitted. In-process inspections are performed for cable laying, facility construction, and handling costly equipment such as servers, workstations, routers, and switches.

Validation

Validation indicates confirmation or corroboration of a claim. Synonyms for the word *validate* include *authenticate, certify, endorse, bear out, substantiate,* and *support,* among others. One definition of validation is *the act of ensuring that something is valid.* Testing connotes running the equipment by supplying the input power and user inputs to authenticate its functionality against the specifications or the design or national/international standards. Expert review and testing are the primary techniques for validation of IT infrastructure projects.

Expert Reviews

Sometimes there is no other person on the project team or in the organization itself who has the knowledge and experience on the domain or technology in which the artifact was constructed. This may become evident while reviewing engineering drawings and bills of material prepared for facility construction or equipment deployment.

In application software acquisition, outside experts may be needed. In large software products, the software architecture plays a vital role in the product's robustness. Once a product is built with a specific architecture, it is impossible to correct without a major overhaul. This aspect becomes all the more crucial when developing a commercial off-the-shelf product because inefficient software architecture can spell doom for product success. In such cases, it is advantageous to employ experts who are external to the project to review the software architecture (or the high-level design).

Organizations use experts for developing and verifying applications and can be any of the following:

1. *Domain experts*—people with many years of experience in a field, having seen all possibilities
2. *Subject matter experts*—people who are experts in a specific subject, such as mathematics (They are typically academics, such as a distinguished college professor. These experts may or may not be experienced in the field, but they have a strong knowledge of the theory and can aid in the development or review of algorithms of the proposed application software.)
3. *Technology experts*—people who are highly skilled in the technology selected for implementing the IT infrastructure
4. *Social experts*—people who have expertise in the areas of social behaviors, market forces, and anthropology (They can assess the suitability of workplace design, workstation design and ambience, and suggest improvements so the best productivity can be realized from the infrastructure.)

Expert reviews are often costly because the expert is external to the project/organization and a fee is paid for utilizing the expertise. Expert reviews should be scheduled carefully to effectively and fully utilize the expert's time. If a postal review (independent review) is used, the expert might need more time to understand the artifact, which will result in extra fees. Still, he/

she might need clarification from the author and hence, interaction between author and expert reviewer is inevitable. Therefore, the guided review is the usual mode of review for conducting expert reviews to save on the costly time of the expert.

Expert reviews can involve a single expert or a team of experts, depending on the artifact being reviewed. Normally, expert reviews are conducted to supplement peer reviews. An expert review is conducted in addition to a detailed peer review to ensure that all lurking defects are uncovered and fixed.

The methodology is similar to that of an independent review and a guided review, except the reviewer is the selected expert. Other aspects remain the same and hence, are not repeated here.

Testing

Testing connotes the running of the equipment to confirm its functionality. We evaluate the equipment while it is functioning and subject it to some preplanned test cases to see that it functions as designed. This examination/corroboration/confirmation of functionality is the main objective of testing. Testing in the context of an IT project is *exercising the infrastructure in a planned and controlled manner to ensure that the implemented infrastructure functions as designed.* The key words are:

1. *Planned.* We have planned how to conduct the test and designed test cases for use while testing.
2. *Controlled.* This indicates all care has been taken to ensure no damage occurs either to the equipment or the individuals involved in testing. Switch on the equipment in the order and method prescribed for it and conduct the test in a careful manner.
3. *To ensure . . . functions.* The objective of testing is to verify the functionality of the infrastructure.
4. *As designed.* We verify the functioning conforming to the designs. It would not be tested using extremes of temperature, humidity, vibrations, voltage, current, impact, and so on.

The following tests are conducted in IT infrastructure implementation projects:

1. Inward testing
2. Network testing
3. Infrastructure testing
4. Application software testing

All IT project testing is *positive* testing. That is, the equipment is not subjected to any function it is not designed to fulfill. The design specifications are strictly adhered to while conducting the tests. Now let us discuss each of these tests in the following sections.

Inward Testing The main objective of inward testing is to ensure the equipment/material ordered is received and adheres to specifications stipulated in the purchase order. Note that the activity of quality control of the equipment/material rests with the supplier/manufacturer. So, it is not necessary to conduct a full spectrum of testing for these products. Let us discuss testing of each component.

Inward testing of servers and workstations: The tests, as depicted in Table 9.1, are carried out on servers and workstations.

Inward testing of networking hardware: The tests to be conducted on this hardware are depicted in Table 9.2.

Other materials may be tested as required to ensure they conform to the specifications included in the purchase order.

Network Testing Network testing involves ensuring that the network is functioning without any hitches. It in part includes the following tests:

1. Continuity between the end points of a connection
2. Connectivity between the servers and the workstations through the networking switches
3. Bandwidth of the Internet connection
4. Connectivity from servers and workstations to the Internet
5. Efficacy of the network security

Table 9.1 Tests carried out on servers/workstations

Test conducted	Expected result
Visually inspect that all the components specified in our purchase order (PO) are supplied	All the specified components are supplied
Visually inspect that no component or wire is hanging loose	No component should be loose and no wire should be hanging
Power up the machine as specified	It should power up and boot the operating system (OS)
Check if the specified OS is loaded on the machine and its version is the specified one	The specified OS should be present
Using the OS utilities, check the amount of random access memory and hard disk capacity	They should be as specified in our PO
Run a few commands and see if the machine is responding correctly	The commands should produce the correct results

Table 9.2 Tests carried out on networking hardware

Test conducted	Expected result
Routers	
Check visually that the model received is as ordered	It should be the same model specified in our PO
Visually inspect that no component or wire is hanging loose	No component should be loose and no wire should be hanging
Power up the router as specified	It should power up and work as expected
Check connectivity to the Internet	It should be connected to the Internet
Configure the router, connect a network switch, and check if the Internet is accessible	Internet should be accessible from the switch
Networking Switches	
Check visually that the model received is as ordered	It should be the same model specified in our PO
Visually inspect that no component or wire is hanging loose	No component should be loose and no wire should be hanging
Power up the router as specified	It should power up and work as expected
Connect the switch to the Internet on one side and a workstation on the other side and check connectivity to the Internet	Internet should be accessible from the workstation at the specified speed
Networking Cable	
Check visually that the model received is as ordered	It should be the same model specified in our PO
Check the number and size of each individual strand of each of the conductors	They should be as specified in the PO
Check the continuity of the individual conductors	All conductors must have connectivity between the two ends
Check the insulation resistance of the cable	It should be as per the ANSI/NEMA standard for the cable
Networking Connectors	
Check visually for the model/type on a sample number of connectors	It should be as specified in the PO

Normally these are conducted to ensure connectivity between all the equipment and security from external threats. No elaborate test plans or test cases are utilized in conducting the network testing.

Infrastructure Testing When the infrastructure is set up, it is essential to test it before it is rolled over for trial runs. Conduct the tests listed in Table 9.3. When all tests are completed, the infrastructure is ready and can be handed over to the user community for trial runs, which would uncover any defects in the infrastructure and facilitate rectification.

Table 9.3 Tests to be conducted on the IT Infrastructure

Test conducted	Expected result
Power up the infrastructure in an orderly fashion	All infrastructure components must power up without any issues
Access a few workstations from each of the servers	The workstations must be accessible
Access servers from a few workstation	The servers must be accessible
Access Internet from the servers	Internet must be accessible from servers
Access Internet from a few workstations	Internet must be accessible from workstations
Test a few functionalities of the application software from a few workstations	Application software must work as designed

Table 9.4 Suggested format to define test cases and log test results

Test case ID	Test case description	Expected result	Actual result	Pass/Fail

All these tests must be conducted as specified in the quality assurance plan described in Chapter 5. For each test, test cases must be prepared in the format depicted in Table 9.4. Normally, an Excel spreadsheet is used to define and record test cases. The actual result and pass/fail columns would be filled in during test case execution.

Application Software Testing Application software is the most crucial component of IT infrastructure. Its quality assurance is the responsibility of the development team, be it an internal or outsourced team. But since its quality is of paramount importance to IT infrastructure, we need to perform the following activities:

1. Verify the review records (peer, managerial, and expert) to ensure the application software artifacts (information as well as code artifacts) were subjected to review and all defects uncovered were rectified. The percentage of the code subjected to peer review will also be known. The best practice is to subject 100% to peer review. If the percentage of coverage is unsatisfactory, it will be necessary to increase the rigor of acceptance testing.
2. Verify the test logs of the project. They will provide information about the types of tests conducted and whether defects uncovered

were rectified. They will also indicate the coverage of the code in independent unit testing. Best practice is to subject 100% of the code to independent unit testing. Based on this information, a decision can be made on the rigor needed to subject the software in acceptance testing.

3. Conduct acceptance testing of the software. Usually, very rigorous acceptance testing is not conducted because it is assumed the development team had been diligent about the software quality they developed. We confirm their diligence by verifying the quality records of the project. Acceptance testing is positive functional testing; that is, we do not implement any actions that are detrimental to the product and only the functionality provided by the software product is tested. The extent and rigor of testing depend on the outcome of the review of the project's quality records. The acceptance test plan and test cases can be prepared by the development team or by the information systems (IS) department, but should be approved by the IS department. Normally, no defects should be found in acceptance testing but if any are discovered, they are tracked through to resolution.

Audits

Audits are record verification systems to ensure business transactions were performed in conformance with an approved process, standards, and guidelines. Audits are used extensively in finance departments, financial organizations, and government departments. With the release of process standards such as ISO 9000, auditing made inroads into operations of business organizations. Audits do not really play a very important role in short-duration projects, but in those of six months or more audits can play an important role in ensuring the project is executed effectively. Audits are basically tools for management to ensure projects are executed in the "right" manner. By "right" manner, I mean it is adhering to the defined process, standards, guidelines, and project plans.

Two types of audits are conducted in organizations:

1. Organization-level
2. Project-level

Organization-Level Audits

Organization-level audits are conducted periodically (e.g, once every quarter, semiannually, and annually) across all projects executed in the organization. The purpose is to ensure the following:

1. All projects are adhering to the defined process of the organization.
2. All projects are executed in conformance with project plans.
3. All quality assurance activities planned for the projects are being diligently implemented.

An organizational audit mainly looks for evidence of implementation of project plans and organizational processes and hence is referred to as a conformance audit. The quality assurance department or another department vested with this responsibility organizes these audits. If the audits find lack of evidence in any aspect of a project, a non-conformance report (NCR) is raised on the project. NCRs require corrective action as well as planning for preventive action to avoid non-conformance (NC) in the future. Audit findings of all projects are consolidated and analyzed to detect patterns or trends and are presented to all project managers and the organization's management so any process improvement opportunities can be discovered and implemented.

Sometimes during organizational audits, all aspects of all projects are audited. When all aspects of a project are audited, it is referred to as a *vertical* audit. At other times, only one aspect is audited but in greater detail. For example, the quality management or project planning process for all projects is audited. This type of audit is referred to as a *horizontal* audit. A horizontal audit is used when a pattern is detected in the vertical audit pointing to uniformly poor implementation in one aspect of project execution.

It is common practice to conduct a mix of these audits in the organization to provide data needed to analyze process implementation and discover opportunities for improvements in the process or its implementation.

Organization-level audits assist the organizational management in identifying slippages and initiate corrective action as early as possible in the projects and put them back on track.

Project-Level Audits

Project-level audits are not period based but rather are conducted when the project is being executed. Normally, they are conducted upon completion of the following IT project phases:

1. Project initiation
2. Project planning
3. Deployment of servers and workstations
4. Completion of networking
5. Deployment of application software
6. Before infrastructure testing
7. Project closure

It is customary to conduct three audits at a minimum for each project. The first is after project initiation, the third is following project closure, and one should be conducted in the middle of project execution. This is one way to scale project-level audits for short-duration projects. For longer duration (e.g., six calendar months or longer) audits after all the phases enumerated above is recommended.

The purpose of audits is to identify, as early as possible, any lack of diligence that could cause serious issues in the later stages of project execution. These audits also ensure the project is ready for the next stage.

Project-level audits assist the project manager in identifying slippages very early in the project and to initiate the corrective actions necessary to bring it back in line with project plans. Audits consist of auditors (persons who conduct the audit) and auditees (persons whose project is being audited). Auditors need to have had specialized training in conducting audits. Auditors within the organization must receive internal audit training.

The usual duration of a project audit is one to two hours. Within this time, the auditor verifies the project records and documents on a sample basis and makes notes of the NCs to prepare an NCR. The NCR is handed over to the auditee. The auditee then must take the necessary action specified on the NCR to address the NCs and have them closed by the auditor within the allowed time. Necessary action as specified by the NCR involves the following:

1. Taking corrective action so the present aberration is corrected and the NC is resolved
2. Putting in place preventive action so the NC does not repeat in the project

Figure 9.5 illustrates the audit process.

Final Words

IT projects are unlike software development projects because the main activity is to put together disparate equipment purchased from vendors and connect it together and to the Internet. There is very little that is produced or developed. If application software is developed as part of an IT project, it is spawned as a separate project. Therefore, quality assurance is to be carried out on the work of assembling and connecting the components. The only testing that can presumably be performed is the system testing of the entire infrastructure near the end of the project. In reality the various quality control techniques described in this chapter can and should be used in IT projects.

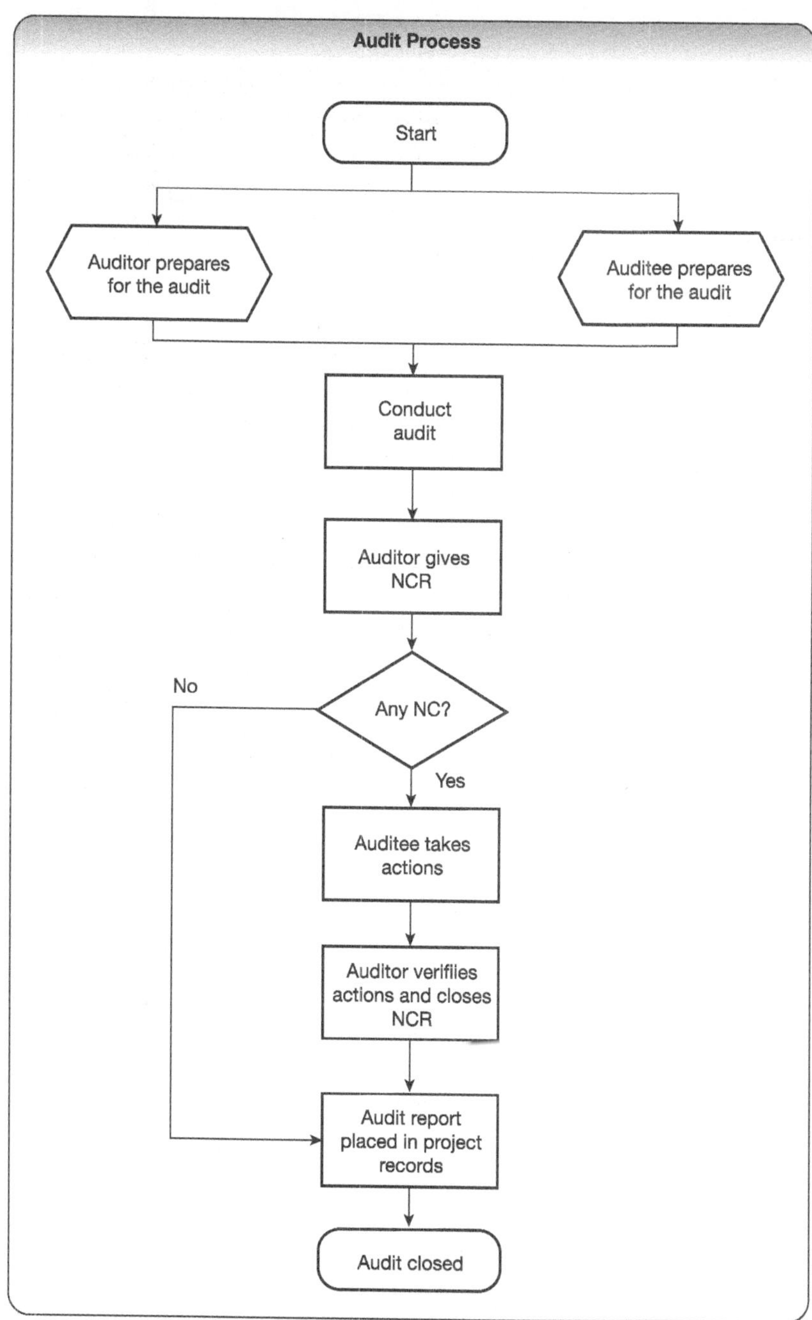

Figure 9.5 Auditing process

10

Project Closure

Introduction

While project initiation looks ahead to ensure successful project execution, project closure looks back at the project execution to take stock of what went right and what went wrong to draw lessons for the future. Project initiation draws from the knowledge repository (corporate memory) of the organization, whereas project closure adds to it. The project closure activity contributes to the continued success of future projects and to the success of the organization. Project closure activities, when conducted methodically, facilitate reduced defect injection and turnaround time and improved productivity and customer satisfaction of future projects. Therefore, project closure is an important activity but it is one of the most neglected areas of project management in organizations.

There are two scenarios of managing IT projects. The first is setting up an IT infrastructure for our own organization. In this case, we may not set up an IT infrastructure again in the near future unless there were plans for expansion. The second scenario is that of an organization offering specialized services in setting up an IT infrastructure for different client organizations. In this case, it is highly likely that we would be executing IT projects concurrently as well as undertaking an additional IT project in the near future.

In either scenario, the project has to be closed upon completion. Some aspects of project closure benefit organizations described in the second scenario more than in the first scenario. In this chapter, we will be focusing on organizations described in the second scenario. Some aspects discussed in subsequent sections may be less/not applicable to organizations in the first scenario, but it would be advantageous to carry out all the actions discussed below.

Let's begin our exploration of project closure activity by answering what should be an easy question, but rarely is.

When Does a Project Really Close?

Most projects include a warranty phase during which the infrastructure is supported by the project team. Usually the warranty support team is drawn from the project team itself but is much smaller. When a warranty phase exists, the project closes only after completion of this phase. When a project moves to the warranty phase, normally the project manager is retained to lead the warranty effort. However, in some cases another person may be designated by the organization to lead during warranty support. If the project manager is moved out of the project during the warranty phase, all project artifacts are handed over to the person leading the warranty support. The project would still be closed on completion of warranty support.

Another possibility is that infrastructure maintenance may also be assigned to the organization/team that set up the infrastructure. In this case, sometimes the IT project would be closed and the maintenance project is initiated. There are advantages and disadvantages for treating maintenance as a separate project. Setting up infrastructure and maintenance requires people with different aptitudes. This is especially applicable in the case of application software. Those who develop software from scratch efficiently may not be able to modify code very well. Those who can repair code efficiently may not be able to develop fresh code effectively. Even in hardware installation and maintenance, there is a difference between those who install and those who maintain. For installation, one need not be proficient in the functioning and troubleshooting. But those who maintain hardware must be proficient in the functionality of the hardware as well as its troubleshooting. Therefore it would make sense that the infrastructure maintenance team be different from the development team.

When the maintenance is spawned as a new project the IT project would be closed as soon as the infrastructure is handed over to the maintenance team. If the same team continues to support the infrastructure during the maintenance phase, the project would be closed only after completion of infrastructure maintenance.

Summarizing the discussion, the project may be closed as follows:

1. Soon after warranty support is completed, if infrastructure maintenance is not assigned to the same organization/team

2. If infrastructure maintenance is assigned to the organization:
   a. The IT project may be closed soon after the maintenance team took over the infrastructure.
   b. The IT project may be closed after completion of the warranty period and infrastructure maintenance work is spawned as another project.
   c. The project (setup and maintenance) may be continued as long as the infrastructure maintenance work continues. It is closed only after the maintenance contract with the customer is terminated.

Project Closure Activities

The following activities are typically performed as part of project closure:

1. Document and deposit best practices in the organizational knowledge repository.
2. Document and deposit lessons learned from project execution in the organizational knowledge repository.
3. Compile and derive final project metrics and deposit them in the organizational knowledge repository.
4. Conduct a knowledge-sharing meeting with peer project managers.
5. Deposit project records with the project management office (PMO).
6. Conduct a project postmortem.
7. Conduct performance appraisals of the project team.
8. Release the project manager.
9. Close the project and celebrate!

Let us discuss each activity in detail, of course, with the exception of the celebration part!

Document Best Practices

Best practices are processes, practices, or sets of activities that yield better than expected results during project execution. Typically, we are interested in capturing practices that are not already part of our organizational processes. These could include:

1. Any engineering methodology that was used differently or developed for improving the quality and/or productivity during project execution
2. A new and effective solution to a tricky issue in the project

3. Any project practice or method for work allocation, quality assurance, motivation, configuration management, and deployment that improved productivity and/or resulted in better quality
4. Use of a new tool or new way of using an existing tool that assisted the project in any manner for achieving better results
5. Design/development of a new tool exclusively for the project that could be used in future projects
6. Any new or modified formats and templates that were used in projects that resulted in improved clarity
7. Any new checklists that were prepared for use in the project that were found to be useful in ensuring comprehensiveness in any project activity
8. Any new procedure or process developed for the project that yielded positive results outside of the norm

It is the responsibility of the project manager to prepare best practice documents, arrange for their review, and implement any feedback. Upon approval, the final step in the process is for the project manager to deposit the new best practices in the knowledge repository.

Document Lessons Learned from the Project

All projects are learning opportunities. The project team and project manager will learn at least a few lessons during project execution. Lessons are typically a mixture of positives and negatives. However, one can only learn from a negative experience after neutralizing the problem and recognizing the lesson. In many cases individuals tend to extol successes but play down failures. As leaders, project managers need to keep an open mind on both the positive or negative impacts to the project. Lessons are only valuable if we recognize them and then carry out a situational analysis using a critical examination technique to draw lessons for the future. When an unexpected impact occurs on a project, the impact and cause need to be documented so others can learn and benefit from the experience. Much knowledge is gathered by the world of science from the documented experiences and lessons learned by others. Project management is no different.

The following areas of project management are typically the most conducive for drawing lessons:

1. Communication with the client, within the project team, organizational management, and other stakeholders
2. Work allocation mechanisms
3. Issue resolution mechanisms

4. Change request resolutions
5. Handling of grievances
6. Engineering, work issues, and resolutions

All these and other areas that have created challenges and opportunities for the project team should be documented, submitted for managerial review, and then deposited in the organizational knowledge repository.

Collect, Derive, and Deposit the Final Project Metrics

Just as best practices and lessons learned represent holistic views of a project, metrics provide a quantitative view. This activity involves computing the metrics for the overall project. These metrics typically include:

1. Productivity metrics for each specialist activity in the project as well as other engineering activities
2. Quality metrics including defect injection rates for each specialty and defect removal efficiency for each quality control activity implemented in the project
3. Schedule variance metrics for the entire project as well as each of the project execution phases
4. Effort variance metrics for the entire project as well as each specialty
5. Personnel metrics including productivity and quality metrics for each project team member
6. Other relevant metrics such as the relative effort spent on various project specialties

All these metrics are reviewed against the organizational baselines. Variances are analyzed to determine if they are purely due to chance (random variance) or assignable causes. Leveraging this type of analysis, the metrics are reviewed, validated, and deposited in the organizational metrics repository for future use

Conduct a Knowledge-Sharing Meeting with Peer Project Managers

Once the above-mentioned activities (of documenting best practices, lessons learned, and deriving the metrics) have been completed, the same information is shared with peer project managers in a knowledge-sharing meeting. The session ensures that all project managers have access to the same rich knowledge base to utilize that knowledge in their projects. This meeting is normally coordinated by the PMO. Representatives of the PMO, process group, and quality assurance department also participate along with all project managers in order to use this information in future projects.

During the session the project manager presents all aspects of project execution including successes and failures. He/she also presents the project execution methodology in detail and the results obtained. During the knowledge-sharing session the project manager also discusses what could have been done better as well as what yielded better results than originally planned.

All in all, this meeting gives a bird's eye view of the project to participants. Participants can elicit more information from the project manager either in the meeting itself or later on to improve their knowledge. One of the goals of a properly conducted session is to ensure uniformity of project execution as well as success of all projects in the organization.

Deposit the Project Records with the PMO

The project records typically include:

1. Request for proposal, proposal, purchase/work order, and order acceptance letter
2. Feasibility report
3. Sizing records
4. Project cost estimates
5. Project plans
6. Work allocation register
7. Configuration register
8. Defect resolution register
9. Change request register
10. Issue resolution register
11. Client communications including commendations and complaints
12. Client-supplied documents
13. Project-specific guidelines
14. Engineering documents including drawings, bills of material, specifications, design documents, and quality records
15. Quality records
16. Audit and non-conformance reports
17. Process waivers and special approvals
18. Process improvement suggestions

It is the responsibility of the project manager to collect all project records and arrange for updating all documents to reflect the "as built" stage in order to represent the final setup of the infrastructure. Finally, the project manager hands over all records to the PMO for record keeping and inclusion in the knowledge repository as applicable.

It should be noted that currently most of the documents are in soft copy form and are handed over on a backup medium such as a CD/DVD or simply copied to a PMO-specified location on the organizational server. Some artifacts such as the configuration, defect, and change request registers may be part of a database in which case only details are handed over to the PMO.

All in all, hard and soft copies or location references are passed on to the PMO by the project manager.

Conduct a Project Postmortem

The novel *The Final Diagnosis* by Arthur Hailey contains a quote from medical circles: "A surgeon knows nothing but does everything; a psychiatrist knows nothing and does nothing; a pathologist knows everything but does everything after the patient died." A pathologist knows all because he/she conducts the postmortem on the dead body examining the internals. Almost all major hospitals conduct postmortems of corpses whenever a death occurs in the hospital (within religious and cultural norms). The postmortem reveals, like no other diagnostic investigation, the efficacy of the treatment and the real cause of death. The postmortem looks at the inside of the body dispassionately, solely with the objective of learning the true cause of death and impact of the treatment. The pathologist along with the lead doctor presents the resulting information in what are referred to as death conferences. There could be many names for these conferences but the intent is the same. During the conference participants discuss the events prior to death including symptoms, diagnostic investigations, treatment, and cause of death. These conferences do not blame the team of doctors who treated the patient, but use the occasion as a platform to collectively learn everything they all can from the unfortunate event. Generally, doctors do not miss these conferences because there is the potential to learn a great deal and increase their own effectiveness. It is not an exaggeration to say the postmortem is the primary platform for arriving at root causes and developing new treatments to improve survival rates.

Project postmortems are also conducted with the same objective of learning to increase the effectiveness of project managers and the organization as a whole. Some organizations combine the postmortem with the knowledge-sharing meeting. This is not always effective as the knowledge-sharing meeting is for the purpose of learning from the project managers' experiences, whereas the postmortem is typically led by an auditor who conducted an investigative audit on the project. The prerequisite for a project postmortem is an investigative audit. The audit reviews the variances in the project and the analysis thereof to determine the efficacy of the variance analysis and the inferences drawn on the variances. Upon completion, the auditor who conducted the investigative audit would present the findings to all project managers along with the project manager of the project. All issues are dissected so everyone will learn from the project. The postmortem findings are included in the project records within the knowledge repository.

Conduct Performance Appraisals of the Project Team

When the project is closed, it is customary to carry out appraisals of the human resources who worked on the project. Normally, the performance review would be carried out organization-wide at fixed intervals of time. Project completion in most cases would not synchronize with the organizational performance review. Therefore, the performance of employees is appraised on project completion before releasing them. The project manager deposits these appraisals with the human resources (HR) department. The HR department will consider these appraisals along with others at the time of the organizational performance review.

Appraisals should be carried out fairly without bias. They are recorded in an organizational performance appraisal format conforming to the organizational process for performance appraisal.

Release of the Project Manager

It is essential to ensure that all project closure activities discussed previously are complete before the project manager is released. The release of a project manager normally occurs gradually. There is typically an overlap of responsibilities for the project manager with the leader of the warranty support. In many cases the project manager is allocated to another project but still, he/she is required to provide assistance to the earlier project during the warranty phase as and when necessary. As the involvement of the project manager gradually increases with his/her newly assigned project, the involvement with the completed project gradually decreases. The project manager should only be completely released from the project when the new team handling the support for either the warranty service or maintenance service is confident of handling the project on their own.

Close the Project

When all the above-mentioned activities are completed and the project manager is released, the PMO closes the project. The PMO issues a note to all stakeholders, including senior management; finance, HR, systems administration, facilities and administration departments; and the customer, informing them of the project closure. Based on the project closure note issued by the PMO, the following occurs:

1. The finance department does not allow any further bookings of effort or expenditures to the project.
2. The HR department does not allocate any further human resources to the project.
3. The facilities department repossesses all the facilities allotted to the project.
4. The administration department does not entertain requests for purchases or any other requests against the project.

The project closure note issued by the PMO marks the end of project execution in all respects. This note is also the last document to be placed in the project dossier.

Organizational Role in Project Closure

Just as the organization plays a vital role in all aspects of project execution, it also plays an important role in project closure. The organizational role is not simply in closing the project per se, but in ensuring that the knowledge gained in the project is captured in the organizational knowledge repository and then spread to all concerned members of the organization. The organization exercises this responsibility primarily through three entities: the PMO, the organizational configuration control board (CCB), and the systems administration department. These activities are discussed in the following sections.

Role of the PMO

During the project initiation phase, the PMO provides important knowledge to the project and the project manager. Now, when the project is closing it collects knowledge gained with the objective of making it available to future projects. The PMO takes over project records and metrics and various analyses performed on the project. After collecting data, the PMO classifies the information into its appropriate categories and stores it in such a way that it can be located and retrieved easily when required. The PMO typically mines all the analyses for assignable causes and includes the validated data for consideration in revising the organizational baselines for the next iteration of the activity.

While taking over the records, metrics, and analyses from the project manager, the PMO ensures that all information is updated to reflect the latest achievements in the project and that all analyses are properly carried out. If any shortfalls are uncovered, the PMO obtains necessary clarifications from the project manager and rectifies the anomalies.

The PMO is the coordinating agency in the organization that maintains the organizational knowledge repository. It is responsible for updating the knowledge repository with information collated from closing projects.

The PMO coordinates the knowledge-sharing meeting, ensures that all concerned persons are present, and ensures that the meeting is conducted effectively. It also coordinates the project postmortem, ensures it is conducted objectively, and ensures that inferences are drawn professionally.

In short, the PMO draws from the organizational knowledge repository while initiating the project and updates the repository with the information collated from the project during its closure.

Role of the Configuration Control Board in the Code Repository

The CCB at the organizational level takes ownership of maintaining the organizational code repository for application software. The organizational code repository contains all code artifacts developed during project execution.

The code repository typically contains the following code artifacts:

1. Source code of all code artifacts
2. Object and executable codes of all artifacts
3. All graphics developed for the project
4. All table scripts, triggers, stored procedures, and procedural language/structured query language routines of the databases
5. All library code including static libraries, dynamic-link libraries, and shared libraries
6. All third-party artifacts procured for use on the project
7. All development and testing tools used in the project
8. All system software including operating systems, databases, integrated development environments, debuggers, and all software tools for use in the project

In the repository all the code artifacts are indexed for easy location and retrieval. They are properly stored to prevent damage or interference. All code artifacts are periodically checked for integrity.

During project closure, the code repository will take over all code artifacts used during project execution, any client-supplied components, and third-party code artifacts procured for the project.

While taking over the code artifacts from the project, the organizational CCB is responsible for ensuring that all documentation necessary for future use is prepared and in usable form. The CCB also conducts sanity testing to ensure code artifacts match the respective documentation in terms of functionality and usage. Another important aspect for the organizational CCB is to ensure the organization does indeed have the intellectual property rights for the code artifacts being deposited by the project. As a final step, the code artifacts should be indexed properly, inserted into the code repository, and made available to future projects.

Role of the Systems Administration Department

The systems administration department takes ownership of the computer hardware and networking resources in the organization. When the project is closed, the systems administration department takes over the computer hardware resources, cleans the computer systems of unnecessary data and software, and makes the hardware ready for allocation to end users. Before cleaning the systems, the systems administration department ensures that all backups are taken and all code artifacts are deposited with the CCB. They will begin coordinating maintenance of the computer and networking hardware.

Final Words

Project closure is an important activity that needs to be performed diligently if we wish to retain the knowledge gained by executing the project. It will otherwise be lost when the project manager leaves the organization. Unfortunately many organizations do not give due importance to this activity. In such organizations, project managers dump the project records on the PMO, code on the organizational CCB and the computer and networking system hardware on the systems administration department, and move on to the next assignment. Project postmortems and knowledge sharing are vital activities, essential for garnering organizational experience and enriching organizational maturity.

As they say in HR, "Did the organization execute one project 30 times or did the organization execute 30 projects?" Project closure is the activity that can make a significant difference.

11

Pitfalls and Best Practices in Project Management

Introduction

Best practices are those methods of working that give consistently good results. Pitfalls are those shortcuts that consistently give poor results. It is a bit difficult to discuss the pitfalls and best practices in project management because there are any number of viewpoints on the subject. All practices are contextual to the organization based on the culture prevalent in that organization. People in an organization often feel that the way they manage is the best in the world because it produces results. Producing results is certainly a most important criterion for management. More important however is that results are achieved in an effective manner with optimal costs, productivity, quality, and morale. Best practices ensure achievement of these objectives and that the organization's performance improves with every completed project and is maintained in an ever-expanding spiral of improvement. Pitfalls bring down the organization from excellence to mediocrity. Therefore, it is necessary for organizations to adopt best practices and avoid pitfalls in order to grow and prosper.

Let us examine some of the common pitfalls and best practices for achieving project success and organizational excellence. Effective project management requires organization-level support in addition to the diligent efforts of project managers. Success is a result of collaborative effort complementing each other between the organization and the individual project manager (PM). Let's discuss pitfalls and best practices at both levels.

Organizational-Level Pitfalls in Project Management

Organization-level decisions, activities, and practices can have a greater impact on or be more responsible for the success or failure of a project than the team assigned to manage and execute it. An organization sets the framework within which the PM manages the project. If the organizational-level activities are not performed effectively, there is less chance for project success. The organizational-level activities are akin to ambience in the theater and the project team members including the PM are the performers. If the ambience is poor, however well the performers execute, the show is not likely to be a success. The following are some organizational-level pitfalls and best practices.

Project Management Process

A process-driven method of working facilitates predictability of results. A person-driven method becomes dependent on the personal capability of the individual leading the effort. Many organizations use person-dependent processes and achieve success only if the PM is highly experienced and knowledgeable. As organizations grow and execute larger numbers of projects concurrently, the use of person-driven processes can lead to unpredictable and non-uniform results. Consistent success is generally achieved by leveraging process-driven approaches. Many organizations have adopted a process-driven approach and have even obtained certifications. Unfortunately, some chase the certification without embracing continued adaptation and implementation of the process-driven approach.

The process-driven approach to project management delineated in Chapter 2 is a strongly recommended best practice, with the rider that you need to define the appropriate process for your organization based on the size and number of concurrently handled projects. Another best practice is to continuously monitor the process for the delivery of results and improve it as necessary in a regular manner. The alternative person-driven method is a common pitfall.

No PMO or Ineffective PMO

This is applicable to those organizations that specialize in setting up IT infrastructure for other organizations. Many organizations fail to see the importance of an efficient and effective PMO. Some organizations do not have a PMO under any name and others create an ineffective one.

Some perceive the role of the PMO as creating the project initiation note (PIN) and nothing more! The PMO is sometimes attached to the delivery manager, and one of his/her secretaries is responsible for generating the PIN and maintaining those documents in a file. In some cases a refugee from one of the technical teams is settled in the PMO with the sole purpose of initiating projects and serving as custodian of project records. This type of PMO is generally ineffective and cannot aid the PM when needed because of its administrative orientation. It cannot provide the right references to the PM during project initiation and every project is started from ground zero. This is very common. Other organizations see this as a role for an entry-level PM or for non-PMs. This type and level of personnel are unable to do justice to this role and are ineffective as well.

The lack of a PMO or creation of an ineffective one is a hindrance to project execution and a significant pitfall.

A PMO can render immense service to the projects being executed in the organization. A well-organized PMO with competent staff goes a long way in ensuring project success. An effective PMO is actively involved in supporting projects. In some cases it is not always possible to get the best project resources, and in such cases the PMO can play an important role by providing expert assistance. During project execution the PMO should be involved, and one aspect of the involvement includes measuring project health with metrics such as earned value, quality and productivity, and assisting the PM in any required course corrections.

An effective PMO performs the following functions:

1. Acts as the central agency for all matters relating to project execution in the organization (It continuously captures the organizational experience in project management, collating all best and bad practices and lessons learned, subjecting them to analysis and maintenance in the organizational repository.)
2. Takes ownership of the organizational repository of project management knowledge (Ownership includes gathering relevant knowledge from internal and external sources, organizing data in a meaningful manner for quick and easy retrieval, and making data available to all PMs as needed.)
3. Initiates projects in such a manner that the PMs can leverage the organization's experience from similar past projects
4. Takes ownership of organizational metrics related to project management, including deriving organizational performance and productivity baselines; collating and analyzing metrics on a regular basis; and

continuously updating the organizational metrics repository with credible metrics data

5. Takes ownership of the project closure process including the post-mortem, knowledge sharing, variance analysis of actual versus estimated/planned values, and possession of project records
6. Scans the technological horizon continuously for developments and improvements in the project management area and ensures the organizational PMs have access to them
7. Mentors PMs in the organization, which includes providing necessary training to effectively perform project management
8. Participates in project progress monitoring meetings and when necessary provides information and assistance to PMs to correct the course of the project

The PMO is a senior staff role providing specialist assistance on projects to PMs. The PMO should be headed by a competent professional senior PM with project execution experience. Some organizations rotate PMs in this role so they understand concerns of both the PMs and the organization. Based on the size of the organization and number of projects being executed, supporting staff may be needed for the PMO to execute projects effectively.

A robust PMO is a highly recommended best practice that generally provides benefits which far outweigh its costs.

Poor Project Initiation

This practice is applicable to organizations that specialize in setting up IT infrastructure for other organizations. Project initiation is a very important step in ensuring successful project execution. In some organizations initiation has become a mere formality. These organizations have fallen into the habit of just preparing the PIN document, filing the purchase/work order and technical specs into the project dossier, and handing it over to the PM.

Poor initiation can significantly impact the possibility of a project succeeding effectively and is a common pitfall.

The best practice is to treat project initiation as an important step to ensure project success.

Poor Cost Estimation

The act of overestimation/underestimation results in an imbalance in the application of project resources. Estimation errors do not augur well for project health during execution. Many organizations do not treat estimation as an important activity. They do not collect metrics on resources actually spent on the project and contrast them with estimated resources or use normalized baselines for estimating. If the estimation process is not diligently performed, the project schedule will not be credible. At most, the team will have a best guess schedule. When the schedule is not credible, it is likely to fail with either the project completion being delayed or the resources experiencing a lot of stress in order to complete it on time. In the ensuing haste, quality takes a beating. In short, the project is rarely completed satisfactorily.

It may not be an exaggeration to say that poor estimation is one of the major causes of project failure and therefore a very significant common pitfall.

The best practice is to treat estimation as an important activity in the organization.

Estimation processes and standards need to be developed and implemented, and the performance of these processes must be monitored and improved regularly using actual values that are collected and analyzed to correct the organizational baselines. All estimates prepared in the organization should be maintained in the organizational knowledge repository and made available to PMs.

Robust cost estimation helps in identifying the right resources and the right amount of resources required for efficient project execution. Training on estimation and the use of metrics to aid credible estimation are aspects vital for project success.

It is a best practice to define an excellent estimation process for the organization and carry it out adhering to that process with all diligence.

Poor Project Planning

The wisdom or importance of project planning is well reflected in the anecdote attributed to Abraham Lincoln that says, "If I am given six hours to fell a tree, I would use the first four sharpening the axe."

In many cases PMs who do not understand the value of planning simply take plans from an earlier project and do a "save as" to arrive at the new project's plans. This shortcut to planning is a risky pitfall. Although one project may be very similar to another, no two projects are exactly the same. However, using relevant portions from previous plans in a "cut and paste" mode where possible saves time and still affords fresh thinking based on the requirements of the current project.

A major pitfall in many organizations is to equate project planning solely with generating a project schedule. Project planning goes beyond a schedule. Plans need to be detailed enough to facilitate implementation during project execution.

Another pitfall organizations get into is to treat project planning as an exercise in creating documents for the sake of meeting process requirements. Such organizations create plan documents and then put them aside and execute the project on an ad hoc basis. Planning is not an exercise in creating documents. It is thinking through the project and making decisions so the project gets executed smoothly without any surprises. Planning is that time in project management when the PM focuses on goals and objectives and how to achieve them.

In some organizations the complaint is that planning requires too many documents with bureaucracy replacing efficiency. This is a common pitfall that can lead to poor planning. All processes should be lean (just enough to meet the needs of the organization) and scalable (smaller projects need less rigor than larger ones). Scalability suggests that for small and short-duration projects, the creation of a single overall plan is adequate with all other plans embedded in it, and for large projects that are especially prone to failure separate plans with greater detail are required.

The best practice is to treat project planning as an important and critical activity rather than an exercise in creating a set of documents required for quality audit purposes.

Poor Standards and Guidelines

Standards and guidelines assist the project team in achieving a predictable minimum level of quality for the deliverable. A high quality set of standards and guidelines will go a long way towards helping the PM achieve efficient and effective project execution. Some organizations pay either lip service to the concept of standards and guidelines or implement them poorly. Organizations that pay lip service to this aspect either totally neglect the definition of standards and guidelines or define sketchy standards and guidelines. They do so at the risk of poor quality in project execution which is a common pitfall.

Some organizations argue that standards and guidelines stifle the creativity and innovation of people and thereby promote mediocrity. This statement is not true. What standards and guidelines stifle is unbridled experimentation in the name of innovation in live projects, but not creativity and innovation in themselves. No organization wants to experiment on live projects. In any process driven organization, there is always a facility to improve processes including standards and guidelines. Every PM is free to offer suggestions for improvement in all aspects of the process including standards and guidelines. They may also volunteer to develop new standards or modify the existing ones and pilot them on their project. In a process driven organization there is usually even the facility of a process waiver request for dealing with emergencies.

Ad hoc or nonexistent standards are a common pitfall that organizations can fall into.

A best practice in EVERY organization is the definition of excellent standards and guidelines. It is also a best practice to facilitate improvement of the organizational standards and guidelines in a structured manner.

Poor Project Oversight

Another common pitfall is poor project oversight by senior management. It can be either too infrequent or akin to breathing down the neck of the PM. Oversight should be at regular intervals short enough to facilitate timely intervention. There is no universally accepted right interval for senior management review of project progress. Oversight needs to be set based on the planned project duration. For shorter duration projects a weekly monitoring may be right, and for longer duration a monthly monitoring may be adequate.

The best practice is to decide oversight timing on a project-by-project basis, record the decision in the project plan, and conform to it.

No PM Training

Project management training is another frequently neglected area. Most PMs grow from one of the technical specialties. A technical specialist grows from a technician to supervisor, to project leader, and then to a PM. During this transition he/she generally learns the basics of project management on the job through observation of superiors. Unless the person works under a number of PMs and on all types of projects, his/her knowledge is likely to be limited by the PM practices they have observed.

In the absence of a formal well-designed training program, newly promoted PMs in addition to conforming to the organizational processes tend to imitate the PMs they worked under. The problem tends to be accentuated when PMs are recruited from outside the organization. They come with their own project management philosophy that in most cases is not in sync with the project management practices of the organization brought into. When various PMs in an organization have different practices of project management, it is likely to give rise to discordance among the human resources.

One argument frequently heard in organizations that neglect project management training is that senior project managers use mentoring to smooth out the rough edges. Another argument is that training has the potential to stifle PM innovation. In essence the argument suggests that given a free hand, PMs will develop new and innovative methods and that discord and conflict are part of any organization and can be managed. Very convincing, aren't they?

Project management training ensures that the organizational philosophy, processes, standards, and guidelines are imparted to trainees based on the project management body of knowledge as implemented within the organization. Course content along with organizational processes, standards, and guidelines are subject to regular improvement. If training is stifling creativity and innovation of resources, something is wrong with the training program and it needs closer examination for improvement. Training brings homogeneity among all PMs in the organization and promotes predictability in project management.

The best practice is to conduct project management training for all PMs before allocating them to manage projects. It is also a best practice to subject the training curriculum to regular improvement in line with that of the organizational process.

Pitfalls and Best Practices at the Project Manager Level

Organizational-level processes and practices set the stage on which a PM performs project management. The PM has a critical role in ensuring the success of the project. Some pitfalls and best practices that can be implemented at the PM level are discussed next.

Contractor Management

Most IT projects include subcontractors, as discussed in Chapter 6. To successfully complete an IT project, it is essential to carefully monitor subcontractors' work. The two extremes of monitoring are to allow subcontractors unbridled freedom and wait for the deliverable or to breathe down their necks. We need to monitor subcontractor work between these two extremes. Progress should be reviewed periodically, perhaps once a week. We need to carry out quality control activities at planned stages. We also need to ensure that subcontractors are performing the quality control activities as expected, have planned activities diligently, and are conforming to that plan.

The pitfall project managers often fall into is to swing to either extreme of monitoring subcontractor performance.

Selection of the right subcontractors using the process discussed in Chapter 6 is a best practice that will help with this issue, together with careful planning, scheduling, and a planned and diligent performance monitoring system.

Quality Control

Quality control often takes a beating in IT projects. For one thing, it is not easy to perform quality control activities without holding up the work for a period of time. The pressure of the completion date looming large on the horizon often forces the project manager to short-circuit quality control.

Why does this happen? It occurs because time has not been provided for conducting quality control activities in the schedule. We need to plan for quality control activities and provide time in the schedule for carrying them out during project execution. The most neglected quality control activities are networking activities, especially the laying of cables and the crimping of end connectors. These two activities together trigger most networking problems including disconnection, poor connection, and the loss of data transmission speed in the infrastructure. As discussed in Chapter 6, they need to be inspected while the work is carried out, not after. It is very difficult to inspect workmanship after the job has been completed. True, we can inspect functionality but if we do not ensure good workmanship, problems are likely to arise over the course of time.

The best practice is to plan quality control activities and implement the plan diligently.

Uniformity of the Pace of Execution

Some project managers are prone to initial procrastination and then a final frenzy of activity in long-duration projects. As there tends to be fewer activities that need to be performed in the initial stages, these PMs often fall into the trap of thinking there is all the time in the world to execute the project. However, this lax attitude can be costly as there are too many loose ends to tie up near project completion. The 90% versus 10% axiom comes into force. It states that in any project, the first 10% of the work consumes 90% of the time and the remaining 90% of the work uses 10% of the time. This happens due to poor planning and by allowing the project to proceed at a slow pace from the start. It is essential to carefully plan so the pace of project execution is spread uniformly across the duration of the project and to then implement the plan diligently. When we allow activity frenzy near project completion, the quality of workmanship can take a beating. Another consequence of this phenomenon is the resentment of overworked, stressed out individuals due to the added pressure. Frenzy and stress can lead to costly and time-consuming errors.

The best practice is to plan and ensure the pace is uniform throughout project duration.

Fair Treatment to Project Human Resources

Project management is the process of getting the work done through the actions of subordinates, peers, and subcontractors. A well-motivated project team can scale unimaginable heights in performance. The PM can add to (or subtract from) the prevailing organizational morale of the team. Fair treatment of team members helps to ensure their organizational level of motivation is maintained. If the project team perceives that the PM is not treating them fairly, morale will deteriorate. A pitfall that some PMs fall into is that of showing favoritism to their cronies, which gets noticed in no time at all.

The best practice is to refrain from giving special treatment to any team member and to treat everyone equally and fairly.

It will serve you well to remember that it is not enough to be fair. You must be seen to be fair too.

Balancing the Workload

Most team members like to perform his/her fair share of the work and achieve the best possible project results. No one likes to see people lazing around while others are working hard. Although the PM may not be able to perceive that team members are keeping tabs on him/her, they actually do. Any imbalance in loading work to the resources gets noticed very quickly. Therefore, it is essential to balance the workload equitably. The following are the best practices in work allocation:

1. Maintain a formal work register for all work allocation. The register will help to quantitatively assess the workload on each team member while allocating work or reviewing individual contributions of the

team members. A formal work register also allows team members to see their individual contributions contrasted with others. A level of formality is needed in large projects. It would be very difficult to ensure a balanced workload using informal methods and to respond to team member accusations of you overloading them.

2. Make the work register available for all team members to see so they can assess for themselves how equitable you are.
3. Measure actual achievements, productivity, and quality for each resource and make it part of the work register.
4. Acknowledge achievement when one team member is allocated with more work and lives up to that level of contribution.

Fair Rewards

Rewards are another area where a project manager needs to be fair. Positive performance ought to receive positive rewards and negative performance ought to receive negative ones. Refraining from recognizing both scenarios and the delivery of appropriate rewards will certainly cause team members to become less motivated. As Douglas McGregor, the famous human motivation author of X-Y Theory suggested, discipline ought to be like a hot stove. It burns whoever touches it; the burn is immediate; the amount of burn is directly proportional to the amount of the touch; it is impartial (it burns everyone irrespective of rank or importance). Positive and negative rewards should also be like that. The saying, "justice delayed is justice denied" suggests that rewards must be in close proximity to the occurrence of performance.

Estimation and Project Planning

Although organizational-level best practices and the pitfalls and ramifications of poor estimation and project planning have been discussed, the role of the project manager in these activities and best practices that can be implemented at this level need to be mentioned at least in brief.

Poor estimation practices are thought to be one of the major causes of project failure. Developing excellent estimation standards and processes that must be diligently adhered to is a best practice at the organizational level. However, it is the PM who ensures that estimation is carried out as diligently and accurately as possible. Estimation must be treated as an important activity at both the organizational level and project level. If estimation goes haywire there is little chance that project planning and execution will be successful.

Best practice suggests focusing attention on estimation and then performing the activity with all diligence.

As noted earlier, some PMs treat project planning as a document creation activity. They take documents from an earlier project and "save them as" plans for the current project. In doing this, PMs fail to think through the project and provide for every foreseeable contingency in their project plans.

The best practice suggests that PMs utilize the project planning exercise to think through the project and carry out the activity with complete diligence.

Resolving Issues

Issues do arise in most projects. A formal mechanism to record each issue and track it through to resolution is recommended. Another important step is to report the status of each issue in the project status report. A common pitfall is not to record or report every issue and then try to resolve them informally. Project stakeholders like to be kept informed of every significant issue that arises in a project and to know it early enough to avoid unpleasant surprises.

The best practice is to use a formal mechanism for issue resolution, record every issue, report them in the weekly status report, and keep all project stakeholders informed about the issue resolution status.

Poor Change Management

One of the most common pitfalls is to handle change management without a well-planned strategy. Projects often begin with overconfidence in the notion that the end users/customer will not ask for changes or the team will have the ability to take care of them informally without impacting the budget, quality, or delivery date.

The best practice in change management is to follow a formal strategy for handling change requests, plan change management in the project plans, and report the status of change requests to all project stakeholders regularly.

Poor Recordkeeping

Project execution generates a host of information that when properly analyzed and included in the organizational knowledge repository can improve the efficiency of the organization manifold. Improved efficiency can generate a significant amount of monetary savings that can end up directly on an organization's bottom line. The PM is the person responsible for ensuring all information is properly recorded in a manner that it can be processed and analyzed. When he/she doesn't keep diligent records, all further analysis is likely to yield wrong results and any modifications of organizational processes based on these wrong indicators could be disastrous for the organization. Remember the adage "garbage in, garbage out?"

Poor recordkeeping is an easy pitfall for a project manager to fall into.

Why do PMs do this? Typically, not because they want to gather bad data but rather because it is easy to see recordkeeping as an overhead activity not directly linked to the deliverable. Typically, this type of activity is not caught until the investigative audit is carried out as part of project postmortem.

The best practice is for the PM to diligently maintain project records so they render useful and worthwhile information about project planning and execution.

Other Best Practices for Project Management

The following are some additional best practices for project management.

A Knowledge Repository

As alluded to previously, a well-organized knowledge repository (not just a dumping ground for records of completed projects) will greatly enhance the chances for success in project initiation and execution. The repository will be of great assistance if the PM can obtain records of relevant projects at the time of initiation and then when needed by the project team. A well-stocked and organized repository will simplify the PM's work significantly and steer the project toward success.

Project Postmortem

In hospitals, if a patient dies, a mandatory postmortem is conducted to find out the real reason for the death. A postmortem helps the doctors to assess if the diagnosis and treatment were in the right direction and allows them to learn lessons for future diagnosis and treatment. Likewise, a postmortem for projects regardless of whether they fail or succeed should also be conducted. The postmortem is often skipped under the argument that it takes a significant amount of time that could otherwise be spent on revenue-earning activities. In some cases the explanation is that the customer satisfaction survey is quite adequate for assessing project performance. These arguments are shortsighted. In other cases a project closure meeting is treated as a project postmortem. Both serve different purposes. The goal of the project postmortem is to identify all the best practices and pitfalls faced by the project. Analyzing and critically examining the causes for these practices will facilitate process improvement.

The best practice is to conduct a postmortem for every completed project.

Training

Training should cover more than the project management training detailed in the above sections; a PM and the project team should be trained in the soft skills required for team effectiveness. Training should include topics of problem solving, communication, interpersonal relationships, conflict management, motivation, and morale. These skills will help the PM and project team to maintain a harmonious atmosphere during project execution. Role-based training is sometimes neglected in an organization. In the absence of formal training, resources tend to imitate their bosses or the most charismatic person, which sometimes may not be in the best interests of the organization.

The best practice is to conduct formal training for all resources involved in project execution.

Information Sharing

The act of formal and informal information sharing among PMs needs to be encouraged. This can be achieved through information-sharing meetings between PMs within the organization, by attending seminars (internal and external), and by providing a bulletin/discussion board where project management issues can be openly discussed. These types of activities can be implemented within the organization without significant cost.

Encouraging and facilitating formal and informal information sharing among PMs is a best practice.

Management Support

Last but not least in importance, management support and funding are vital to any success in the organization. Management must recognize project management as a specialist discipline and as essential to the success of the project as engineering activities. All best practices cited above can only be implemented if sponsored by management.

Is It Essential to Implement the Best Practices?

Many senior managers argue that best practices are for large organizations and big/important projects, and that others don't really need them. This thinking connotes that best practices add overhead and extra cost. Nothing could be further from the truth. Best practices ensure getting it right the first time, to avoid costly mistakes and minimize rework. In larger projects, the rigor of process implementation and oversight should be higher, but best practices should not be compromised on any project.

Another argument against implementing best practices is in the definition of project success. If a project is completed on time, some consider it a success. This argument is obviously flawed given that not meeting expectations or a commitment receives a less than satisfactory or failing grade in any other work environment. Satisfactory is defined as good enough to meet a requirement, but not all requirements. Is a project satisfactory if it is completed on time, but fails to deliver planned results and costs exceed budget?

Success is defined as the achievement of something planned or attempted. So at the minimum, a successful project is one which is completed on time and within budgeted cost and delivers the planned results committed to. To put it into perspective, this level of performance in other work environments is often referred to as "meets expectations or commitments."

In most any human endeavor and particularly in business, we generally attribute the term "success" to those who exceed expectations. Therefore, a more consistent definition of project success would be one where planned results are achieved ahead of schedule and/or below budgeted cost. To meet this definition of project success, planned results must be achieved in an efficient and effective manner with optimal costs, productivity, quality, and morale.

Best practices are those methods of working that give consistently good results and help ensure achievement of these objectives and successful project execution. They should be applied in every project to the degree needed to achieve project success, assuming you want consistently good results on all projects.

Appendix A

Management for Project Managers

Background

Numerous articles, books, and other types of literature are available on the topic of management. Many management models, tools, and theories are also available. These models, tools, theories, and literature are all largely derived from and focused on manufacturing organizations, with modifications to some extent based on the services industry (e.g., retailing, banking, and insurance). Most manufacturing organizations started out being "person-dependent," but over time they grew to be "technology-dependent," with a goal of leveraging their processes to reduce dependency on the *inscrutable* resource—human beings.

Appendix A explores management from the standpoint of a manager, particularly a project manager. In this appendix, I give as much information as I can on the subject of management, and briefly touch upon a number of topics covering the following:

1. Project planning
2. Project execution and control
3. Motivation and morale
4. Interpersonal relationship management
5. Communication

What Is Management?

There are three angles from which to view the term "management:"

1. The first angle is the set of people responsible for running the affairs of an organization. Here the word "management" is used in its personified form.
2. The second view of the term "management" is an art and social science practiced by people to get things done through others where the authority is not absolute and there is vagueness in the procedures/processes (e.g., matrix management). Here the word "management" is used as a process.
3. The final aspect of "management" is a body of knowledge on the subject of managing. Here the word "management" is used as a part of social sciences.

This appendix looks at the term management from the point of view of the second aspect, as a process, that of the art of getting work done through others. Why did I use the word "art" when describing the word "management"? There is a large body of knowledge under the topic of management. This body of knowledge has been collected empirically by practitioners themselves or through studying practitioners. Adopting this body of knowledge generally produces predictable results. Many mathematical models, such as linear programming, transportation problems, management games, and other topics have been developed to assist managers in making objective decisions and to obtain predictable results. Even though many aspects of management are scientific, many are still not measurable and there are no formulas that can objectively predict precise consequences. Regardless of slow and steady progress evolving management into a science, it is, as yet, at least partially an art.

Evolution of the Discipline of Management

The word management itself signifies the fact that something is *not* under control! Consider the adage: "If we can, we control it. If we cannot, we manage it." This brings to mind a second adage: "If you cannot surmount it, then circumvent it." So, management can have a number of varied objectives, such as to:

1. Deliver what you had originally set out to deliver
2. Attain your goal; reach your target
3. Not win the race, but finish it
4. Keep all concerned stakeholders from becoming unhappy/dissatisfied

Perhaps, we should also have said that the word *management* signifies that if something is not desirable to be controlled (or is not controllable), then it is better for it to be managed. But *control* can sometimes beget a penalty-avoidance type of performance. At times therefore using control is not always desirable—letting things happen and then managing (maneuvering) to get innovation and thus better-than-average performance is better: "If we can, we administer. If we cannot, we manage!"

Management has evolved from a base process of oversight and ensuring that everyone worked to their full capacity. From this base process, Frederick Winslow Taylor (1856–1915) proved that full capacity is not really the same as maximum output. Taylor used physical experiments and coined the term *scientific management*. He advocated studying the work being carried out and then using that study to design the proper methods for carrying out the work. Taylor also advocated that providing rest breaks increased output. Taylor's work has lead to new fields of "work study" (method study and work measurement), industrial engineering, ergonomics, "a fair day's work for a fair day's pay," productivity, and quality assurance. Taylor's work caused significant evolution in work design and workstation design.

The evolution of management continued with Henri Fayol (1841–1925). Fayol's work vastly influenced the process of management and was the forerunner of present-day management thought. Fayol began as an apprentice engineer and went on to become the managing director of a mining company in France. His management background is reflected in his later theories. (Fayol wrote a book entitled *Administration Industrielle et Générale* in 1916. This book was translated and published in English as *General and Industrial Management*.) Fayol classified management functions into five categories:

1. Planning
2. Organizing
3. Commanding
4. Coordinating
5. Controlling

These were later modified to:

1. Planning
2. Organizing
3. Staffing
4. Directing (Leading)/Coordinating
5. Controlling

These were further refined later to:

1. Planning
2. Organizing
3. Leading
4. Controlling

Henri Fayol also propounded 14 principles for management:

1. *Division of Work (Specialization)*. This principle suggests dividing the work into packages that can foster specialization among workers. This principle may be said to be the harbinger for the assembly line in manufacturing leading to reduced cost of goods.
2. *Authority.* Those who have responsibility for results should have authority to issue commands and exact obedience.
3. *Discipline.* Personnel should be disciplined and perform their functions diligently.
4. *Unity of Command.* Each employee should have only one boss. An employee should not receive commands from multiple individuals. (In organizations using matrix management, especially software development organizations, practice of this principle seems to have dropped significantly.)
5. *Unity of Direction.* Each position should have a single objective. In today's business environment almost every executive position has multiple objectives.
6. *Subordination of Personal Interest* (to that of the organization's interest). Pursue organizational goals while at work and do not look for personal aggrandizement. Although this seems to be directed more at management personnel, the principle applies to all.
7. *Remuneration.* Fayol advocated fair pay. This principle may have been the harbinger for the "need-based minimum wage" concept.
8. *Centralization.* This principle advocated making decisions at the top of the hierarchy and that everyone else would follow orders.
9. *Line of Authority.* This principle defines hierarchy of management as a pyramidal structure for the organization.
10. *Order.* This principle suggests that there is a place for everything and everyone and that everything and everyone are in their place. The concept of segregation of work and strict order is still followed in the armed forces.
11. *Equity.* All personnel should be treated in a fair and just manner. Fayol advocated kindness in treatment.

12. *Tenure for Personnel.* This principle advocated ensuring that employees work longer for the organization. The basis is the recognition that the loss of a trained employee has a substantial impact. Job insecurity is not good for the organization. Fayol suggested putting in place steps to lessen the chance that a good employee does not leave the organization.
13. *Initiative.* All employees should show initiative.
14. *Esprit de Corps.* This principle advocated promoting esprit de corps, which is the team spirit in which the team pulls together to achieve a goal.

As can be seen, these principles are still very relevant even though we cannot practice all of them fully in the current labor/management environment.

Management in Present-Day Context

Present-day management is understood to be:

1. Planning
2. Organizing
3. Leading
4. Controlling

Present-day managers are expected to perform these four tasks as primary responsibilities. The scale, however, differs for each type of manager: a project manager performs these tasks at a project level and a senior manager performs them at a group or organizational level. We will now briefly discuss the four tasks.

Planning

Planning is defined as the intelligent anticipation of resources required to perform a predefined endeavor successfully at a future date in a defined environment.

The key terms contribute the following meanings:

1. *Anticipation* indicates that the planning precedes performance and is a best guess however scientifically the guess is derived.
2. *Resources* refer to the 5 Ms—Men (persons), Materials, Methods (includes information), Money, and Machines plus time (duration).
3. *At a future date* indicates that the work is not already performed and is consistent with the anticipation of resources.

4. *In a defined environment* suggests that where the work is going to be carried out is known and defined. Any variation in the environment would have an effect on the plan. The environment refers to the working conditions including work and workstation design, methods of management, prevailing morale at the workplace, etc.
5. *Predefined endeavor* suggests that the scope of the work is known.

In order to accomplish planning, we need to perform the following activities:

1. Scheduling to estimate the calendar time resource within the constraints of existing facilities and availability of other resources
2. Cost estimation to define the monetary resources needed; this is also referred to as *budgeting*
3. Planning the deployment, quality management, and other plans as needed
4. Documenting all estimates and plans
5. Reviewing and approving the plans

Organizing

Organizing refers to creating the work environment that breaks into the following tasks:

1. Breaking down activities of the organization into departments/sections/teams so that work can be performed efficiently and effectively
2. Designing and arranging the workstations (a workstation is a combination of machine and human resources required to accomplish the work assigned) that will be used to accomplish the work
3. Breaking the work down into its constituent components such that they can be allocated and executed at a workstation
4. Defining and developing methods, standards, and processes for all types of work including quality assurance to be carried out in the organizations

Leading

Leading is concerned with guiding the team that works for the manager/leader toward achieving the objectives. More specifically, the tasks are:

1. Providing direction
2. Providing guidance
3. Providing assistance/removing obstacles to performance

4. Providing the motivation and ensuring team morale
5. Setting targets:
   a. Productivity targets
   b. Quality targets
   c. Schedule targets
   d. Technical targets
6. Performance evaluation
7. Pursuing and tracking the team goals until they are accomplished successfully
8. Coaching and mentoring team members

Controlling

Controlling involves ensuring that project execution adheres to the plan. Tasks include:

1. Continuously measuring progress
2. Comparing the actual against the planned performance and identifying the gaps in achievements, if any
3. Taking corrective actions to align actual with planned performance:
   a. Adding resources
   b. Providing expert assistance
   c. Providing better tools/methods
   d. Changing the plan when required
4. Taking preventive actions so that future occurrences of slippage are prevented and the time lost is made up so that final deliveries are not adversely affected

Primary Responsibilities of Managers

There are four primary responsibility categories for managers:

1. **Work Management:**
   a. *Division of work* is the breakdown of the deliverable into work packages that can be allocated to individuals for execution. The breakdown of the deliverable should ensure that it could be assembled/integrated later into the specified final deliverable in an efficient manner. The division should also facilitate inspection/testing of the packages to ensure quality is built into the product. The work packages must also facilitate measurement of

productivity. When breaking the work down, a manager should ensure that the packaging does not necessitate frequent work allocation (although there is no minimum duration, it is better that the allocated work takes at least one day).

b. *Allocate work for execution* in such a way that the person has the ability to execute it. The allocation of work to an individual should be done in a manner that the targets for schedule, productivity, and quality are achievable. The targets must be commensurate with the skill level of the person given the work. Where possible it should be seen that all people have similar workloads; fair allocation to all available people.
c. *Integrate the deliverable* (arrange work) so that the assembly, testing, and delivery of all the components are as designed and are ready for delivery to the client.
d. *Ensure quality* through implementing all planned quality control activities that ensure that work is executed in conformance to organizational standards and quality norms.
e. *Ensure productivity* by implementing all measures necessary so that work is carried out meeting or exceeding organizational productivity levels.
f. *Deliver, install, commission, train, and hand over* the deliverable to the customer while meeting the schedule and quality specifications. Delivery typically includes assisting in the implementation and rollout of the product and finally in obtaining acceptance from the client.
g. *Get paid* by arranging for billing and collection for services rendered. This may include any follow-up with the client if applicable.

2. **Expectation Management:**
   a. *Senior management expectations* are that the project is executed with a minimum necessity for their intervention; with maximum client satisfaction; while meeting or exceeding the organizational norms for schedule, quality, and productivity; and that there is access to the correct project information when needed; that managers maintain team morale; and finally that the project earns a profit.
   b. *Client expectations* are to have access to progress information; that the team adheres to the agreed schedules and quality norms; that there is cooperation on the resolution of issues and change

requests; and finally that the team pays attention and provides quick turnaround for their communications.

c. *Peer expectations* include the sharing of knowledge and experience; assistance in reviews; assistance when interviewing recruits; and finally assistance in process improvement initiatives.

d. *Team expectations* are for fair work allocation; assistance in troubleshooting issues; fair performance appraisals; transparent and fair performance targets; fair recognition including rewards and punishments; and finally that grievances are redressed.

3. **Morale Management:**
   a. *Self-morale.* A central component of your own morale is self-confidence. Confidence is the personal belief in one's ability to deliver expected results and that management would support your actions.
   b. *Team morale.* Central to team morale is the confidence of your team that they can together achieve their objectives and the strongly held belief that you (the manager) would support the team.
   c. *Organizational morale.* Organizations, like people, have a culture and morale. The organization's morale should invigorate you or your team and provide confidence in the organization's ability to support the team.
4. **Resource Management:**
   a. Human resources are the team members. The goal is to use them effectively, efficiently, and wisely.
   b. Time resources boil down to one critical resource: calendar time. Calendar time is a resource that is consumed and rarely can be recovered if used poorly. Therefore, optimize the utilization of time in order to meet targets and schedules.
   c. Equipment resources are equipment and tools. Use them efficiently and maintain them at their peak capacity.
   d. Monetary resources are to be managed and accounted for. These include both expenses and revenues. The goal is to use them optimally.

These are the responsibilities that need to be kept in mind while performing *project management.* Translating responsibilities into action requires specific tactics. These are discussed on the following pages.

Delegation (Utilization of Subordinates)

The job of a manager is to get things done. This means that unless you manage a one-person project, you, as a manager, will need to work with and through other individuals. You will therefore need to delegate work to subordinates. An important aspect to keep in mind is that although you can delegate authority, you *cannot* delegate responsibility! As a manager, the responsibility for results always remains with you. In other words, you may delegate something to a subordinate to do, but if this subordinate goofs up, you are still responsible for getting the delegated task done. As a manager, however, when you delegate authority to your subordinates, you also extract accountability from them.

Consider this exaggerated example: a cashier in a bank steals some money. Who is responsible for answering to the customers and depositors? Will the depositors only shrug their shoulders and say, "That poor bank manager—what can he do if a cashier just runs away? It's just our bad luck. Let's not blame the manager." No way would that ever be the case! Bottom line: the bank manager is responsible for his subordinate's actions. But will the subordinate get off scot-free? No. The cashier will be accountable for his or her actions. The bank manager will file a report with police to track down, arrest and jail, and recover the stolen money from the cashier.

People Management

People management is a vast topic, which is beyond the scope of this appendix. We will therefore devote a separate appendix to people management (Appendix C). A few points related to people management, however, are pertinent for inclusion in this appendix: interacting with subordinates, peers, and superiors.

Interaction with Subordinates

At times, you will need to deal with subordinates in ways that are similar to how a concerned and disciplined father treats and disciplines his teenage children. We use teenage children as an example because a teenager:

- Is not yet fully "grown-up"
- Is sharp and smart, but immature
- Is capable, but likely to be somewhat irresponsible
- Requires proper handling (firmness coupled with love)

Proper handling of these characteristics can produce astounding results. Treat subordinates with firmness that is coupled with compassion—you will see them respond to (not react to) you.

Interaction with Peers

Treat peers as a true friend treats his friends. We use the word *friend* because a true friend:

- Is still a friend even when you are in need (Likewise, when a peer has a need, you step in to help—no invitation necessary.)
- Listens patiently and gives complete attention to a friend's ideas and views
- Bridges gaps in a friend's performance
- Is willing to teach a new skill to a friend
- Does not expect anything in return from a friend

Friendly interaction with peers, however, does not include gossiping and sharing personal information. Life (as well as the workplace) is full of competitors. Be careful what you share. (Refrain from gossiping and inappropriate sharing of information. Your career might end with a note on Facebook!)

Interaction with Superiors

Treat superiors like a responsible son or daughter treats their father. We use the comparison of a father and a child because generally a child:

- Has no suspicions about the father's intentions (i.e., believes the father)
- Wants to take care of the father
- Takes reprimands better from the father (child's ego and self-confidence are not affected as much)
- Wants to do better than the father
- Wants to please the father and get words of praise from him

By exhibiting these characteristics, your superiors will slowly but surely begin to exhibit fatherly behavior with you.

But are these recommendations sure to get results always? Difficult people are everywhere. So, you may not always get the results promised from following these recommendations. (This topic is discussed in more detail in Appendix C.)

Work Management

As a manager, you have the responsibility for conducting certain activities that are necessary to ensure that work is carried out by your subordinates. Activities performed for getting the work done and for making delivery to clients include:

1. Allocating work

2. Assisting and facilitating to subordinates who are carrying out the work
3. Arranging quality control activities such as inspection, walkthrough, review, and testing to ensure that the executed work and deliverables conform to the organizational standards and design
4. Arranging for integrating disparate components into a single whole; product or deliverable

Management Levels

The first level of management is often called technical management or line management. Line managers are the conduits between people who work and people who manage. Therefore, they are very close to where the work is carried out. Their day-to-day job is more concerned with the technical aspects of the work (the *how* of getting things done) where they provide technical leadership. Frequently, the planning role for technical management is primary work allocation. The control aspect of management is focused on guiding work.

The second level of management is typically called middle management. This level directs first-level managers and interacts with other layers of management. It often has multiple levels and names including manager, senior manager, deputy general manager, general manager, etc. The primary concern of this layer of management is to ensure integration, cohesion, results' delivery, and firefighting and to be the bridge between senior and first-level management.

Senior management is concerned with profitability of their unit. They take full ownership of a unit or division, group, or company. The key measures of success are the *results* expected by top management.

Top management (highest level officers and executives) sets and manages strategy and establishes the ultimate goals of the organization. Top management is concerned with direction, survival, and growth of the entire organization.

The IT project manager falls into the middle management level in large organizations or projects and into technical or line management in smaller organizations or projects.

What Does a Project Manager Do?

I put this question to myself and came up with the answer . . . *plenty*. Then I tried making a list:

1. Delivery functions:
    a. Manage work:
        i. Plan
        ii. Organize
        iii. Allocate work
        iv. Progress chasing
        v. Complete individual assignments
        vi. Integrate
        vii. Deliver
    b. Manage quality:
        i. Plan
        ii. Implement verification and validation
        iii. Allocate verification and validation activities
        iv. Progress chasing
        v. Complete quality assignments
        vi. Monitor and measure quality continuously
        vii. Improve quality continuously
    c. Manage productivity:
        i. Plan
        ii. Monitor and measure productivity
        iii. Improve productivity
    d. Team morale:
        i. Plan
        ii. Monitor morale
        iii. Motivate team continuously
    e. Manage schedule:
        i. Plan
        ii. Monitor work progress vis-à-vis schedule
        iii. Implement preventive and corrective actions as required
        iv. Deliver on schedule
2. Reporting functions:
    a. Report to the management
    b. Report to the client

    c. Report to the quality department
    d. Participate in meetings
3. Organizational assistance functions:
    a. Participate in strategic initiatives
    b. Participate in quality initiatives/certification:
        i. Process improvement activities
        ii. Participate in audits
        iii. Conduct audits
        iv. Verification and validation assistance to peers
    c. Recruitment/interviews
    d. Human resource development (training, recruitment)
    e. Assist in project acquisition
4. Miscellaneous functions as required: in other words, do what is needed to deliver value.

The factors that are critical to success of a project manager are the *delivery* and *reporting functions*.

Final Words

In Appendix A, I have tried to present the art and science of management in a nutshell that is relevant to project managers. Many books address this subject. To learn more about the art and science of management, I strongly recommend that you read a few books. The good ones are usually available through professional management/leadership associations and college libraries.

This book has free material available for download from the Web Added Value™ resource center at *www.jrosspub.com*

Appendix B

Decision Making for Project Managers

Introduction

Decisions, decisions, decisions . . . making decisions, postponing decisions, and sometimes jumping to decisions—occasionally we are faced with tough decisions and, at times, we delegate them. Sometimes we make hasty decisions and repent later. From time to time we delay decisions to see the world, move on, and our decisions are no longer relevant.

Decisions are part of everyday life, even more so for a manager whose ability to make successful, quality decisions is a required core competency. Many aspects of decision making will be presented in this appendix. Some of the materials covered will be very brief and might induce you to further study in order to master the subject. First, let us attempt to define decision making:

> *Decision making is choosing between alternatives in a volatile environment, while having incomplete/unreliable information about the scenario at hand and with uncertain and unpredictable outcomes from the available alternatives, mainly for the sake of expediency.*

During a project, we describe the environment as *volatile* because project execution is never stable. Humans are inherently nonlinear systems and therefore chaotic. A project by definition is not a continuous endeavor; it is a temporary one with a defined beginning and ending. Any specific project is executed only once and for the first time, people are temporarily assigned to the project, the client is new, and mid-project changes are certain. How can we define this as anything but a volatile environment?

I included the terms *incomplete and unreliable information* in the definition because in a project environment, we do not have the time to wait until perfect information is received. Deadlines always loom large on the horizon and completeness of information cannot be ensured. Therefore, the information at hand will always be incomplete and unreliable though the degree of unreliability and incompleteness would certainly vary. We cannot hope to have better than a 90% level of completeness and reliability of information. If you have complete and reliable information, you can pass judgments.

Similarly, we use the terms *uncertain and unpredictable outcomes* because the volatile environment as described above is not conducive for predictability of outcomes. Again, if you know the outcome and its certainty, they would have been called judgments.

We also said *expediency*, which is not justice. Decisions are made in organizations to tide over the present situation/difficulty, to solve the immediate problem/issue, and to get things moving. Therefore, sometimes decisions may render injustice. We do not condone this but merely state the facts of decision making.

One prevalent misunderstanding is that decisions are judgments. This is far from being universally true. While judgment is used to make a decision it is rarely synonymous. With this definition we can move forward. Decisions can be classified into the following types for better understanding.

Classification of Decisions

1. Strategic and periodic decisions:
   a. Selection decisions:
      i. Products/services
      ii. Process
      iii. Locations
      iv. Layout
      v. Equipment
      vi. Workforce
   b. Design decisions:
      i. Product design
      ii. Service design
      iii. Job design
      iv. Process design

        v. Control system design
        vi. Capacity design
2. Recurring decisions:
    a. Target setting
    b. Scheduling
    c. Sequencing
    d. Inventory control
    e. Cost control
    f. Maintenance
3. Planning decisions:
    a. Planning the system
    b. Planning the usage of the system
4. Organizing decisions:
    a. Organization structure
    b. Organizing the jobs
    c. Staffing
    d. Work and workstation design
    e. Standards of performance
    f. Compensation systems
5. Controlling decisions:
    a. Quality
    b. Quantity
    c. Schedule
    d. Productivity
    e. Inventories
    f. Costs
    g. Maintenance

All of us make some of those decisions. However, it is very rare that any given decision maker will make all the above-mentioned decisions except, perhaps, the entrepreneurs.

Decision-Making Styles

Decision-making styles differ from person to person. It will help to know what the decision-making styles are in order to understand our own style and improve upon it if necessary. It is also obvious that the same style of decision making is not appropriate for every scenario. Although individuals may have their own style of decision making, the knowledge of decision-making styles allows the flexibility to adopt the appropriate style that fits the scenario at hand. Let us look at the styles of decision making:

1. *Judgment-/hunch-based decision making.* This style is utilized by those who use experience in decision making. Experience builds knowledge and possible consequences that result from a decision. Experience hones the hunch to a fine edge. Some of us are also inherently *convergent thinkers*. This means that we look for one single best solution for any situation. Convergent thinkers tend to use this type of decision making. This style is best suited for situations where the experience/knowledge gap is wide between the decision maker and decision implementers. Some scenarios that come to mind are:
   a. Decision implementers are trainees/novices and the decision maker is more experienced/knowledgeable
   b. Emergency situations such as a battlefield-like or fire-fighting scenario
   c. Breakdown maintenance
   d. Negotiations
2. *Analytical decision making.* This style implies that a thorough analysis is carried out in which all possible alternatives are considered along with their costs and probable results. All possible paths are analyzed and the optimal decision is selected. This type of process is used by knowledgeable people who are somewhat less experienced in their field. The scenarios that come to mind where this style is appropriate are:
   a. The decision is strategic and has long-term impact, especially a selection and design decision.
   b. There is time available for developing all alternatives and making the decision.
   c. The decision maker is from a premiere educational institution but is not experienced in real-life situations.
3. *Precedence-based decision making.* This type of decision-making process uses established practices and policies for making decisions. A well-repeated precedence is also called "organizational policy." This style is used to ensure uniformity in decision making between different decision makers, perhaps at different locations. The scenarios that come to mind are:

   a. Senior management sets the policy and middle managers make decisions.
   b. Headquarters sets the policy and branches make decisions.
4. *Participative decision making.* This style is also sometimes called consultative decision making. The decision maker consults the stakeholders to get their perspective on the scenario at hand to ensure that all concerns are taken into consideration before making the decision so that those concerns can be addressed in the decision. Possible scenarios are:
   a. Target setting
   b. Sequencing
   c. Scheduling
   d. Inventory control
   e. Preventive maintenance
5. *Democratic decision making.* This is a style of decision making in which the decision maker simply lets the decision implementers make the decision. This is especially useful in public-interfacing scenarios. The decision maker formulates guidelines (or sets the boundaries) and allows the decision implementer to make the decision. This type of decision making is prevalent in knowledge realms like research and development, educational institutions, high-tech fields, and aid distribution work.
6. In *consensus building*, a decision maker generates acceptance for a decision from persons with different and sometimes conflicting interests in the matter at hand. The decision maker consults all the involved persons and discovers their concerns and level of acceptance for the proposed decision. He/she then negotiates to arrive at a consensus and rolls out the decision. This type of process is normally followed in committees where peers come together to discuss and finalize a decision that concerns all. The trick is in arriving at a win-win situation for all. Everybody has to give and get something. This type of process requires a decision maker who is acceptable to all and is thoroughly knowledgeable in the field and the decision scenario.

Dominant Factor

Sometimes there is a dominant factor that influences the decision making. For example, for a mining company there is no alternative but to open a plant near the mine. A shipping company needs to be near the seacoast. Location of market is another dominant factor. For example, while it is possible for a company to locate away from its market, it is typically more efficient to be close to its customers. Other dominant factors in decision making may include emotional factors of the entrepreneur, such as the preferred location when opening a company, or the expertise of the entrepreneur when it comes to selecting the product, and many others. In day-to-day affairs, customer preference usually becomes a dominant factor. We have to manage around dominant factors (they guide and direct). In some cases like Y2K, the calendar becomes the dominant factor. In some cases the statutory obligations become the dominant factor. When a dominant factor is present in a decision scenario, the decision will be affected by the factor and our understanding of it.

When a dominant factor isn't present, or is not preferable to use, we can then utilize some of the tools/techniques described below.

Available Tools and Techniques for Decision Making

The following are some of the tools and techniques developed over a period of time for improving the quality of decision making and reducing the dependency on the individual capacity to arrive at a good hunch-based decision.

Critical Examination

Critical examination is an excellent technique for bringing more clarity to a scenario and evaluating the available alternatives. This tool can also be used in combination with other tools. Critical examination is based on two sets of questions as follows:

1. Primary questions—*what* and *why* are used to clarify a scenario.
2. Secondary questions—*what else* and *what should* are used to discover alternatives and to focus on a selection.

Five aspects of any scenario can be illuminated by the use of the above-mentioned questions:

1. Purpose (Why)
2. Means (How)
3. Place (Location)
4. Sequence (When)
5. Person (Who)

Table B.1 summarizes the questions.

The entry in the column captioned "What should" gives the decision. Critical examination can be used all by itself or it can be utilized in combination

Table B.1 Critical examination

Question	What	Why	What else	What should
Purpose	What is done? Is it necessary?	Why is it done?	What else could be done?	What should be done?
Means	How is it done?	Why this way?	How else?	How should?
Place	Where is it done?	Why there?	Where else?	Where should?
Sequence	When is it done?	Why then?	When else?	When should?
Person	Who does it?	Why them?	Who else?	Who should?

with other tools in any decision-making scenario. We can use other tools for evaluating alternatives (column captioned "What else") and to arrive at the best possible decision.

Queuing Theory

Queuing theory facilitates analysis of the workload at a workstation in order to plan the number of workstations to optimize capacity utilization and service levels. Possible examples include checkout counters, a workstation in the organization, ticket-issuing counters, and mechanics. These are places where the application of queuing theory can be seen and used for decision making. Queuing theory allows us to visualize the work arrival and execution rates at a given workstation and provides us with a set of equations for making decisions, especially with regard to building capacity that is adequate to execute tasks at hand effectively and economically.

Linear Programming

Linear programming (LP) is a mathematical optimization technique that allows us to define objectives and constraints. LP provides a procedure to optimize the process to meet the objective. Optimization includes either maximization (e.g., revenue or profit) or minimization (e.g., cost and tardiness). The solution is derived by a procedure called *simplex programming*. It is not practical to carry out simplex programming by manual means and computer assistance is more or less necessary to utilize this technique.

Transportation Problem

The *transportation problem* deals with reaching a number of places (m) starting from a number of places (n), while optimizing the travel usually by reducing distance or time. Typically, this type of decision making was originally applied to determining how to distribute from a number of warehouses across the country (or for that matter, the world now) to a number of sales points across the country (or the world). This problem is solved using a number of iterations. Each iteration involves making an assignment of originations and destinations and computing the costs between the points. The assignment is iterated until a satisfactory solution is found. For real-life problems, assistance of a computer is necessary to be able to use this technique.

Program Evaluation and Review Technique/Critical Path Method

Program evaluation and review technique (PERT) originated in the research and development field as a tool for visualizing the activities to be performed for completing a program. The PERT process also supported handling the uncertainty involved in the research and development domain using probability theory. The critical path method (CPM) originated in the construction industry for determining the completion time for projects and identifying the critical activities (activities that should not be delayed if the project is to be completed on schedule). Both techniques are based on developing a network diagram. Over time both came to be referred to and used together. These techniques help in visualizing the activities, their sequence of performance to complete a project, and deal with uncertainties as well as identify the critical project activities. PERT/CPM is best performed with the use of computer assistance, and is discussed in greater detail in Appendix D.

Management Games or Game Theory

Management games (or game theory) are a tool that helps to analyze the competition's strategy. Game theory helps us to know the outcome of strategies between two or more parties. The basic form of the game theory decision-making tool is expressed in the popular example of the prisoner's dilemma. In the prisoner's dilemma, two men are caught at the scene of a theft. They are taken to a police station and interrogated in two separate rooms. Now, if neither confesses, they might go scot-free or be given only the minimum sentence. But if either one (or both) confesses and implicates the other, one of these men will certainly receive the maximum sentence. The dilemma is that neither prisoner knows the strategy of the other. More often than not, a manager finds himself (or herself) in a similar situation. But instead of a jail sentence, the dilemma concerns the consequences of profit/loss or gaining/

losing a deal. Game theory helps us to work out the possible outcomes for a number of strategies/counterstrategies and to then select the optimal strategy.

Delphi Method

The Delphi method consists of consulting knowledgeable persons in an anonymous manner and soliciting a response or a decision from each; comparing the answers and sharing the rationale for all or at least the outliers; and then iterating until a consensus has been reached on the decision at hand. Crowdsourcing is a variant of the Delphi method.

Decision Trees

Decision trees allow us to graphically explore the possibilities for the consequences of our actions. A typical decision tree is depicted in Figure B.1. The branches can contain any number of actions and outcomes. One side benefit to the graphical nature of decision trees is that they help organize seemingly disparate thoughts that can grow in any direction.

Interpolation and Extrapolation

Historical data are a source of substantial information. Interpolation and extrapolation are statistical techniques for forecasting future trends using historical data. Interpolation is for forecasting an intermediate value and extrapolation is for forecasting a future value. These techniques are also referred to as time series analysis.

Sampling

Sampling is a technique for gathering information for a decision. The underlying assumption that a randomly drawn sample truly represents a homogenous population is the basis for using sampling plans. This technique of data

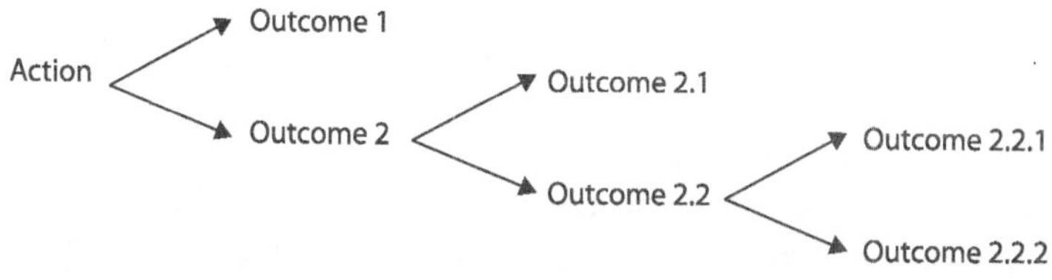

Figure B.1 A decision tree

gathering is used to test assumptions, theories, proposed decisions, and quality control. The key terms used in the context of sampling are:

1. *Universe* or *population* includes the whole range of data of all relevant candidates that can be included. A population is generally very large, so large that it is not practical to cover every member of it.
2. *Sample* is a small section of the population or universe drawn at random.
3. *Candidate* represents each data item in the population or universe that can be considered for inclusion in the sample.

The key aspects for sampling to be successful are (1) the population or universe is homogenous and (2) the sample is randomly drawn. On many occasions, we find that the population is not homogenous and the sample is not truly random. Therefore, we use many techniques for drawing samples. Some of these are:

1. *Random sampling* is used in a homogenous population. We draw sample candidates based on a lottery or using random numbers.
2. *Judgment sampling* is a technique in which the selection process is based on our judgment about the candidate's ability to truly represent the population.
3. *Convenient sampling* is a technique in which we select the candidates who are available to us without much exertion.
4. *Stratified sampling* is a more powerful manner of sampling and is used in populations that are not truly and fully homogenous. We divide the population into various strata and draw a random sample from each stratum.
5. *Cluster sampling* is a technique that is similar to stratified sampling in which we divide the population into representative clusters and then draw sample candidates from each of the clusters using the random sampling technique.

We use strategies such as a single-sampling plan or double-sampling plan in the context of sampling.

In a *single-sampling plan* we draw one sample from the population and use it to draw conclusions about the population. *Double-sampling plans* have two typical methods. In the first method we draw one sample, test it, and then draw another sample from the same population if the results of the first sample are somehow found to be unsatisfactory, and test it again. Based on the outcomes of the two samples, decisions are made. This is popular in lot testing. Lot testing is performed when there are large numbers of products to be tested; a sample is drawn and tested. A second sample is drawn if the first sample fails the criteria for lot acceptance. If the second sample confirms the findings of the first sample, then the lot is rejected. But if the first sample failed the lot and the second sample passed the lot, the organizational process is followed. The process can be to accept the lot or carry out 100% testing, or take another sample and take the majority outcome.

In the second method, we draw two samples from the same population and test them concurrently with two independent agencies and compare the results. One popular example that comes to mind is testing for cancer via biopsy. In this example two samples are sent to two laboratories and the findings are compared.

Statistical Analysis

Statistical analysis is a set of tools that allow managers to extract information (and perhaps knowledge) from the data. (Every manager should take a basic course in statistics if he/she is interested in making good decisions.) I would go so far as to say that every manager uses statistics, at least to the extent of using averages and trends. The following are the few statistical techniques that I think are the most valuable for decision makers. The descriptions provided below are not comprehensive and you should educate yourself in these techniques by studying more elaborate material on these topics:

1. *Measures of central tendency, dispersion, and skewness* are helpful in drawing inferences about the population. There are three measures of central tendency for data: mean, mode, and median. The arithmetic mean (normally called the average value) is used to summarize data for us. We use terms such as mean time between failures, average defect density, and average duration of a project (to name a few common metrics) for describing population attributes. The mean is a good measure when there are a large number of observations, but use of the mean may not be appropriate for small numbers of observations. In small samples of data the use of the statistical mode (modal value or most occurring value) is typically more suitable. The other measure of central tendency is median or the middle value. The measures of dispersion describe the variability of data. Most commonly used measures of dispersion are standard deviation (represented by the Greek letter σ—Sigma) and variance. Other measures of dispersion are quartile deviation, percentile deviation, etc. Skewness is a measure that tells whether the data are uniformly distributed or skewed in some

way. We have to check for this skewness, as we cannot make normal decisions from data that are skewed in any way.

2. *Correlation* or *covariance* is a method to determine if one set of outcomes is related to another set of inputs. A common question can be examined/confirmed by this measure: "Would increased inspection ensure higher quality? We compute the coefficient of covariation and, based on this computation, draw an inference about whether one is dependent on the other or not. But remember one important thing about correlation: correlation and causality can be two very different things!
3. *Probability distributions* include three popular distributions:
   - *Normal* probability distribution assists us in making inferences about normally occurring values. In many populations, for example, there is one central tendency with an equal number of observations occurring on either side of this central tendency, but with fewer observations occurring the further away they are from the central point.
   - *Binomial* probability distribution assists us in making inferences about values that are binary in nature, such as in tossing a coin: in a coin toss, only two possible values (outcomes) are possible (we will ignore the possibility of the coin standing edgewise!).
   - *Poisson* probability distribution assists us in making inferences about rare events, such as fires, floods, and earthquakes.

   There are other probability distributions such as Beta, Gamma, and T distributions that are used for specific purposes. Please refer to a statistics handbook for more information.
4. *Goodness of fit* testing uses a set of techniques to validate the results obtained from statistical testing. We compute the measure of goodness of fit from the interaction of expected values and the actual values (χ^2, chi-square; pronounced with "ch" as in "kay").
5. *Hypothesis testing* uses a set of techniques that assist in designing tests and using sampling of data to determine if our hypothesis is valid.

Consultants

More often than not, managers have to manage a knowledge area in which they do not have as much information as they would like. It is also a possibility that a manager does not have sufficient experience in the decision scenario he/she is being faced with to be able to define and assess the alternatives, the possible outcomes, and to properly define the problem in the first place. That is where consultants come in handy. A properly chosen consultant brings in his knowledge and training to assist in all areas from defining the problem, developing the decision scenario, enumerating the alternatives, generating possible outcomes, and enabling the selection of the optimal decision.

The Decision Postmortem

We should learn from the outcomes of all the decisions made. The decision outcomes could be:

1. *As expected*. In this outcome, we need to examine if we made a really good decision or if control of the decision's implementation ensured the expected result.
2. *Better than expected*. In this case we need to analyze what caused the improvement so we can use that aspect in all our future decisions.
3. *Worse than expected*. In this case we need to analyze what caused the decision to fail and how that failure could have been prevented so we can avoid these pitfalls in the future.

Should we conduct a formal postmortem with all concerned and then document it? We would suggest that if the decision was important enough to approach formally, then the answer is "yes." Documenting is always good because it is available for future reference, even if only for us.

When the decision involves others, documentation is optional. Having the documentation allows flexibility in the future as we may or may not involve others. In all cases a postmortem on important decisions is a good idea. Get the facts/data, analyze the decision, and decide what to do in the future.

Final Words

Everyone makes decisions. We therefore need to be aware of decision-making theory, techniques, and tools. Mastering as many tools and techniques as possible enriches a project manager's skill set.

Appendix C

People Management

Introduction

People management is the oldest form of management. The word *management* itself contains the word *man,* which represents human beings as being at the beginning of the word. Ever since humans have organized themselves to accomplish a task, they have required some form of management (some would say manipulation) to achieve a desired result. The endeavors of management can vary from waging wars to building edifices or growing food. Any endeavor requires that some form of organization be performed (even if it is done inefficiently). To accomplish any task with more than just a few people also requires some combination of exhorting (motivating), judging/measuring performance, rewarding, promoting, punishing, and possibly even demoting individuals or groups.

In project management, as in all other endeavors, people are managed to achieve the objective, while meeting the goals of being on time and being within the allocated budget, and at the same time maintaining and improving the morale of the team members. People management includes carrying out several activities:

1. Estimating the human resources requirement
2. Acquiring the required human resources for project execution
3. Allocating work to team members so that project execution is efficient and effective
4. Motivating team members to higher levels of achievement
5. Maintaining team morale at desirable organizational levels

6. Disciplining team members as necessary
7. Developing and mentoring people who are suitable for higher responsibilities
8. Releasing human resources when the project is completed

Let us look at each of these activities in greater detail.

Estimating the Required Human Resources

We arrive at the requirement of people from the effort estimate of the project in conjunction with its technical specifications. A project needs people of varying skill sets. Normally, the following skill sets would be needed depending on what activities are carried out in-house:

1. Hardware engineers to deploy the machines and test them
2. Networking engineers to run the cables and connect the machines
3. Electricians and electrical engineers to provide electrical outlets for supplying power to various infrastructure equipment
4. Construction engineers, skilled workers, and labor if undertaking facility construction
5. Facility designers if undertaking facility design work
6. Software development team including software engineers, project leaders, business analysts, database administrators, software architects, and a project manager (PM) if undertaking software development
7. Any other resource required for a specific project activity

We apportion the effort estimated for the project among these categories and round them off to the nearest day. Although it is ideal to allocate people for part of a day, it is often impractical to allocate a person for less than a day. Based on the effort required for each category, we will determine the people who are required full time and the people who can be allocated part time. Full-time people are required for those activities that take significant duration continuously. Part-time people are best applied to those activities that are required for only a short period of time or those that are needed intermittently over a long period of time, but each requirement is for a short duration.

The PM will also need to develop the project execution schedule in such a way that the period for which each of the skill sets required is both understood and effectively communicated.

We can request the human resources from the organizational HR department. Our request should include the number of people, the dates for which they are required, and the skill sets needed. The elements of a sample resource request form are presented in Figure C.1.

Request No.	Resource requested	Resource type	Qty	Required by date	Probable release date by phase

Figure C.1 Elements of a sample resource request form template (template exhibited in Appendix I)

Acquiring the Required Human Resources to Execute the Project

People required for the project need to be acquired either from within the organization or from external sources. Sources internal to the organization are:

1. People on the bench, that is, those who are not currently allocated to any project (They could be de-allocated from a completed project and awaiting allocation to another project or new recruits waiting to be allocated to their first project.)
2. People working on other projects who are likely to be released by the required date
3. People in the recruitment pipeline who are likely to join and be available by the required date

Sources external to the organization can include:

1. Consultants from consultancy organizations taken as temporary hires
2. Freelance consultants taken as temporary hires
3. New recruitment for the regular rolls of the company

It is the responsibility of the project management office (PMO), if there is one, or the human resources department to acquire the required number of people with the desired skill sets for the project and arrange allocation. Based on the resource request, the PMO or the entity vested with the responsibility of making people available to projects would perform the allocation.

One issue that plagues many PMs is the difference in skill levels of people in the organization. The skill level in any organization varies from poor to superior. The other levels are fair, good, and very good (Chapter 7 provides more details on this). When effort is estimated we assume average (good) skills. When the actual allocation takes place, we may get a mix of skill levels ranging from poor to super. The total number of allocated persons would equal the number of requested people when skill levels have been factored into the equation. For example, if we requested five people with average skills, the actual allocation may be one person with very good skill, two with good skills, and four with poor skills. Although the total number of people allocated is seven, when we normalize the allocated number based on the individual skill levels, the allocation would be five as requested. The PMO needs to ensure that the allocation matches the normalized request for personnel and to convince the PM that a fair allocation of people has been made to the project.

Allocating Work to Team Members

When human resources are acquired and allocated to the project, work is allocated to them and project execution begins. The following activities are carried out as part of work allocation:

1. Work is organized into work packages that can be executed by one person or a small team of two to three persons working together. Each work package will include its scope and instructions for carrying out the task. Work packages typically include execution as well as quality control work.
2. Effort to complete the work based on the skill of the persons putting in average (good) levels of effort is estimated.
3. Work is allocated to those responsible for completion. Allocation includes:
    a. Entering the work allocation in a work register
    b. Providing the scope of work and instructions to people performing the tasks
    c. Providing targets for schedule, effort, and quality
    d. Negotiating the targets with the assignees and finalizing
4. Monitor progress and ensure completion.

Motivating Team Members

The subject of motivating people to put forth superior effort has received significant attention in both industry and academia. When people come to work, they typically have two primary objectives:

1. Earn a livelihood
2. Perform the assigned work

Then there are a host of secondary objectives such as the possibility of advancement and earning more money, job satisfaction, respect in society, and others. Regardless of the secondary objectives the first objective is to earn a livelihood!

There are, of course, exceptions that prove the rule. Take the example of people whose livelihood is already taken care of by their forefathers or spouses; still they come to work. In these cases the primary objectives might include:

1. Personal respect that comes with working
2. Acquiring knowledge, for instance, to learn about the business in order to start a similar one
3. Social interaction to pass the time productively

Thus, the work is generally a means to an end rather than a goal unto itself. In addition to the objectives for working, people can be classified in several simple ways:

- By their *purpose*:
  - Straightforward (open)
  - Scheming (closed)
  - Normally straightforward (unless in a situation that affects them personally)
- By their *pleasantness*:
  - Pleasant
  - Disagreeable
  - Neutral (no pronounced inclination to either characteristic)
- By their *expectations*:
  - Easy to please
  - Difficult to please
  - Usually easy to please, but can be difficult
- By their level of *desire*:
  - Ambitious
  - No ambition
  - Somewhat ambitious
- By their level of *acceptance* (of you):
  - Willing
  - Reluctant
  - Usually willing (except when you have bad news)
- By their level of *responsibility*:
  - Responsible by nature
  - Irresponsible by nature
  - Mostly responsible
- By their *age*:
  - In the prime of life
  - Well past the prime of life
  - Slightly past the prime of life

Classifying people by age, the last category, is illegal, especially for recruitment or advancement, in North America and in Europe at a minimum. Nevertheless, individuals in any organization naturally fall into certain age categories. In all of these classification schemes, however, notice that types one and two are the extremes. Type three is typically found in most organizations, but an individual can be any combination of these classifications:

- Straightforward, pleasant, easy to please, ambitious, willing, responsible, and in the prime of age (obviously a best-case scenario!)
- Scheming, unpleasant, difficult to please, no ambition, reluctant, irresponsible, and well past prime

The list can (and does) go on with a multitude of combinations and permutations. Given this level of complexity, how do we motivate people to perform their tasks to the best of their ability?

History is replete with examples of ordinary people performing extraordinary feats when motivated by necessity, fear, or some reward. Motivation schemes include:

Carrot and stick. One of the most common and effective techniques is *the carrot and the stick*. (Why? It works with many types of people!) The carrot and stick technique rewards excellent performance and punishes poor performance. This reward/punishment process can go a long way in maintaining performance in ordinary situations. A cardinal rule for this technique, however, is that the technique must be exercised fairly, without fear, and without favoritism. Any perception of bias or hesitation when exercising this technique renders it ineffective (including taking umbrage during extraordinary situations and avoiding application of policy). (*Note*: A limitation to the carrot and stick technique is that PMs are rarely in a position to reward or punish on their own or with the desired immediacy, which might mean using this technique in modern, progressive organizations is not all that feasible.)

Stimulus-response. The second most effective technique is the *stimulus-response theory*. This technique is based on the assumption that people will respond visibly and positively to a positive stimulus. The alternative is also true: people respond negatively to a negative stimulus—albeit not always in an explicit manner (which can be misleading). In most cases, for example, a negative response comes sooner rather than later, but maybe not when we are ready for it or at a time that we would prefer. So, take care to ensure that a negative stimulus, when given, is administered in such a way that a positive response is generated—doing so is very important. (Remember the words of Mario Puzo in his novel *The Godfather*: "It is not easy to say 'no' and one needs training in administering negative stimuli.")

Expectancy. Another theory we need to learn about is the motivational theory proposed by Victor Vroom (Yale School of Management) in 1964. According to *Vroom's Expectancy Theory*, people have expectations when they come to an organization and put in the effort required to complete their assignments. In addition to earning a salary, these expectations can include fair treatment, career advancement, recognition, rewards, and punishment (e.g., for lack of performance, violations, errors, etc.). In Vroom's Expectancy Theory, when positive performance results in a realization of positive expectations and negative performance results in a realization of negative expectations, an individual will be motivated to better performance. (*Note*: A point of interest is that most individuals watch how the expectations of others are being met. If they perceive that certain individuals are getting more positive or fewer negative rewards, they are likely to become demotivated.)

Laissez-faire. The *laissez-faire* philosophy is a "hands-off" style in which a manager provides little direction concerning the assignment and completion of tasks and gives team members as much freedom as possible. The team members have the power to make decisions and solve problems on their own. Having this added responsibility can be a source of motivation to the team. The manager does not, however, ignore the team. The manager is available to answer questions and provide/supply information as required. But even in laissez-faire management, a manager must still be fair, and also be perceived as being fair, in all of his/her actions by all concerned parties. (If a manager is unfair, yet seen as being fair, or vice versa, any motivational actions taken tend to result in failure.) The laissez-faire philosophy is sine qua non (absolutely indispensable) in people management and motivation situations.

Behavioral correction. An important aspect of motivation is delivering *behavioral correction* to people who are not performing in a way that is commensurate with the exigencies of the work, the abilities of the person, and the compensation being given to the person. Behavioral correction is best achieved through coaching and counseling. Coaching provides expert guidance to a person on how to achieve better performance. The "how to" is provided by training (either classroom or on-the-job) and expert assistance by a senior person that is followed by periodic progress assessments. Counseling is resorted to when the skills are present, but an "attitude correction" is necessary. The first form of counseling is typically friendly—counseling in which the correction needed is pointed out in nonconfrontational manner. Nonconfrontational counseling may be used when an individual is unintentionally exhibiting an undesirable behavior—the individual does not realize the consequences of his/her behavior and is therefore receptive to counseling. Even after friendly counseling, sometimes an individual's undesirable behavior continues. When an individual knows that he/she is exhibiting an undesirable behavior, confrontational counseling is used. Confrontational counseling involves presenting the individual with the expected behavioral correction as well as irrefutable evidence of the undesirable behavior and the consequential damages. Confrontational counseling also includes outlining the consequences to the person if the required behavioral correction does not materialize. (Outlining the consequences of not making the desired behavioral correction requires management's approval.) We recommend training in the art of confrontational counseling for all PMs so that they will be equipped with the skills necessary to better deal with difficult situations. Training can be through formal training or by self-study.

Maintaining Team Morale

Team morale is extremely important if the project is to be executed successfully. Remember the "Charge of the Light Brigade"? Even underdogs can be exhorted to incredible actions if their morale is very high. It is often seen in sports that the team with higher morale wins over the team with lower morale even if their skills are similar. Even if every team member is positive, team morale can still be low. Some reasons for low team morale include:

1. A perception that the project is not important to higher management or that it is not important within the organization
2. A perception that the technology used in the project is obsolete
3. A perception that the human resources are being treated unfairly by the project's management
4. A perception that team meetings and reviews do not receive adequate importance
5. A view that the targets are either too lax or too tight
6. The presence of rumormongers and gossips on the team

Many other reasons lead to lower morale. But what is important is that a PM should continuously monitor team morale and strive to maintain it at a desirable level.

Disciplining When Necessary

Although all precautions and actions are taken to motivate team members and to maintain team morale at higher levels, sometimes disciplining an errant subordinate becomes necessary. Disciplining a team member is usually necessary, however, only if the team member is found to be willfully indulging in some act(s) that is detrimental to the health of the project and to the morale of the project team. For example, an unintentional delay in an assigned task or a task taking more effort than has been estimated might necessitate counseling and coaching, but not disciplining. A subordinate might also act out as a result of some unresolved grievance. So, before subjecting a subordinate to disciplinary action, ensure that:

- All grievances have been resolved.
- Some reasonable expectations of the individual have not been met by the organization.
- The infraction is not the result of an innocent action(s).
- The offending act is indeed willful.
- Other persons are not engaged in a conspiracy against the employee.

When these criteria have been addressed, disciplinary action(s) can be taken with the assurance that a mistake is not being made. Remember a cardinal rule: the punishment should be commensurate with the infraction. Terminating the services of an individual is akin to capital punishment. Additionally, recruiting a new employee and training this person costs much more than correcting and retaining an existing employee. The result of a disciplinary action therefore should be targeted at correcting the behavior (if possible) rather than being punitive. If discipline is inevitable, we recommend that a manager should carry out the disciplinary procedure/policy of the organization, diligently giving the errant individual every opportunity to redeem himself/herself.

We should also note that infractions typically do not just "crop up overnight." Most behavioral issues tend to be the culmination of a number of incidents that have occurred over a period of time. We typically find that the need to discipline is a failure of management: it could have been prevented through the proper use of motivation and behavioral correction.

Developing and Mentoring Suitable Persons for Greater Responsibilities

PMs are uniquely positioned in the organization for spotting talent for leadership in software engineers. Once leadership potential is discovered, the PM is usually the first person in the organization who can develop the potential into reality. By getting the person to exercise a latent leadership talent, the PM creates an opportunity to develop the employee. Mentoring involves making the employee part of decision making, providing leadership opportunities beginning in a small team environment, continuously coaching the person, and then increasing independence gradually over a period of time. We also suggest exposing the new leader to senior levels of management so that he/she can be evaluated, as well as to continue the person's development by enhancing the opportunity for the new leader to be allocated to other projects in order to work with other PMs within the organization.

Release People Upon Completion of the Project

As discussed before, projects follow a cycle described roughly below:

1. Projects start with a minimum set of people to carry out project initiation activities.
2. More people are added to carry out initial preparation activities.
3. Even more people are added to carry out project execution.
4. As execution progresses it may be necessary to ramp up inspectors/testers to carry out quality control activities.
5. As the project execution nears completion, it is generally necessary to release some of the people because they may be needed in smaller numbers toward the end of project completion.
6. Once quality control is completed fewer inspectors/testers are required.
7. After project completion, most of the project team may need to be released except those assigned to warranty service activities.
8. At the close of the project everyone is typically released.

IT projects are not static. They generally require that human resources be continuously ramped up and down to be both effective and efficient. *Ramping up* involves conducting induction training for new team members. *Ramping down* involves conducting a performance appraisal for employees so they can understand their project performance. Releasing persons from the project involves a set of activities such as the following:

1. Carry out the performance appraisal for the employee and after agreement with the employee submit the performance appraisal to the HR department.
2. Update the skill database of the organization with the new skills acquired by the employee during the period of project execution.
3. Take over all project-related artifacts including documents, tools, and any other artifacts that may be with the person.
4. Archive the project-related communication that may need preservation as part of project records for future reference and possible use. (Note: this is a legal requirement in some countries.)

5. Prepare the project release communication (a formal letter or an e-mail) and hand over the person to the PMO (or whoever is in charge of reallocating the employee to another project).
6. Document best and worst practices or any events deserving special mention and forward to concerned management personnel.
7. Update the project information to reflect the release of the employee.

This completes the release of the employee (contractors would be similar).

Best Practices in People Management

The following suggestions will help manage the human resources of the project effectively:

1. Communicate continuously and coherently with all team members. In the absence of official communication, team members will listen to the organization's grapevine, which can distort facts so that they become detrimental to the project's (and organization's) well being.
2. Monitor morale continuously. Strive to keep morale at a sensibly high level. *Remember*: A team with high morale can scale unimaginable heights.
3. Motivate continuously. Learn about the team members and try your best to motivate them. To some extent, motivation is unique to an individual. It pays to show team members individual attention.
4. Discipline only when you are absolutely sure you are taking the correct action. Make every effort to not only be fair, but to also appear to be fair to the entire team. *Remember*: Unless you administer discipline very skillfully, your actions can end up demotivating the entire team.

Handling Difficult People

As a PM, you will need to deal with various individuals, ranging from your own team members to peers, superiors, and customers. Typically, all of these individuals are well educated and highly intelligent. Most of them are good individuals and will perform well what is expected of them, but a few will be "difficult." Will these few difficult individuals really matter? Consider what George Bernard Shaw once said: "The reasonable man adapts himself to the world; the unreasonable one persists in trying to adapt the world to himself. Therefore, all progress depends on the unreasonable man." Also noteworthy to consider is the effect of the "insignificant majority and significant minority." Identifying the significant minority and insignificant majority is commonly used in ABC analysis (Always Better Control), VED analysis (Vital,

Essential, and Desirable), etc. (Although ABC analysis and VED analysis are beyond the scope of this section, we refer to them to forewarn you of the significant minority so that you can more effectively manage people.)

Our discussion of difficult people reminds us of an amusing anecdote: a psychiatry professor was giving a lecture to her students about the behavior of the abnormal man. This was the fifth time in a row. When the professor began a continuation of the lecture the sixth time, a student raised his hand and asked her: "Professor, when are you going to start telling us about the behavior of the normal man?" She replied, "When we find him, we cure him."

So, are any people easy to handle? The answer: "Yes, but often only for a period of time." People who are easily managed for a short time include:

- *Trainees*: until their training has been completed and they are on the permanent rolls of the company
- *New employees*: until they have successfully completed their probation period
- *Employees*: until they have received an expected promotion (and still wish to receive it)
- *Employees*: who are low on performance, but high on pleasing the boss (and thus survive)
- *Eager beavers*: who always want to please their bosses (just for the sake of pleasing)

Wise individuals, however, understand their role as well as yours as a manager and perform their duties diligently, irrespective of your provocation (e.g., at times when the message from upper management is not good or the tasks are challenging, etc.), and are always easy to handle. The percentage of these people in an organization is usually miniscule. The remaining percentage is to some degree difficult to handle.

Classifications of Difficult People

We can classify difficult people into the following categories:

1. Two-timer
2. Backstabber
3. First chapter expert
4. The martyr
5. Prima donna
6. The manipulator
7. The gossip
8. Breather-down-the-neck

9. Buck-stopper
10. No man
11. Mr. Justice
12. The carrier pigeon

So, where do you find these people? You find them everywhere. They are among your subordinates, your peers, and your superiors.

Two-Timer

Here is a person whose stand depends on the situation and people involved. He puts on a "public smile and a private snarl." What he says in public differs from what he says in private. This person is completely undependable. We can spot him the first time we are two-timed. Do not treat the first time as coincidence. No one two-times unintentionally. These people could be found in your subordinates and peers as well as in superiors. How do we handle this person? When he makes a private commitment to you, do not depend on it unless you get it in some form of writing such as e-mail, and if he chats on a messenger save the conversation. Try to have witnesses when dealing with him. Maintain minutes of the meeting whenever you meet with him.

Backstabber

Backstabbers betray confidence, especially if it can get them some positive points with the upper echelon. They are not your enemies but your friends. It is very difficult to spot these people or prove that they backstabbed you. We can spot these persons only through secondary sources. When a boss-type person is exhibiting animosity toward you for no apparent reason, realize that somebody backstabbed you. And that somebody is suddenly friendly with this boss-type person. These people could be found in your peers and subordinates and rarely in superiors. Backstabbers obtain the information that assists them to backstab you, from you, using charm, encouragement, and sympathy to egg you on to criticize senior persons. *Remember*: "Loose lips sink ships." In your workplace, never offer criticism in the presence of others of a senior person who is especially powerful. Backstabbers can backstab only when your back is turned toward them. Never show your back to anyone, including your most charming friend.

First Chapter Expert

This person knows something about every scenario, technology, and person in the organization. She never allows anyone to go into detail about something because her knowledge is limited. Her knowledge is limited to the introductory chapter of some book on the subject at hand. So she ends up using her limited knowledge to shoot down any positive proposal by "picking holes" in it—holes which are plugged in subsequent chapters in the book. Arguing with a person with half-baked knowledge on a subject is extremely difficult. First chapter experts are also easy to spot. You see her discussing new topics everywhere, but she disappears as soon as someone else goes into detail about the topic. First chapter experts are mostly found among your peers. You can deal with a first chapter expert by giving the details first and then by giving her some credit, saying something like: "As Jane can probably explain to you because she knows…." This usually shuts her up.

The Martyr

People who are overlooked for promotions often become martyrs, particularly the people who have a long tenure in the organization, who lack the academic credentials to allow them to reach the top echelons, or who are not on the career progression fast track. These people often exhibit the attributes of a martyr. Martyrs have a negative spin on everything, especially in private. They usually do not express a negative spin in public for fear that they will be fired from the organization. Martyrs are easy to spot. When something goes wrong, a martyr comes to you and says, "I told you (thought) so." If there is a new initiative, he will tell you privately that it is going to fail. Although a martyr is harmless, he can discourage you from coming up with new initiatives or taking up a challenging opportunity. Martyrs are found among your peers and superiors. You handle a martyr by indulging him, but never taking his discouraging words seriously. He is actually a great source for pointing out the other side of your proposals. So use him as your personal quality assurance person for proposals and initiatives.

Prima Donna

Prima donnas are sticklers for rules, regulations, conventions, practices, and so on. Often a prima donna is a petty-minded person. Prima donnas are found in the security department, as secretaries to bosses, as auditors, as parking lot attendants, etc. For example, have you ever had an experience with a parking attendant who waits until you have parked your vehicle, locked it, and are ready to go before he slowly ambles over to tell you that you have parked wrongly or are in the wrong place and that you have to park where he says. You think (and maybe say): "Why didn't you just tell me before I parked"? This parking lot attendant is a prima donna. Perhaps you are visiting a client and his secretary tells you to wait. But you soon see that she is polishing her nails and not making any attempt to communicate your arrival to her boss. You then remind her gently, only to be reprimanded. She is a prima donna. These people have limited power, and just to annoy you, they use it to its full extent. So how is a prima donna handled? Give the parking lot attendant a friendly greeting when you enter the parking lot. Put on your charm and best manners with the secretary. The trick is to give them the impression that you respect their position and power, and you can get along well with them.

The Manipulator

Manipulators act as if they are very busy either to avoid work or to pass it on to you. Manipulators always look haggard and as if they are under pressure. Often they are slow workers or do something else during working hours. A manipulator eventually comes to a peer saying something similar to: "I'm really busy right now. Can you help me by doing this?" Sometimes a manipulator goes so far as to tell her boss: "Even though it's my job, Mark is the best person because of his experience and special skills (real or imagined) and he seems to be free of any work right now." Manipulators are mostly found among your peers. To handle a manipulator, put on that same haggard look yourself when you notice the "always busy-as-a-bee" person and approach her to see if she is free to help you out. But wait—are we telling you to become a manipulator yourself? You bet we are! No medicine is better suited for a manipulator than to give her a dose of her own medicine.

The Gossip

The problem with gossips is that they hear the words of someone thinking out loud or they hear part of a conversation and then put two and two together to make eight and pass the result off as fact. If they cannot find anything worth circulating, they often invent some piece of juicy information. The impact of a gossip is best illustrated by a quote attributed to Mark Twain: "A lie travels half-way around the world before truth gets its boots on." Gossips sow distrust, prejudice, and suspicion among other people. They also waste a lot of time—your's, their's, and everyone else's. For some reason, a gossip seems to have a lot of spare time. He is also a very good conversationalist and can narrate with great skill to hold your interest—so well that listening to him can even become somewhat addictive and make you want to ask for more information. Gossips are found among your subordinates and peers. The best way to handle a gossip is to avoid him or avoid being drawn into a gossip session with anyone. Remember that if a gossip is giving false information to you about someone else, then he surely will do the same about you with others when you are not present.

Breather-Down-the-Neck

The breather-down-the-neck is an uneasy delegator. She is usually in a supervisory position (a boss). Perhaps due to some past bad experience with her subordinates, she is not comfortable delegating work. She is also insecure about her position. When a person who normally works alone is promoted to the position of a boss, that person also often becomes a breather-down-the-neck until he/she attains maturity. Even a boss with a few subordinates will resort to breathing down the necks of their subordinates because they have little else to do (or nothing else better to do). If a boss is a breather-down-the-neck, understand that she may just be maturing into the skills needed to be a boss and give her some space. Something that gets a breather-down-the-neck off your back is to meet a deadline the first time and a few more times so that she becomes more confident with your commitments. Then she will not be so overbearing. The trick is to give her a sense of confidence about your commitments.

Buck-Stopper

Anything that goes to a buck-stopper stays there. It never comes out. If you want the buck to be moved, you have to chase down the buck-stopper. A buck-stopper never says "no," but neither does he give a commitment or an actual response. His desk is a bottomless pit. You can put something on it, but getting it back will be very difficult. A buck-stopper generally dodges all of your queries about the status of a task or for a commitment to a date for completion of any action expected from her. You find buck-stoppers among your peers and handling grievances or complaints in service departments. A buck-stopper's thinking is that "if it's really urgent, someone will come and ask about it in person." To get something done by a buck-stopper, you need to push him. Pay a visit to him to get what you need.

No Man

A "no" man is able to say "no" to everything you say. A no man uses excellent logic to deny your proposal or a request. Even if you were to say, "The sun rises in the east," a no man would say, "No—the sun does not rise in the east." If you press on with an argument, he will say that the east itself is ill-defined, that the physical north pole and the magnetic north pole are not the same, that the Earth itself is slanted, etc. A no man is easy to spot. The most frequent word spoken by him is either "no" or "not." No men are found among your peers, particularly in service departments. Although negative, no men are eager to make proposals. So, to get a no man to say "yes" (or something similar), ask him to make proposals on your behalf. Instead of telling him what needs to be done, consult him and make suggestions, but let him think that your proposal is in fact his proposal.

Mr. Justice

Mr. Justice has grown up hearing the stories of class struggle. Mr. Justice therefore divides the world (and the organization) into the "haves" (those who have power or the management) and the "have nots" (staff, workers, professional workers, etc.). Mr. Justice sees injustice in every action taken by management. He denigrates the benefits, but always accentuates the side effects. More often than not, Mr. Justice (or Ms.) is active, directly or indirectly, in a trade union and some other similar type of association. Mr. Justice also opposes the recognition of meritorious persons. He instead advocates seniority for receiving awards and rewards. Consequently, Mr. Justice types are low performers. They hover around the penalty-avoidance level of performance. Mr. Justice is mostly found among your subordinates. Rarely is he found in your peers. Confrontational counseling, using quantitative data, is the best way to bring Mr. Justice in line—and it will be a continuous and periodic chore. If you miss a single confrontational counseling session, Mr. Justice will revert to using trade union jargon.

The Carrier Pigeon

The bearer of good news is always well received and rewarded. You have seen this scenario in movies when the heroine hugs or kisses the postman who brings a letter from her distant lover or from someone informing her of good news. Some people in an organization take on this role of the postman. When some achievement is made or something great is done, the carrier pigeon immediately visits the boss to inform him—before the person actually making the achievement has a chance to talk to the boss. A carrier pigeon always keep her antennae up, scanning the horizon for newsworthy items to report to the boss. This behavior is harmless, but the excitement for you, the achiever, is gone—you have been beaten to the punch! Your success is already "old hat" to the boss. Carrier pigeons are easily spotted by observation. They constantly poke their noses into other people's affairs. If something important is going on in the organization, a carrier pigeon always manages to be in close quarters irrespective of whether she is involved. She is usually at places where she is not needed. Carrier pigeons are mostly found among your peers. Obviously, carrier pigeons have the ear of the boss. So, be careful about what you say to a carrier pigeon. She not only carries good news, but she also carries tales. If you criticize the boss in a carrier pigeon's presence, know for certain that your message will be carried. Discretion is therefore your best safeguard. If you are on the verge of some success, keep it to yourself. Remain calm and wait to show your excitement in the presence of your boss.

Final Words on Handling Difficult People

Humans are basically difficult to handle because humans are unpredictable. Most of the time, another person's response is not commensurate with your stimulus. A person's personality attributes can also change over time. So not necessarily is "once a thief always a thief" always correct, but "forewarned is forearmed" is certainly better than being ignorant. As a PM, you need to know how to motivate people toward success and you need to practice motivating them diligently, but being prepared to handle difficult people is also necessary. The purpose of Appendix C is to "forewarn and forearm" you.

Appendix D

Introduction to PERT/CPM

Project managers have been relying on PERT/CPM techniques to plan, schedule, and control projects for the last 60 years. PERT stands for program evaluation and review technique while CPM stands for critical path method. PERT has its origins in research projects having been used successfully in the development of Polaris ballistic missiles launched from beneath the ocean's surface. Owing to the success of the Polaris project, PERT gained popularity and was adopted in project-based manufacturing organizations. CPM had its origins in the construction industry. Both techniques became prominent after World War II, and over a period of time were used together. Today, they are referred to as PERT/CPM.

A Network Diagram

The backbone of both techniques is a network diagram. A network diagram is a graphical representation of the relationships between activities performed in order to execute and complete a project. Originally a network diagram was composed of *events* (also referred to as *milestones*). An event denotes reaching a milestone or completion of an activity. These events are connected by arrows representing *activities*. An event (or milestone) represents a significant point in the project such as completion of a set of activities. By definition, an event is the culmination of one or more activities and it does not consume resources. It is represented by a circle in classical network diagrams.

An activity is the smallest unit of productive effort to be planned, scheduled, and controlled. It consumes resources, namely, human effort, time, money, material, equipment, and information. It is represented by an arrow in classic network diagrams and by a circle or other shapes in modern network diagrams. In such diagrams, arrows are used to represent precedence relationships. Activities are also referred to as "tasks."

The entire network is embedded between two events, namely, the "Start" and the "End" events. A Start event signifies project commencement and an End event signifies project completion. Figure D.1 shows a traditional network diagram.

In this figure the circles represent the events, which are also referred to as "nodes" in common parlance. These nodes are numbered but can also be named. Activities are represented as arrows and are referred by the predecessor and successor events. In this example the activities are 1-2, 1-3, 2-4, 3-5, 4-6, 5-6, and 6-7.

With the passage of time, the orientation of network diagrams changed from an event orientation to an activity orientation. The activity orientation shifted how activities are now represented (circle in the modern network diagram). The arrows represent the relationship between activities. These network diagrams are referred to as activity on node (AON) network diagrams or precedence network diagrams. Today, precedence network diagrams are used predominantly. Figure D.2 depicts an AON network diagram.

Construction of a Network Diagram

The first step in constructing a network diagram is to develop the work breakdown structure (WBS) for the project. A WBS is a functional breakdown (decomposition) of the project into successive levels of activities that need

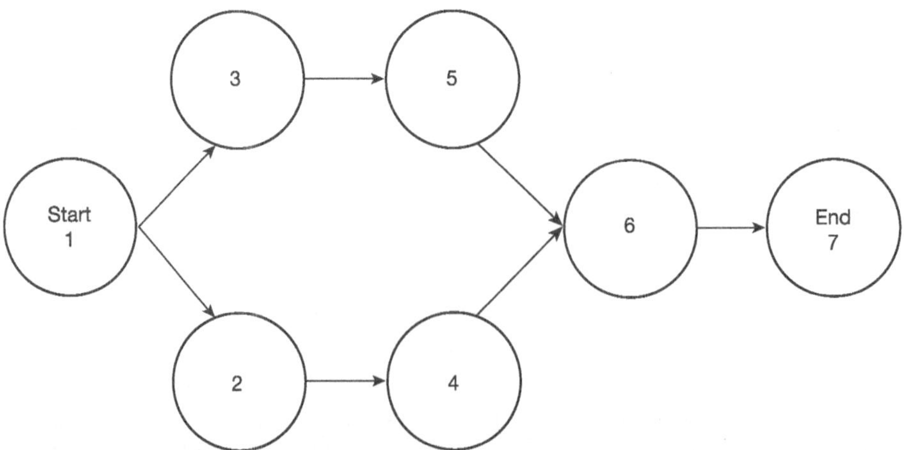

Figure D.1 Traditional network diagram

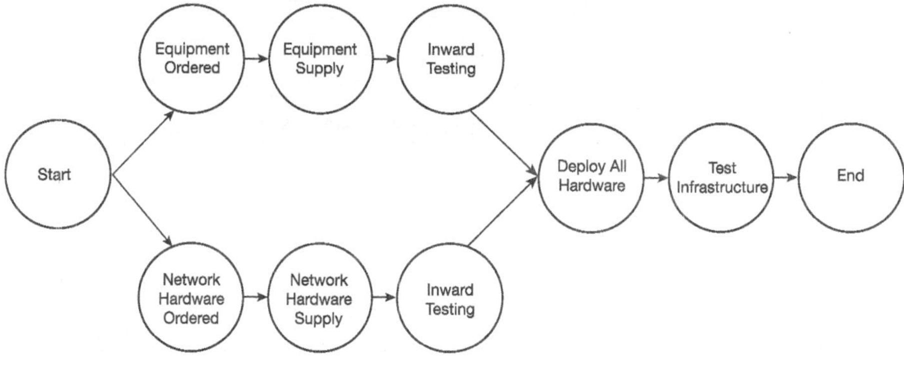

Figure D.2 AON network diagram

to be performed in order to complete the project. We will use a start-end or end-start approach to construct a network diagram. In a start-end approach, the steps are:

1. Enumerate all activities to be performed to begin the project.
2. Enumerate all activities to be performed upon completion of the initial activities.
3. Enumerate the next level of activities to be performed.
4. Iterate Step 3 until all activities have been defined.
5. When all activities are listed the WBS is ready.

This approach can be visualized as an upright triangle as shown in Figure D.3.

The end-start approach to building a WBS is the exact opposite of the start-end approach. The steps are:

1. Enumerate the last and final activities to be performed before completing the project.
2. Enumerate the activities to be performed in order to begin the final set of activities.
3. Enumerate the activities to be performed to begin the previous set of activities.
4. Iterate Step 3 as long as we can foresee the previous set of activities to be performed until the stage is reached where no previous set of activities exist.
5. Now the WBS is ready.

This approach can be visualized as an inverted triangle as shown in Figure D.4.

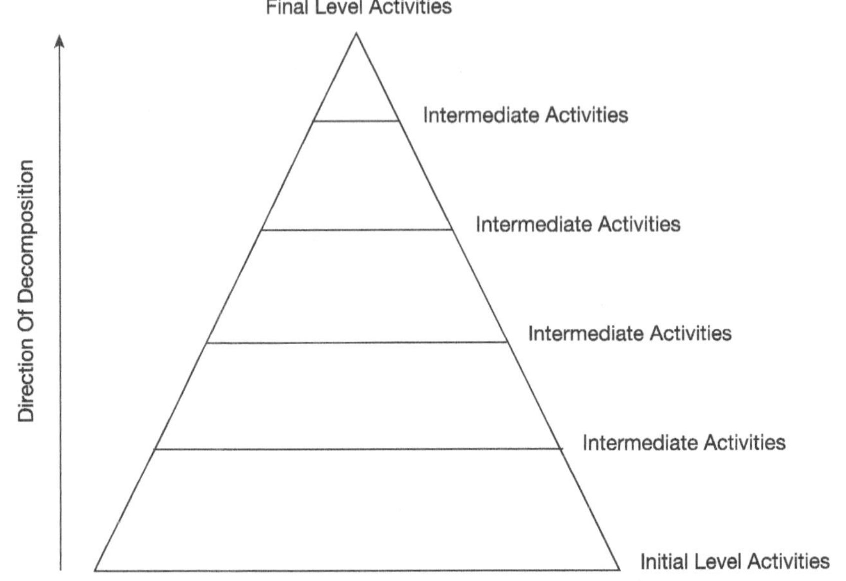

Figure D.3 Start-end approach to WBS

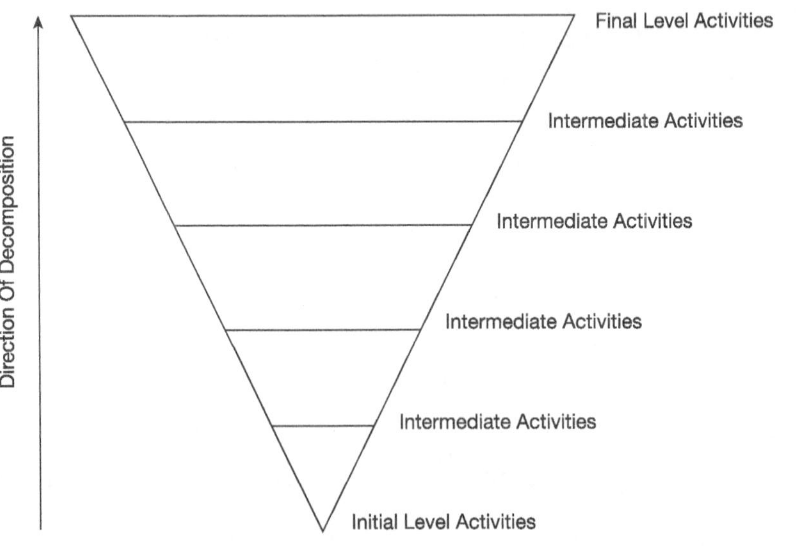

Figure D.4 End-start approach to WBS

Once all activities are identified, establish the precedence relationships between the activities in the WBS. *Remember*: it is possible to perform some activities parallel (concurrently) to each other. Some have to be performed in sequence (one after the other) with each other. In the diagram shown in Figure D.2, activities of equipment and networking can be performed concurrently but the activities "Deploy All Hardware" and "Test Infrastructure" need to be performed in sequence. In other words, testing can begin only after completing the deployment activity. To illustrate, let us build the WBS that would have generated the network diagram shown in Figure D.2. It is shown in Table D.1.

Using this WBS (above), we can draw the network diagram shown in Figure D.2. The following guidelines help in drawing the network diagram:

1. Draw the "Start" node at the leftmost place.
2. Add nodes to the right of the first node until the diagram is complete.
3. Number the nodes for easy identification/reference purposes. Thus, we increment the number from left to right and top to bottom.
4. Do not cross the arrows unless it is unavoidable. Figure D.5 shows an example of the crossing of arrows to be avoided.

Table D.1 WBS example

Activity ID	Activity description	Predecessors	Successors
1	Start	None	1. Equipment ordered 2. Network hardware ordered
2	Equipment ordered	Start	Equipment supply
3	Equipment supply	Equipment ordered	Inward testing of equipment
4	Inward testing of equipment	Equipment supply	Deploy all hardware
5	Network hardware ordered	Start	Network hardware supply
6	Network hardware supply	Network hardware ordered	Inward testing of network hardware
7	Inward testing of network hardware	Network hardware supply	Deploy all hardware
8	Deploy all hardware	1. Inward testing of equipment 2. Inward testing of network hardware	Test infrastructure
9	Test infrastructure	Deploy all hardware	End
10	End	Test infrastructure	None

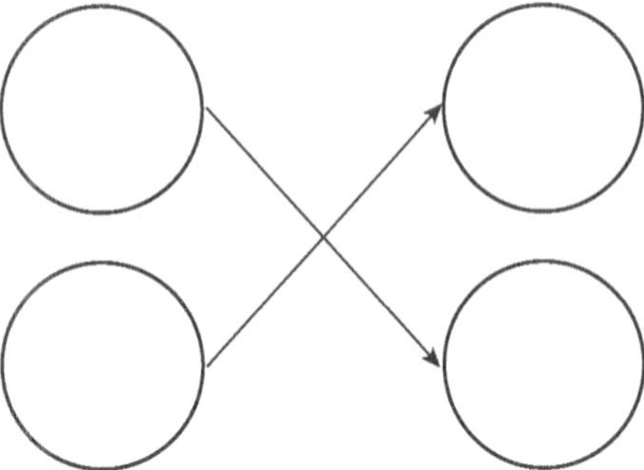

Figure D.5 Avoid crossing arrows in network diagrams

5. Avoid loops in the network diagram. Figure D.6 shows an example loop that must be avoided.
6. Distinguish each level of concurrent activities and draw the network diagram in tiers.
7. Allow no dangling activities. (Allowing no dangling activities means that every activity, with the exception of the Start and the End, should have a minimum of one predecessor and a minimum of one successor.)

The next step in the PERT process is the estimation of the duration for each activity. PERT recognizes uncertainty inherent in estimation and suggests estimating three values of duration for each activity:

1. *Optimistic time* (t_o) is the best-case-scenario duration. An expert performs the activity and all resources are available on time and no unforeseen incidents cause delays, and so on. It is the shortest duration in which the activity can be completed.

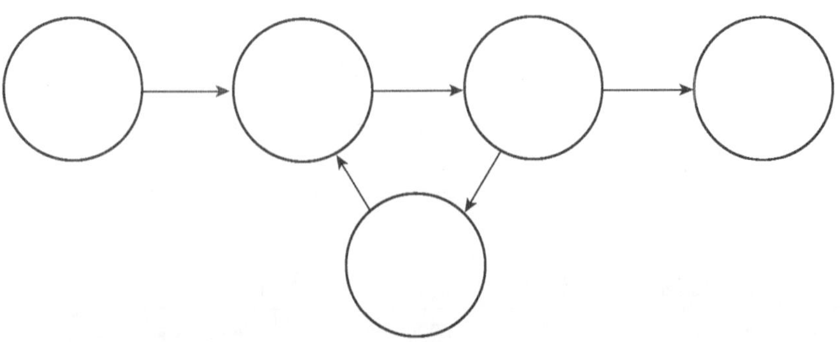

Figure D.6 Avoid loops in network diagrams

2. *Pessimistic time* (t_p) is the worst-case-scenario duration. A novice performs the activity, all possible delays occur, and resource availability is delayed. It is the longest duration needed to complete the activity.
3. *Most likely time* (t_m) is the normal-case-scenario duration. An average skilled person performs the operation, some delays occur, and most resources are available on time. It is the duration normally taken to complete the activity.

From the three values above, we compute the expected time (t_e) using the formula:

$$t_e = (t_o + 4t_m + t_p)/6$$

Table D.2 shows an example computation of expected times for the activities of the network diagram shown in Figure D.2.

Now let us calculate the duration required for project completion. We compute this value using the t_e, the expected times of each activity. We do this on the network diagram shown in Figure D.2. We place the values of start and finish near the node, which is shown in Figure D.7. In Figure D.7, ES stands for Earliest Start, which signifies the day on which the activity can begin as counted from the first day on which the project started. EF stands for Earliest Finish signifying the day on which the activity can be finished earliest as calculated from the day on which the project started.

Table D.2 Estimated durations

Activity ID	Activity description	Optimistic time	Pessimistic time	Most likely time	Expected time
1	Start	0	0	0	0
2	Equipment ordered	4	8	6	6
3	Equipment supply	5	11	8	8
4	Inward testing of equipment	10	16	13	13
5	Network hardware ordered	3	7	5	5
6	Network hardware supply	4	10	7	7
7	Inward testing of network hardware	10	18	14	14
8	Deploy all hardware	5	9	7	7
9	Test infrastructure	3	5	4	4
10	End	0	0	0	0

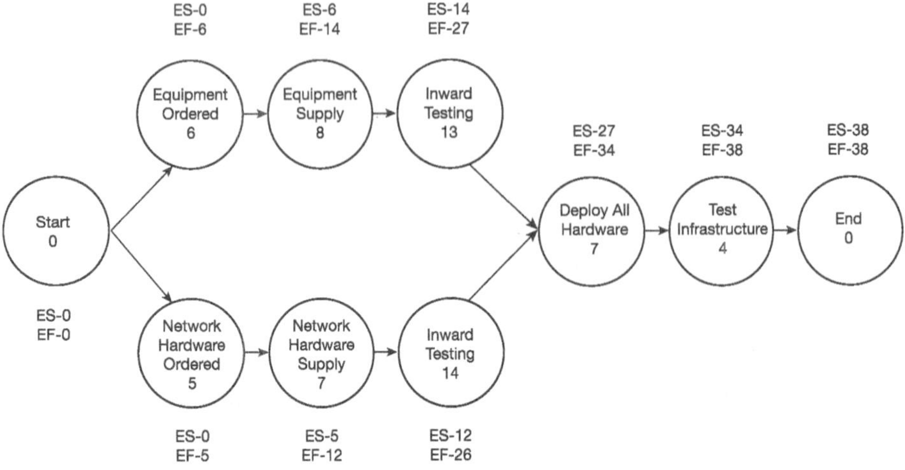

Figure D.7 Forward pass: a network diagram with the earliest Start and Finish values for each activity

Earliest start is computed as the earliest finish day of the preceding activity. For example, the activity of Equipment Supply can be started on the sixth day. It is the day on which the preceding activity of Equipment Ordered is finished. Now consider the activity Deploy All Hardware, which has two preceding activities, namely, Inward Testing of Equipment and Inward Testing of Network Hardware. Inward Testing of Equipment finishes on the 27th day and Inward Testing of Network Hardware finishes on the 26th day. Therefore, the activity of Deploy All Hardware can start on the 27th day only. Therefore, the rule for computing ES for an activity is the latest of the earliest finish times of all its predecessor activities. The rule for computing the EF for an activity is simply the ES of the activity plus its duration. The above method of computing the earliest times of project duration is referred to as the *forward pass* or earliest time computation. Based on the above computation, the End event finishes on the 38th day. This is called the earliest finish duration of the project.

Now the times for the activities beginning from the end event can be computed. This is called the *backward pass* and is used to compute the "latest time" as shown in Figure D.8. In this figure, LS stands for the Latest Start time for an activity. LS is the time by which the activity must start so that the successor activity is not delayed. LF stands for the Latest Finish time for the activity.

For computing the latest times, begin at the End event and work backward. For the Test Infrastructure activity, the LF should be 38 so the End event is not delayed. The LS for the Test Infrastructure activity is (LF—duration),

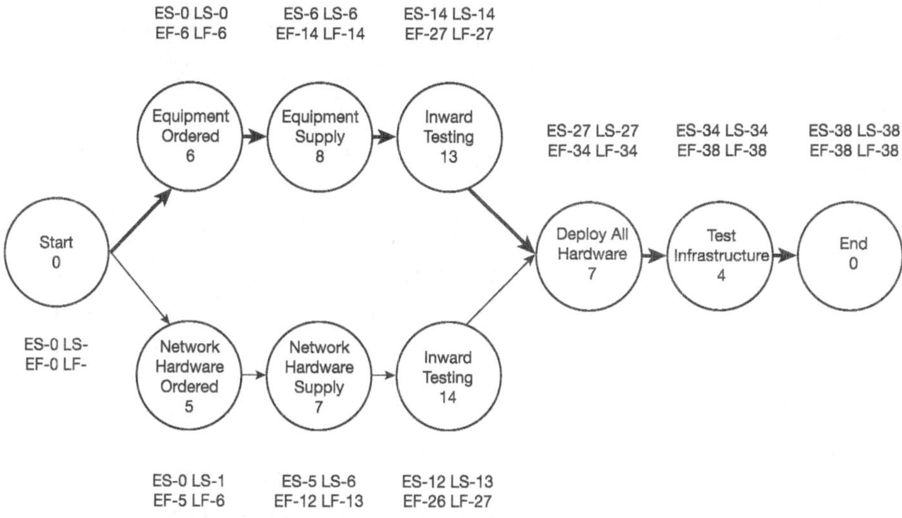

Figure D.0 Backward pass: a network diagram with the latest Start and Finish values for each activity

that is, 34. Work backward in this manner and compute latest times for all activities. The difference between the earliest time and the latest time for an activity is called the "slack" or "float." For example, for the Network Hardware Supply activity, ES is 5 and LS is 6 (alternately, EF is 12 and LF is 13). Therefore, the slack for that activity is 1. Slack is the amount of time by which the activity could be delayed from its earliest time without delaying its successor activities.

From Figure D.8, note that some activities have slack and some do not. Those that have none are known as *critical* activities. Critical activities are those vital to timely project completion. Any delay in completing the critical activities would directly and proportionately delay project completion. The path from the Start to End event connected by all critical activities is called the "critical path." In the network diagram, all critical activities are normally connected by a red arrow. Figure D.8 shows the critical activities are connected by a thick black line.

To arrive at the duration of the project, simply sum up the duration of each of the activities on the critical path. There is an alternate way of arriving at the critical path. Trace all the paths from the Start activity to the End event and compute their durations. In Figure D.8 there are two paths.

Path 1 is Start-Equipment Ordered-Equipment Supply-Inward Testing-Deploy All Hardware-Test Infrastructure-End. This path has duration of 38 days. Path 2 is Start-Network Hardware Ordered-Network Hardware Supply-Inward Testing-Deploy All Hardware-Test Infrastructure. This path has duration of

37 days. As seen, path 1 has longer duration. Therefore, it is the critical path for Figure D.8. The critical path in a network is the path that takes the longest duration from the Start event activity to reach the End event.

Probability

PERT recognizes the uncertainty inherent in estimating project duration and provides a methodology for estimating the probability for project completion for a given duration:

- The formula for computing the standard deviation for an activity is finding the difference between the optimistic time and the pessimistic time for the activity and then dividing the result by 6. The formula is *standard deviation* = $(t_p - t_o) \div 6$.
- Variance for an activity is the square of the standard deviation. Compute variance for all activities on the critical path.
- The standard deviation for the project is the square root of the sum of variances of the critical activities. The formula is *standard deviation for the project* = *square root* (sum of variances of all activities on the critical path).

Let's use the data in Table D.2 and work out the values (shown in Table D.3).

Table D.3 Computation of standard deviation

Activity ID	Activity description	Optimistic time	Pessimistic time	Standard deviation	Variance
1	Start	0	0	0.00	0.00
2	Equipment ordered	4	8	0.67	0.44
3	Equipment supply	5	11	1.00	1.00
4	Inward testing of equipment	10	16	1.00	1.00
5	Network hardware ordered	3	7	0.67	0.44
6	Network hardware supply	4	10	1.00	1.00
7	Inward testing of network hardware	10	18	1.33	1.78
8	Deploy all hardware	5	9	0.67	0.44
9	Test infrastructure	3	5	0.33	0.11
10	End	0	0	0.00	0.00

The critical path, computed as discussed earlier and identified by the values in the above table, is 1, 2, 3, 4, 8, 9, 10. The sum of the variances of the critical activities is (0 + 0.44 + 1 + 1 + 0.44 + 0.11) = 2.99 or 3. Therefore, the standard deviation for the project is the square root of 3 or 1.732.

To compute probability, we determine the value of Z using a formula:

$$Z = (D - t_e)/\textit{standard deviation}$$

where:

D = the required due date for project completion
t_e = the expected time of completion of project according to the critical path

Then, we look up the probability for the value of Z (from probability tables that are available on the Internet, in mathematical tables, or in any book on statistics).

For the project shown in Figure D.8, let's now compute the *probability* of completing the project in 36 days:

$D = 36$
$t_e = 38$
Standard deviation = 1.732
$Z = (36 - 38)/1.732 = -1.15$

When we look up the value of Z from probability tables, we get a value of 0.12507 or about 12.507%. Thus we can say that the probability of executing the project (whose expected time of completion is 38 days) in 36 days, is about 12.5%.

Critical Path Method

The CPM is also a network diagram-based technique, similar to PERT in most respects except in the matter of handling uncertainty. CPM treats durations of activities as deterministic. Deterministic activities are those whose durations are known with a certainty. CPM uses a single time estimate for each activity. However, CPM assumes there is a possibility that by spending more money by pumping in more/better resources, the duration of the activities can be reduced within certain predefined limits so that the total duration of the project can be reduced.

This aspect of pumping in more/better resources to reduce the duration of activities and thereby reduce the total duration of the project is called *crashing* the project. Crashing is the systematic reduction of duration of the entire project with the least possible increase in the project cost.

Before proceeding further, we need to answer why it is necessary to resort to crashing the project. We assume that the project completion date arrived at using the forward pass and backward pass computations would be acceptable to the client. Often, the project completion date arrived at by our computations and the completion date demanded by the client may not be the same. If the completion date demanded by the client falls after our date, then all is well. But if the date demanded by the client occurs before, we are faced with a difficult situation. This is often the reality. Crashing helps to try and advance the initial project completion date to meet client demands.

Each activity is associated with two sets of values, namely, normal duration and normal cost as well as crash duration and crash cost. It is assumed that the relationship between these two sets of values is linear. As an example, assume that the activity of ordering equipment has a normal duration of five days with an associated normal cost of $1000. Its crash duration is three days and its crash cost is $1500. Then its crash cost per day is [($1500 – $1000)/2] = $250. This value is referred to as "cost-time slope."

An example of crashing using the project is depicted in Figure D.8. The initial data for crashing are given in Table D.4. Using these data we compute the number of crashable days and the cost-time slope for each activity, which is shown in Table D.5. Crashing is an iterative process because it takes a number of iterations to achieve the objective. In this example, let us crash the project to its minimum possible duration for a better understanding of the process.

In the first iteration, there are two paths: the first is 1–2–3–4–8–9–10 with duration of 38 days, and the second is 1–5–6–7–8–9–10 with duration of 37

Table D.4 Crashing example—initial data (time in days and cost in $)

Activity ID	Activity description	Normal time	Normal cost	Crash time	Crash cost
1	Start	0	0	0	0
2	Equipment ordered	6	9000	4	12000
3	Equipment supply	8	12000	7	15000
4	Inward testing of equipment	13	13000	10	16000
5	Network hardware ordered	5	7500	4	10000
6	Network hardware supply	7	10500	6	14000
7	Inward testing of network hardware	14	14000	11	17000
8	Deploy all hardware	7	14000	5	18000
9	Test infrastructure	4	6000	4	6000
10	End	0	0	0	0

Table D.5 Crashing example with crashable days and cost-time slope

Activity ID	Activity description	Normal time	Normal cost	Crash time	Crash cost	Crashable days	Cost-time slope
1	Start	0	0	0	0	0	0
2	Equipment ordered	6	9000	4	12000	2	1500
3	Equipment supply	8	12000	7	15000	1	3000
4	Inward testing of equipment	13	13000	10	16000	3	1000
5	Network hardware ordered	5	7500	4	10000	1	2500
6	Network hardware supply	7	10500	6	14000	1	3500
7	Inward testing of network hardware	14	14000	11	17000	3	1000
8	Deploy all hardware	7	14000	5	18000	2	2000
9	Test infrastructure	4	6000	4	6000	0	0
10	End	0	0	0	0	0	0

days. Thus, the critical path is 1–2–3–4–8–9–10. To reduce the duration it is necessary to crash critical activities. Consider the critical activity with the least cost-time slope for crashing first. As seen from the above table, activity 4 has the least cost-time slope of $1000 per day, so this activity can be selected for crashing. The next question is how much duration do we crash? Select the duration in which this critical path does not become shorter than any other path in the network diagram. Knowing that the difference between the two paths is one day, this activity can be crashed for one day.

Now formulate the rules for crashing in the first iteration:

1. Select an activity on the critical path that has the least cost-time slope.
2. Select the duration such that the duration of the critical path after crashing is not shorter in duration than any other path in the network diagram.

It is necessary to redraw the network diagram again with this new information. Figure D.9 shows the network diagram after the first iteration of crashing. Now carry out the second iteration. As seen from the network diagram, there are now two critical paths. When there is more than one critical path in the network diagram, the first rule in selecting the activity for crashing is to choose such activities that are common to all the critical paths. There are two

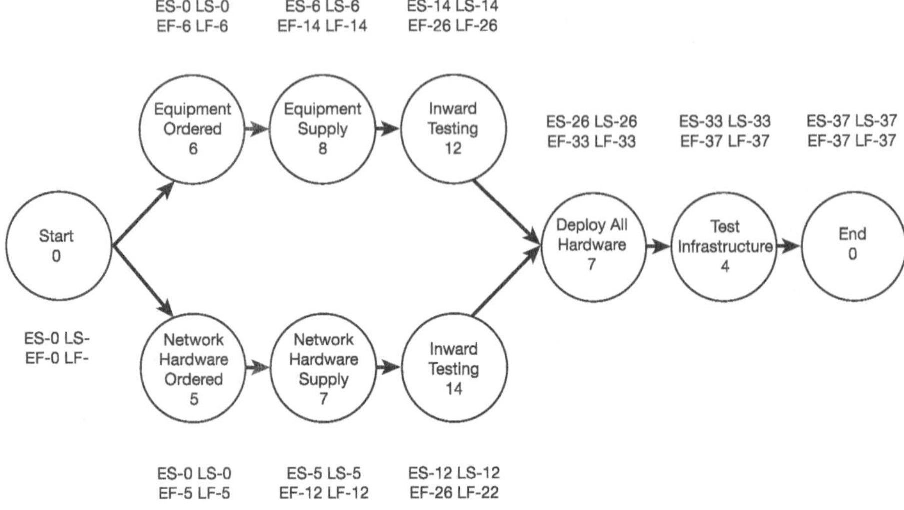

Figure D.9 Network diagram after first crashing

such activities, namely, Deploy All Hardware and Test Infrastructure. When we have multiple candidate activities for crashing, we need to select the one with the least cost-time slope. In this case, only one activity can be crashed: the Deploy All Hardware activity, which can be crashed by two days at an extra cost of $4000. Now the question to be answered before crashing is, would full crashing (i.e., reducing the duration of the Deploy All Hardware activity fully) reduce the entire project duration in the same linear amount? In this case, yes. Crash the Deploy All Hardware activity fully and redraw the network diagram. The revised network diagram is shown in Figure D.10. Now the project duration is reduced to 35 days. Would further crashing be possible? Look at the activities that can be crashed further:

1. Activity 2 can be crashed by two days with a cost-time slope of $1500.
2. Activity 3 can be crashed by one day with a cost-time slope of $3000.
3. Activity 4 can be crashed by two days because this activity has already been crashed by one day with a cost-time slope of $1000.
4. Activity 5 can be crashed by one day with a cost-time slope of $2500.
5. Activity 6 can be crashed by one day with a cost-time slope of $3500.
6. Activity 7 can be crashed by three days with a cost-time slope of $1000.

In order to reduce project duration by one day, we have to select one activity from both paths. As seen, activities 4 and 6 both have the least cost-time

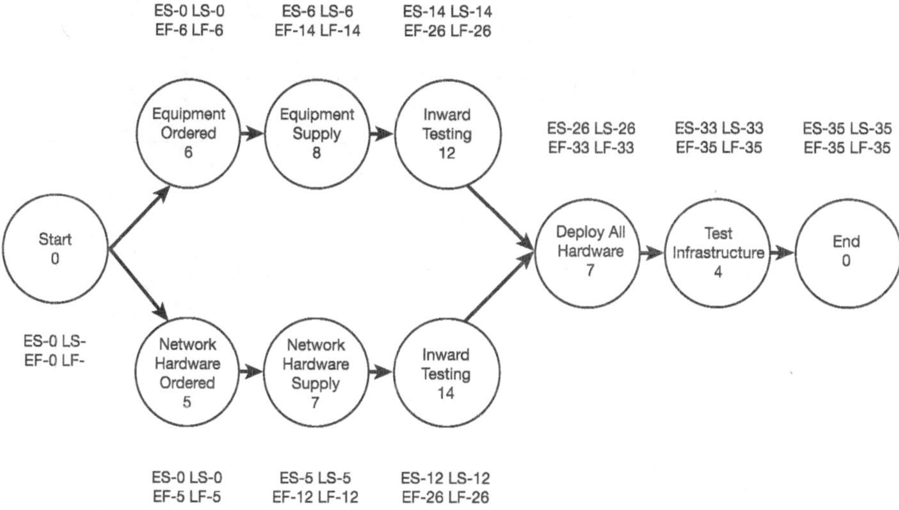

Figure D.10 Network diagram after second crashing

slope of $1000 per day. Activity 4 allows for crashing of two days but activity 6 allows crashing by three days. We can draw one more network diagram crashing these two activities, compute the critical path once more, and continue to iterate. But before we do so, we need to ask whether the desired duration is reached. If it is reached, it need not be crashed further.

But since we set the objective of crashing to reach the limit of possible reduction in duration, we need to check the maximum possible crashing. For this, enumerate all critical paths along with their durations and evaluate the extent of crashing possible, as seen below:

1. Path 1–2–3–4–8–9–10 has a duration of 35 days with a maximum crashability of five days (activity 2 with two days, activity 3 with one day, and activity 4 with two days).
2. Path 1–5–6–7–8–9–10 has a duration of 35 days with a maximum crashability of five days (activity 5 with one day, activity 6 with one day, and activity 7 with three days).

Note that both paths allow a reduction of five days each. This will be the limit to which this project can be crashed. Draw the final network diagram. It is depicted in Figure D.11.

The project is now fully crashed, that is, the minimum duration has been reached. No further crashing is possible. Table D.6 gives final durations with costs. From the network diagram we see that the normal duration is 38 days

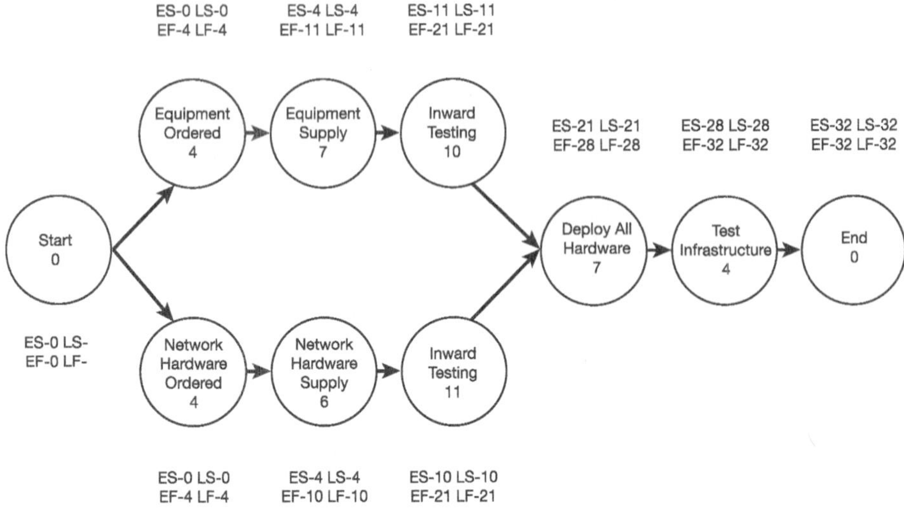

Figure D.11 A network diagram showing a fully crashed project

Table D.6 Project fully crashed (time in days and cost in $)

Activity ID	Activity description	Normal time	Normal cost	Crash time	Crash cost
1	Start	0	0	0	0
2	Equipment ordered	6	9,000	4	12,000
3	Equipment supply	8	12,000	7	15,000
4	Inward testing of equipment	13	13,000	10	16,000
5	Network hardware ordered	5	7,500	4	10,000
6	Network hardware supply	7	10,500	6	14,000
7	Inward testing of network hardware	14	14,000	11	17,000
8	Deploy all hardware	7	14,000	5	18,000
9	Test infrastructure	4	6,000	4	6,000
10	End	0	0	0	0
	Total cost		86,000		108,000

with a normal cost of $86,000 and crash duration of 32 days with a crash cost of $108,000.

Summarizing the discussions on crashing:

1. Crashing is a systematic exercise in reducing project duration with minimum increase in project cost.

2. Before attempting crashing, it is imperative to set an objective in the reduction of project duration or the maximum cost increase that is permissible.
3. Crashing is an iterative process; it is iterated until the objective is met.
4. In any iteration, the rules for selecting the candidate activities for crashing are:
   a. If there are multiple critical paths, then the activities common to all critical paths are to be selected. Otherwise, all activities on the critical path are candidates for crashing.
   b. In all the candidate activities for crashing, it is necessary to select those activities that have the least cost-time slope.
5. Crash the selected activities and recompute the critical paths.
6. Check if the objectives in terms of duration and cost are met.
7. If they are met, redraw/update the network diagram and close the exercise. If the objectives are not met, again iterate Steps 4 to 6 until the objectives are met.

In practice, a manual crashing exercise for even a moderately large project having 500 activities may not be practical. It takes a number of iterations and would need a large number of computations. Therefore, use computer-based tools like Microsoft Project or Primavera that automate the process of crashing. Before making use of tools for crashing it is important to understand how the process works.

Resource Leveling

You may have noticed that we used duration while computing the critical path in the previous examples. Both PERT/CPM are duration-based techniques for arriving at the project completion date. It is assumed in both techniques that all the required resources (namely, human resources, monetary resources, equipment resources, methods, material, and information resources including necessary approvals) are available for performing the activities when the activity is scheduled to start. But in reality, resources are often limited, especially for costly resources shared by many projects and perhaps by many activities within the same project itself. If any of the required resources are unavailable, that activity would be delayed by the period of the unavailability of that resource.

Resource leveling refers to that iterative exercise of systematically reducing the overload of the resources with the objective of maintaining the existing project completion date, and if not feasible then delaying the project to the minimum possible extent.

Therefore, follow these steps while computing the project completion date:

1. Initially, assume that all resources are available for all activities and compute the critical path and project completion date.
2. Allocate the required resources to each activity.
3. Plot the resource loading for each resource for the entire duration of the project:
    a. Resource loading is computing the number of hours of workload in terms of the activities to be performed by each resource.
    b. Draw the resource loading graph.
4. Identify the resources that are overloaded, which are the following:
    a. Those that have more than eight hours of workload for the day pertaining to human and equipment resources.
    b. Those that are not available or are in short supply for material and monetary resources.
5. Attempt to reduce resource overloading (namely, human and equipment resources) by:
    a. Ascertaining if the capacity can be temporarily expanded by:
        i. Having resources to work extra time for the required days and paying overtime.
        ii. Hiring temporary workers for the required period.
        iii. Subcontracting a portion of the work.
    b. Providing all of the required resources to the critical activities and delaying the noncritical activities using each activity's available slack
    c. Computing the critical path to assess the impact on the project's completion date (We also recalculate resource loading for all of the resources for all days of project duration and assess the remaining resource overloading if any.)
    d. Performing Steps 5b and 5c iteratively until all overloading of resources is leveled to normal loading levels without delaying the project completion date
    e. Resorting to iterating Steps 5b and 5c and trying to minimize delay in the project's completion date when eliminating resource overloading is not possible without delaying the project's completion

When resources such as monetary and material resources are in short supply, we need to just go ahead and procure them. Otherwise, the resources in short supply will only delay the project by the amount of time procurement is delayed. Information resources also delay a project if their availability is delayed. Monetary, material, and information resources, however, cannot be leveled by delaying the noncritical activities.

Just as crashing is an iterative process, so is resource leveling. For real-life projects that have 500 or more activities and 25 or more resources, resource leveling is very difficult and tedious. Usually computer-based tools such as Microsoft Project and Primavera are used for resource leveling, but these tools usually perform "resource-constrained" scheduling rather than leveling the resources. Our recommendation is that you do not commit to a project completion date until resource leveling or resource-constrained scheduling is performed.

Final Words

A brief outline of the techniques of PERT/CPM has been presented here. However, this introduction is adequate for project managers who use computer-based tools such as Microsoft Project and Primavera. The background information will enable them to perform scheduling effectively.

This book has free material available for download from the Web Added Value™ resource center at *www.jrosspub.com*

Appendix E

Problem Resolution in IT Projects

Introduction

What is a problem? There are many definitions that apply to different contexts. For our context of managing IT projects, this definition of Merriam Webster's dictionary is apt: a problem is "something difficult to deal with; something that is a source of trouble." Other definitions offered by the same dictionary are "difficulty in understanding or accepting something," "feeling of not liking or wanting to do something," and "an intricate unsettled question." We will define it "as an undesirable event raising its ugly head at an inconvenient time. A problem is an unforeseen impediment to the progress of a human endeavor." When a problem crops up, the workflow stops or slows down, everyone concerned is stressed out, harsh words are used, voices are raised, and in short, the environment is not harmonious anymore.

But problems are common to every human endeavor. We cannot avoid them. It is by dealing with problems and resolving them that so much progress has been achieved by humankind. Problems crop up in IT projects too. Problems are the springboards that launch us to the next level by making us better and more capable individuals. Handling problems is the vehicle by which we gain valuable experience. Problems are the reason we invent better methods and tools. It would be hard to imagine progress and improvement without facing problems. In fact, it is better to view problems as challenges.

In this appendix, we will discuss the sources of problems in IT projects and some strategies to tackle and solve them.

Now let us look at the term "solution." It is necessary to understand this word because of the various and often erroneous connotations attached to it. Discarding the connotation of a liquid mixture of multiple ingredients, the definitions offered by Merriam Webster's dictionary are "an action or process of solving a problem" and "an answer to a problem." The popular connotation of the term "solution" is that it provides a resolution that is acceptable to all; that it satisfies all the involved parameters and concerned stakeholders. But it is not possible to reach a solution to every problem situation in project management! For one thing, projects do not have all the time it takes to find the right solution that is acceptable to all. We have the pressure of time and the limitation of the resources. Second, the objective of the project is to expedite the work and not to conduct research to come up with the best possible solution. There is a limit on the amount of resources we can spend to develop a solution that is acceptable to all concerned, which is why we do not use the popular phrase "problem solving" and instead use the phrase "problem resolution."

Resolution is defined by Merriam Webster's dictionary as "the act of analyzing a complex notion into simpler ones," "the act of answering," and "the act of determining." The term "resolution" connotes a course of action to move forward which has been accepted by all even with some of them having reservations. With a "resolution," the problem is taken off the table. All concerned stakeholders agree to a course of action and are moving forward. We do not engage with it any longer. Well, it may not be the "best" solution for the problem at hand but it allows us to move forward. The impediment is removed.

Sources and Nature of Problems in IT Projects

Problems crop up from three sources, namely:

1. Work-related technical problems
2. Environment-related problems
3. People-related problems

Work-Related Technical Problems

Work-related problems arise for the following reasons:

1. *Poor design or an error in the design of the infrastructure.* Technical problems halt progress temporarily. We need to provide clarification or circumvent the issue. For example, when routing network cables, a

concrete beam may obstruct the route. We need to either drill a hole through it or route the cables around it. Sometimes there is no space for maneuvering while installing equipment. In such cases we need to rearrange the equipment so there is space for maneuvering. There could be similar issues arising out of poor design. All these are temporary impediments and can be quickly resolved.

2. *Poor workmanship*. Suppose the network connectors are not crimped on the cable ends properly. It will cause connectivity and network speed issues. Locating such problems is very difficult. If the electrical connections are not made tightly, they may cause blackouts or brownouts. Quality assurance and quality control are the solutions to such problems.
3. *Bad tools*. Bad tools or tools that are in need of maintenance can cause problems. We need tools for drilling holes in walls, crimping connectors, screw drivers and wrenches to tighten bolts and nuts, and so on. If these tools are not in good condition, they slow down the progress of work and cause fatigue to the technicians, which could lead to quality problems. Ensuring that the tools being used on the job are in good condition alleviates this problem. Periodic calibration and maintenance of tools are vital to keeping tools in the right condition.
4. *Malfunctioning of equipment*. If the hardware malfunctions initially, or functions in a way it is not expected to, it will delay progress. This can even be due to wrong usage! So, we need to ensure that only trained people operate the equipment. The other reason is that equipment is malfunctioning. When equipment malfunctions, we need to record the actions that led to the malfunctioning and then interact with the supplier to resolve the issue. Sometimes it may involve repairing equipment or even replacing it. Whatever it may be, there is a solution although it consumes additional time and perhaps some money too. Inward quality control when properly carried out can alleviate hardware malfunctioning to a large extent.
5. *Equipment breakdown*. Breakdown connotes proper functioning initially but then malfunctions later on after some usage. Equipment used in setting up the infrastructure or the hardware itself can break down. When the equipment used in setting up the infrastructure, such as test equipment, breaks down, we need to repair it at our cost. We can repair it and use it but we lose time. If the hardware used for set up breaks down during testing or pilot runs, we need to interact with the supplier because it would still be covered by the product

warranty. It would take a comparatively longer time to bring it back to working condition and move on with the testing or pilot run.

6. *Malfunctioning of software.* Either the system software or application software can malfunction. The probability of system software malfunctioning is much less than the malfunctioning of the application software because the system software is much more thoroughly tested than the application software. System software can malfunction if the medium on which it is supplied is corrupted. It is also possible that the software may be corrupted during the download process. Application software malfunction during on-site testing is a common phenomenon, especially if it is custom developed. We need to build some buffer duration for the testing activity of application software into the schedule, but the malfunctioning can exceed our expectations. In such cases, we need to interact with the development team of the application software and get it to work as quickly as possible.
7. *Equipment mismatch.* The IT infrastructure consists of multiple disparate pieces of equipment procured from different vendors. The design activity ought to take care that each piece of equipment interfaces with the others, but infrastructure designers normally take care of this aspect. Sometimes one or two pieces of equipment cause problems and do not interface as expected with other equipment. Another problem often faced during the testing of the infrastructure is that one or two pieces of equipment function slowly and become a bottleneck in delivering the expected throughput. In such cases, the problematic equipment needs to be replaced with the right equipment. This not only entails additional expenditure but also additional time. This can be prevented if the validation of the infrastructure design is carried out diligently.
8. *Equipment tuning.* Equipment tuning is a vital aspect in setting up IT infrastructure. Some of the equipment needs setting/adjusting of its parameters either through its software or hardware interface for it to function at its peak capacity and speed. If the individuals are not well trained in this aspect, the tuning may not be accurate. Wrong tuning of the equipment causes throughput to fall during operation. This causes delays to the project progress. This can be prevented by diligent quality control of the activities of installation and commissioning of the system software. When this problem is detected during testing, the tuning needs to be corrected by an experienced individual to suit our infrastructure. The occurrence of this problem delays testing and requires additional time for rework.

9. *Issues with application software.* Normally, the application software is tested in a simulated environment. It can malfunction when loaded on the actual equipment in the real operating environment. All the defects lurking inside the application software start surfacing when tested in a real environment. Most IT projects have on-site warranty support persons during testing who will correct the issue immediately. We can include some time in our schedule for rectification of malfunctioning application software during the planning stage itself. When the problems overshoot expectations we are faced with delay in completing the project.

Technical problems have solutions, but they consume the time resource and cause delays. When technical problems are encountered, we typically come out unscathed except for the loss of time and some extra cost. The lost time needs to be recovered if we wish to meet the final delivery schedule. How to recover the lost time is described in a following section.

Environment-Related Problems

Environmental problems arise from outside of the project team. These could be from suppliers, management, subcontractors, customers, or the purchase of equipment. The environment-related problems are described below.

1. *Receipt of wrong equipment.* Receiving the wrong equipment is not a normal occurrence but it does happen occasionally. By wrong equipment, I do not mean receiving a PC instead of a minicomputer. Some of the specifications may not match between the equipment ordered and received. Sometimes the model ordered may be phased out by the supplier and the next model may be supplied. Sometimes, even if the model is the same as the ordered one some of the specifications like the amount of RAM or hard disk or processor speed may differ. We might get better or worse specifications than what we ordered. We may be able to accept the equipment supplied if it supports better specifications, but not if the specifications are worse. Whatever it is, some time is lost in resolving the issue during inward quality control. This issue will result in cascading delays in the project. However, it can be alleviated by selecting the right suppliers and diligently following up until the right equipment is received.
2. *Not receiving some of the components.* Sometimes suppliers fail to ship the required components ordered. If we do not receive routers or networking switches on time, quite a bit of our work will be delayed.

Supplier follow-up is an important activity. If we fail to diligently follow up with the suppliers, we may receive wrong components or none at all. If we wait until the promised delivery date to start following up, our supplies may be delayed. Some of the components are likely to be available off the shelf but some may be made to order. Another aspect to be considered in these days of offshoring, especially with regard to the made-to-order components, is that they may be coming from a far-off location such as China. The shipment may be delayed or lost in transit and getting another piece may take weeks if not months. We need to follow up diligently or absorb the delay and try to recover the lost time.

3. *Delayed receipt of equipment*. We may receive equipment later than what is indicated in our schedule. Sometimes the original date promised by the vendor itself may be beyond our scheduled date. Other times, due to conditions beyond the control of the supplier, the delivery may be delayed. There are umpteen reasons for a delay. I am not suggesting that all deliveries are likely to be delayed. Even if the delivery of *one* piece of crucial equipment is delayed, it could negatively impact project progress. Diligently follow up with suppliers, and if delays still occur, absorb them and try to recover the lost time.
4. *Money being in short supply*. Money can become scarce without notice. It may be used for some other urgent needs. Even cash-rich organizations may face a liquidity crunch now and then. When cash is in short supply, we cannot make payments to various agencies executing the project and it can lead to serious consequences, including work stoppages. As discussed in Chapter 8, cash management is a very important part of IT project management.
5. *Subcontractor delays*. IT projects require multiple specialties and typically have a few subcontractors. Most subcontractors perform their activities diligently and complete their assignments on time, but sometimes delays can occur. By regular follow-up, the delays from subcontractors can be prevented. But sometimes, even with diligent follow-up, the subcontractor may delay the completion of the assignment. This would hamper the project progress. But we may be able to take phased deliveries so that the subsequent activities can be started and the delay can be absorbed. We may levy penalties for delays to recover some of the money lost due to delays. But all the same, we need to factor the subcontractor delays in the execution control and recover the lost time when delays occur.

6. *Accidents at the site.* Even though these are rare occurrences, all the same, an accident may occur on the site anytime. We need to strictly enforce all safety procedures and precautions. But when an accident occurs, it will have severe consequences for the project. We may incur extra and unplanned expenditures in addition to project delays. We must prevent accidents during project execution by all means. There is no easy resolution to accidents.

Environmental problems are caused by random occurrences, not the project team, but the team often has resolutions. The project team inherits those problems and has to resolve them to move forward without impacting the project schedule and cost. We might be able to recover the lost time but sometimes the cost escalation becomes unavoidable.

People-Related Problems

The problems that crop up from technical and environmental causes do have solutions. They are temporary impediments (except for accidents). We need to handle their impact on cost and delays in project progress. But problems that arise due to people-related causes often do not have clear solutions, and sometimes it is even difficult to recognize them as problems. People are ingenious and can camouflage their problems as either technical problems or environmental problems. It is best to prevent people-related problems than have to resolve them. Appendix C is dedicated to *people management* detailing how to manage them well so that these problems can be avoided. The following are some problems that can arise due to human causes:

1. *Ego clashes.* These do occur between peers on the project, especially between peers who depend on each other for the effective performance of their own activities. It is more often the perception than reality that causes the ego clash. One or both perceive that the other person is working in such a way as to affect the individual's performance or make him/her look bad in the eyes of the superior. The other individual's actions are perceived as detrimental to self-interests. Competition to excel is healthy in the organization and in the project. But if the competition is not maintained at healthy levels, it can degenerate into conflict. When ego clashes occur, the involved persons start acting against each other and start complaining about trivial issues. Communications become the means to build defenses rather than to share information. Concern for each other's issues evaporates and is replaced by gloating at each other's embarrassment. There will

be more meetings only to resolve issues rather than to review progress or to share information. The firefighting becomes more frequent than fire prevention. The atmosphere will be one of distrust, noncooperation, and defensive, instead of trust, cooperation, and outgoing. The individuals will be demotivated and team morale will reach its lowest point. The best way to handle ego clashes is to prevent them by creating an environment of harmony, trust, and cooperation. If and when ego clashes occur, it is better to replace one or both persons so that the atmosphere is protected from further pollution.

2. *Poor communication, instructions, and understanding*. Poor communication is one of the reasons often quoted for people-related problems and ego clashes. Even in well-intentioned people, communication gaps can lead to problems. Poor communication includes the absence of communication of vital information, the assumption that the concerned have all the information, delayed communication, wrong communication, and ambiguous communication. Poor communication results in not executing the required work, wrong execution, or delayed execution. This would negatively impact the schedule and sometimes even escalate the cost of the project. Having good work methods and plan documents in place avoids poor communication. Another aspect that leads to poor communication is the PM being too busy to communicate well. Sometimes the project manager is inundated with too many important/not-so-important activities and does not have adequate time to communicate well. The project manager needs to delegate activities and dedicate his/her time for communication, progress review, and such other activities rather than to try doing things all by himself/herself.
3. *Absenteeism*. Personal absences due to leaves, accidents, religious occasions, family needs, and ill health of self/family members is a real problem in projects. Projects are bound by tight deadlines and cost constraints. Having spare resources for catering to absenteeism should be limited to 15–20%. This would be adequate to fill the gap due to expected absenteeism. But it becomes a problem when we have unforeseeable absenteeism, which can be due to attrition, illnesses, accidents, natural calamities, deaths, and such other reasons. We cannot fill the vacancy for this type of absence instantaneously. This kind of absenteeism will have an impact on the project progress. We can however plan ahead for these kinds of occurrences. We may identify agencies that supply human resources for temporary assignments and draw the required resources from them at a short notice. Another

alternative is to draw from other projects within the same organization if possible. Sometimes projects fall behind for a variety of reasons and the allocated people may be idle for want of assignments. Another possibility is to assign an existing subcontractor with some additional work that should have been performed by the absent resource. We have possible resolutions but sometimes none may work. In such cases, we lose some time and we need to recover the lost time or delay the project completion.

4. *Union activities*. Unions and strikes, though, are rare in IT projects, but we still need to cover them here as a possibility. The best resolution for a strike, tool-down, or work-to-rule is to prevent such situations. When such situations arise, the best way to handle them is to bring in the specialists in industrial relations from within the organization as early as possible. Strikes cause a visible impediment to project progress and are fraught with serious consequences. Therefore, the earlier the specialists are involved, the better it is. A strike is like a fire. The earlier the fire department is called, the quicker the fire can be put out.

When you really evaluate any problem deep enough, there will be a human being behind the problem. If the preventive maintenance is not carried out on schedule, or a supply is delayed because someone has not followed up diligently, or a tool was misused, certainly there is an individual responsible. Most problems can be traced to individuals with the rest being truly due to random causes. So handling people is a very important aspect of project management. Appendix C covers this in more depth.

Tools for Problem Analysis

As can be seen from the above narration, there is a resolution for every problem but this can impact project completion and project cost. The true difficulty, however, is not in the resolution but in its diagnosis, just as in medicine. Rarely does one disease alone attack an individual. It normally comes coupled with other diseases. The symptoms and sometimes the individual's description thereof could be misleading. There could be errors in the results of the diagnostic procedures. All these put together make it difficult to accurately diagnose the disease and thereby make it difficult to cure. The same thing occurs with problems in IT projects. When you look at a problem as it surfaces, it is rarely so clear as to be classified into its proper category (except for maybe environment-related problems). Equipment and human-related problems often come together. When a piece of equipment is reported to be causing problems, it can be repaired quickly and put back to use. But why did the equipment get damaged in the first place? Was it because its preventive maintenance was not carried out? Was it misused? Or was it a random breakdown? All of these could be the reasons!

So, on receiving a problem report, the first action to be taken is to analyze the problem. Here are some tools to do that:

1. *Analogy*. This is a good tool. When a problem is reported, look for an analogy from the relevant past history. It will give us an understanding of the problem, its possible causes, and what actions were taken to rectify the situation, as well as the consequences of those actions. We can learn from the analogy and apply the resolution appropriate for the present problem. The prerequisite for using this tool is that earlier projects should have documented best practices and pitfalls at project closure.
2. *Brainstorming*. This is a technique that is utilized in baffling problems. A few people knowledgeable in the problem space and who are concerned with the situation gather together in an informal environment and give free rein to their thinking about the problem at hand. This facilitates understanding the problem as well as possible resolutions to the problem.
3. *Divide and conquer*. In divide and conquer, we breakdown the main problem into smaller subproblems that can be resolved.
4. *Means-ends analysis*. In means-ends analysis, we identify the ends (goals) for our present situation and try to identify the means (actions) that are necessary to resolve the problem situation. Means-ends analysis is a versatile technique and is used in engineering designs, artificial intelligence, etc.
5. *Research*. This technique is also used in technical problems. When a piece of equipment does not work as expected, we are confused. The equipment should perform the intended action and we have tuned the parameters correctly to the best of our knowledge. But still it is not working! In such cases, we conduct research on the problem trying to find someone who faced such a problem and solved it. We may post in discussion forums on the Internet or contact other project managers or academics and try to elicit their opinion. The research may yield an understanding of the problem and probable approaches to resolve it. This research is not basic or applied research as in the scientific community, but a search for problem resolution.
6. *Root cause analysis*. Root causes are the underlying reasons for the problem. Root itself connotes invisibility and the reason for supporting

something. For a tree, the root is underground and is the support for the very existence of the tree. Therefore, when a problem crops up, the real reason does not become obvious at first glance. We need to dig deeper to find the real (root) cause of the event. We use tools such as cause-and-effect diagrams, a causal factor chart, root-cause map, and root-cause summary tables to analyze the problem and identify the root cause. Once the root cause is identified, we can fix it appropriately. However, root-cause analysis takes some time and cannot be used in situations that require a quick fix.

7. *Critical examination.* Critical examination is described in detail in Appendix B. It can be used in problem analysis also, either in stand-alone mode or in combination with other techniques.

Problem Resolution

When a problem is reported we take the following actions:

1. When a problem surfaces, the first action is to douse the fire immediately. Visit the site where the problem surfaced and find out what the problem is and what could be the immediate resolution. The immediate resolution may not be the best solution. Apply your experience and judgment and put a temporary resolution in place. The temporary resolution may not be the one suggested by the individuals involved; it may be a variant of the suggested one, or it may totally be yours. But, convey to the concerned individuals that it is a temporary one and the full fix will follow soon. The temporary resolution is to ensure that the work does not stop abruptly. It is to keep the work moving. If it is impossible to continue the work, assign the crew to other work. Also, see if it is possible to keep the problem piece of work pending and continue on to the next task. Ensure that the crew is gainfully employed. Focus on keeping the work moving. Do not focus on placing the blame on someone at this point in time.
2. Assign someone from your team who is knowledgeable about the work to analyze the problem and apprise you of the facts. The people who analyze tend to jump to make a judgment of why it happened and what should be the next course of action. Ensure that the assigned person collects data as factually as possible but does not jump to conclusions by informing him/her right in the beginning about what is required and what is off limits.
3. Once the facts are available, analyze the problem. Involve some of the concerned individuals and some experts. The purpose of this analysis

is not to apportion blame. That comes much later when the problem is resolved and the project is once again on firm ground. The purpose is to find what should be done moving forward and how to deal with the impact on the schedule and cost of the project. The techniques of analysis described in the preceding section may be utilized for carrying out the analysis.

4. Once this analysis is completed and the resolutions are available, you can implement them. Try and minimize the impact on the schedule and the cost of the project. Although it is difficult to recover lost money, it is possible to recover the lost time.
5. Once the project has recovered from the problem and is moving forward smoothly, now carry out further analysis to find the root cause for the occurrence. The problem could be due to environmental issues, genuine technical reasons, or a random occurrence. There may not be any malicious intentions on the part of anyone. If there are no malicious intentions, then let the issue go. But if you find that the problem was caused due to ego clashes, willful negligence, or malicious intent, take disciplinary action appropriate to the situation in consultation with the HR department. If it comes out that there is an individual responsible for the incident, find out if it is due to lack of expertise or training. If the person lacks the necessary expertise, ensure that the individual is trained by making him/her work under a more senior or expert resource until he/she gains the acceptable level of expertise.
6. Record this event in detail and make it part of the documentation to be included in the project records and shared with others during the project closure meeting.

It is possible that sometimes we allow the offender to go scot-free if the resource is critical to project success. At the moment, yes, we do allow the offender to go scot-free but only so long as the project needs that individual. Make sure that the individual receives the due negative reward in the course of time. If you do not, it will send a wrong message to the rest of the project team: you can cause problems and get away with it.

Recovering the Time Lost Due to Problems

Money is a nonrecurring resource. It is exhausted when we use it and is not recoverable. It is not elastic. But time within limits is elastic and stretchable. Although we have 24 hours in a day, the work day is only 8 hours. So we can work a few more hours every day and recover some, if not all, of the time we lost in resolving problems. Here are ways that allow us to recover lost time:

1. *Work extra time on workdays and on holidays*. Working extra time on normal working days or holidays undoubtedly causes stress to the employees. But in emergencies and when we lose valuable time because of an unforeseen problem, we may ask the concerned team members to endure some stress for a limited period to recover the lost time. Resort to this alternative with caution. Resort to it too often and for too long, and the employees may get stressed out and their regular productivity levels will fall. It is better to couple working extra time with an incentive like equivalent time off, or double wages, or some other interesting incentive so that the employees will be psychologically motivated to put in the extra effort.
2. *Allocate more resources*. The work may not always be amenable to utilizing more resources than a preset limit. If we have already allocated existing resources to that preset limit, we cannot allocate any more resources to reduce the duration. But sometimes it may be possible to allocate additional resources to the work at hand and utilize the extra resources to reduce duration. The effort (person-days/hours) may not be reduced but the duration (calendar days/clock hours) could be reduced. If this alternative is feasible, it is better than making the existing resources work extra time because this does not cause stress or fatigue to the employees.
3. *Allocate more expert resources*. It is well accepted in the industry that all resources will not have the same level of skill. The skill level may be poor (as in the case of a trainee), fair (an employee with one year of experience on the job), good (an employee with two to three years of experience), very good (an employee with four to six years of experience), and super (more than six years of experience). Needless to say, a person with a higher skill level can produce more than a person with a lower skill level during the same amount of time. Therefore, we can allocate better skilled people to the task and execute it faster to recover the lost time. If the team already has super-skilled people, we may not be able to utilize this alternative. But usually, a team has a mix of skill levels and there is room for allocating resources with higher skill levels. Of course, the assumption here is that there are better skilled resources than those already available to the team for allocation.

4. *Provide an incentive to finish assignments earlier.* Experiments have proven time and again that people focus and execute assignments at a faster rate if they are assured of an incentive, be it financial or nonfinancial. We can offer some such incentive to existing employees to recover the lost time. As incentive schemes have worked well in the past, they will work well in the future too. We might need to involve industrial engineers in working out an incentive scheme and implementing it. One side effect of this approach, in the context of recovering lost time, is that other employees to whom the incentive scheme is not applicable may resent being left out. It is usually advisable to implement any incentive scheme for all employees and not just a subset.
5. *Subcontract part of the work.* We can subcontract a downstream piece of work that otherwise would have been executed by the team whose work is delayed due to a problem. This is equivalent to allocating more resources to the task, but now the persons allocated are from a subcontractor. The difference is that the activity of supervising those additional resources is also passed on to the subcontractor. The constraint is that we should have a stand-alone piece of work that can be subcontracted and a subcontractor that is willing to take on the work at short notice should be available.
6. *Make phased deliveries.* This is not really recovering lost time but delaying certain project deliverables. We do this in such a way that the downstream activities are not negatively impacted. Obviously, the downstream activities are rarely started in one day like a big bang. So, there may be a possibility to delay certain deliveries and still not impact the downstream activities. We need to assess the situation carefully and redraw our delivery schedule in such a way that the delayed deliveries do not affect the downstream activities. This way, the end users/customer may not have any objection to delays.

Recovering all the lost time is not always possible. But what is always possible is the ability to recover some of the lost time. Another aspect to be noted is that all the above alternatives of recovering lost time will cost the project extra money. Reduction in duration is associated with an increase in cost. We must be ready to spend more money if we wish to recover the lost time. Most projects experience some problems, lose some time, and face the prospect of having to delay the project. Knowledge of the alternatives available to recover lost time enables us to implement them and recover the lost time to deliver the infrastructure on time.

Creative Problem Solving

The best example of creative problem solving can be seen in the design of the airplane. Before the airplane became common place, many people attempted flight. Everyone imitated the birds. What the birds have that humans do not are wings. So it was recognized that wings are necessary if you wish to fly. Various wings were designed, fabricated, and many trials were conducted with them, including jumping off cliffs and flapping wings. It was assumed that levitation was achieved by flapping wings. But keen observers found that flapping was not necessary for levitation by observing eagles circling high in the sky without flapping their wings. It was deduced that forward movement and levitation were both achieved by the wings and that forward movement was achieved by flapping and levitation was achieved by the shape of the wing. Wing shape can be imitated. But how does one achieve forward movement in the air where friction-based movement is not possible? The movement on the ground was achieved by the friction between the wheel and the earth. Then some people, among them the Wright brothers who were the most successful, came up with the idea of using an airscrew, taking a cue from the propeller of ships. That did the trick. The airscrew achieved the forward movement and the wing shape achieved the levitation. We now have transoceanic flights carrying 450 passengers! That innovation of the airscrew for forward movement, replacing the friction principle, solved a big problem and air travel became natural for human beings. A creative solution solves a tedious and vexing problem permanently and in a manner that is accepted all around.

A story that illustrates the concept of creative problem solving goes something like this. A traveler in a desert came across three brothers quarreling among themselves. He gets involved and inquires about what the trouble seems to be. One of them replies, "Our father left us seventeen camels. He stipulated that the youngest one gets half the camels, the middle one gets one third of the camels, and the eldest one gets one ninth of the camels. Now how do we divide up the camels?" The traveler thought for a moment and came to a decision. He added his camel to the 17 and made them 18. He gave nine (half) to the youngest one, he gave six (one-third) to the middle one, he gave two (one-ninth) to the eldest one, and the traveler rode on the remaining camel that was his. You may find variants of this story elsewhere. But the gist is that it is an example of creative problem solving by the addition method.

A creative solution is one that has not been thought of or implemented earlier in a similar scenario. Solutions implemented in wars have been used in manufacturing and logistics profitably. It is possible to implement creative problem-solving techniques in IT project management too. There are many techniques for creative problem solving and the central idea of all those techniques is to come up with an original idea to solve the problem.

One technique that we all follow is to imitate some relevant aspect of nature. Submarines imitate fish. Sharks are being keenly studied for their motion and the ability to generate high speeds so that this can be implemented in submarines. Observation of nature can give us great ideas for practical use.

Horizontal thinking is akin to daydreaming. Vertical thinking is conforming to existing practices. Lateral thinking, another tool, is a combination of vertical thinking and horizontal thinking. Vertical thinking presupposes knowledge of the subject matter because unless you know the subject, you cannot conform to it. When you couple horizontal thinking with knowledge, you are likely to come up with original ideas.

Generating a number of ideas is another technique in creative problem solving. Brainstorming is often used to generate ideas fluently. From the ideas thus generated, we can find some original ideas. We can derive originality from ideational fluency.

Abstraction is another technique for creative problem solving. You reduce the problem by adding, subtracting, multiplying, or dividing it. The camel-sharing story discussed previously is an example of abstraction by adding. Similarly, we can abstract by subtracting or multiplying or dividing something from the problem space.

Creative problem solving is a large subject deserving a full chapter for its treatment. It is advantageous for every manager including IT project managers to get an introduction to the art of creative problem solving so that some tough problems presented in the management of IT projects can be resolved effectively.

Appendix F

Stakeholder Expectation Management for IT Projects

Expectations are unstated requirements. They are typically implicit assumptions of performance that are construed as requirements for the project by the stakeholders other than the project manager (PM). Because they are unstated and implicit, it is not possible for the PM to make these expectations explicit by documenting them.

The first aspect of expectation management is to recognize that there are expectations in all stakeholders, not just customers. The second aspect is to set the "right" expectations with stakeholders. If we do not set the right expectations, the stakeholders may develop unreasonable expectations. Reasonable expectations can be met but not unreasonable ones. When stakeholders express that their reasonable expectations (some of which could be unreasonable in our view) are not being met, we need to discuss them and set the right expectations. Lastly, we need to strive to meet all reasonable expectations of all stakeholders without being asked.

Let us discuss what the expectations from various project stakeholders could be. At a macro level there are five classes of stakeholder expectations to be managed in any project:

1. Customer or end-user expectations
2. Organizational management expectations
3. Project team expectations
4. Subcontractor expectations
5. Supplier expectations

Table F.1 provides a set of typical expectations to use as a basis for translating expectations into requirements.

Expectations translate into requirements unless they are not set "right." Not all expectations are unreasonable nor are they always reasonable. An example of reasonable expectations can be from customers when they expect courtesy, lucid communication, and accommodation of change requests, but can be unreasonable when "the customer is always right" no matter the situation. If expectations are reasonable and can be accommodated in terms of cost and schedule, we should accommodate them.

Table F.1 Expectation requirements summary

Stakeholder	Requirements	Expectations
Customer/end users	The infrastructure functions flawlessly	The project team ensures that the equipment selected is robust, easy to use, and subjected to all possible quality control activities comprehensively.
	The application software is defect-free	The application software is user friendly with an intuitive user interface and has a built-in context sensitive help facility for guidance. It was subjected to all the possible quality control activities comprehensively.
	Timely delivery	Delivery means all components. It should not be the beginning of deliveries. Delivery should not be delayed by even a day. Training is provided to end users before delivering the infrastructure.
	Professionalism	Be polite. Remember "the customer is always right."
	Customer service	Take our calls on the first ring. Arrive within the hour. Show patience if payments/approvals are delayed and absorb the delays when we ask for changes.
	Customer service	Never escalate issues to higher levels especially those in which we are wrong.
Organizational management	Execute the project successfully	Avoid complaints from customer/end users.
	Deliver on time	Deliver a referable customer and obtain a commendation letter from the customer.
	Control changes	Use price-escalation clause to get the client to pay extra for every change request received from the customer.
	Deliver defect-free deliverables	Test, smartly, infrastructure against stated and unstated requirements. Do not escalate costs with interminable/comprehensive testing for all possible events.

Organizational management (*continued*)	Raise invoices as specified in the work/purchase order	Make sure that you deliver the invoice on the first day allowed for raising invoices and then follow up with the client and obtain payments as quickly as possible.
	Good internal teamwork	Release your resources if they are required in another project or for any other use without complaint and without impacting your project. Spare your time willingly for organization initiatives.
	Be a communicator	Be the channel of communication between management and the project team especially for conveying bad news.
	Be a leader	We can't reward all deserving people so find a way to maintain team morale even though some injustices are inevitable.
Project team	Fair allocation of work	Allocation of work ought to consider my likes and dislikes.
	Fair assessment of work completed	Fairness ought to be tempered with understanding of human frailties and exigencies.
	Fair performance appraisals	Fairness ought to be tilted towards the employee.
	Fair rewards	I should get the reward!
	Fair treatment	We have the right to criticize you but you ought to be restrained in your criticisms. Leaders should never be insensitive.
		Project urgencies and deadlines are usual, but my need for leave is unusual. You should grant me a leave of absence when I require, not when you can spare.
		Your targets/norms are too unrealistically tight.
Subcontractors	Clear specifications	The specifications should be self-explanatory.
	Timely payments	Payment should be released the next day the invoice is submitted.
	Timely approvals	Approvals should not be stretched until the last day of the service-level agreement (SLA).
	Fair quality control	Rework should not be asked.
	Fair treatment	We are also part of the project. We ought to be treated as members of the project team and not as second class citizens.
Supplier	Clear specifications	Specification of a national/international standard is preferable.
	Timely release of payments	Payment should be released before the last day of the SLA.

Which of the above expectations are reasonable and which are not? Unfortunately, there is no standard sieve to sift what is reasonable. Reasonability depends on the circumstances of the project.

My suggestions for handling stakeholder expectations are as follows:

1. Customer or end-user expectations:
   a. Be a professional, show all the courtesies due to a customer/end user. After all, the customer/end user is paying for all the expenses of the project, which include our salaries too. The end user is usually represented by the head of the department whose operational requirements are going to be fulfilled by the infrastructure.
   b. If the customer insists that they are right, when you think otherwise, take their decision in writing and accept their decision. After all, they are left with the baby so to speak when the project is completed!
   c. Ensure that all communications are lucid and timely.
   d. Extend cooperation in all matters including change requests. Come to an understanding with the customer/end user about the impact of the change requests on the project. Create a set of rules to evaluate each change request in order to meet your specific project needs and the organizational culture. Each change request may be innocuous but their cumulative impact may be sizable. An example set of criteria to evaluate change requests is enumerated below:
      i. A change request that consumes less than 8 person-hours would be absorbed without impacting the project schedule or cost. But the cumulative impact of such changes may impact the schedule or cost. So set a limit on the number of such absorbable requests or set a limit on the cumulative effort that would be absorbed.
      ii. For a change request that consumes more than 8 person-hours but less than 24 person-hours, the cost would be absorbed if the schedule impact is acceptable. Again, there should be a limit on the number of such change requests (or on the cumulative effort that would be absorbed) so that the cumulative impact would not affect project profitability.
      iii. For a change request that consumes more than 24 person-hours, both the cost and schedule would be impacted and therefore would be addressed only if additional time and budget were provided.

   e. Put in all efforts to bridge gaps in specifications and then raise issues for clarifications after you have done your homework.
   f. Escalation of issues to higher levels is done only as a last resort. Do not resort to escalation unless absolutely imperative.

2. Organizational management expectations:
   a. Plan for the time needed to support organizational initiatives. Some of the initiatives like recruitment and training benefit the project too. These initiatives can enhance capabilities for everyone in the organization. Develop a second tier in project management that can hold the fort during your short-term (one or two days) absence for attending to organizational initiatives.
   b. Negotiate when required to release resources for other projects and reach win-win solutions.
   c. When price escalations are required, base them on fact and create a set of criteria to guide you in various project circumstances. Meticulous recordkeeping would be of great help in such scenarios.
   d. The project manager is a channel of communication between the management and the project team. Use this channel wisely. Communicate good news as well as bad news. Learning and mastering counseling would be of help especially in conveying bad news. Always add that the future is bright when conveying bad news, portraying the bad news as a temporary setback.
   e. Keep the organizational imperatives in mind when demanding promotions and rewards for you or your team members.

3. Project team expectations:
   a. Allocation of work for team members should take into consideration the personal aspects as well as skill sets. If it becomes necessary, as it happens many times in real life, you may need to allocate work to a team member against his/her liking. Present it in such a way that it is perceived as a challenge or a learning opportunity. Sometimes the right way is to make the request and let the person know that you don't have other choices. It is also good to make it known that for the team to succeed, they need to succeed and take on assignments that need to be completed just like other members of the team.
   b. Negotiate leaves of absence when in a tight spot on project schedules. Get team members to come out with a solution so that the work is not impeded by their absence. They will come out with solutions.

c. Try to ensure that performance appraisals are based on objective criteria and meticulous recordkeeping. Benchmarking between the team members is feasible and should be implemented so that there can be no reasonable objections raised by the team members.

d. Recognize that the team members are junior to you and hence may be less mature than you in the matter of handling criticism, either giving or receiving. If you are fair and competent, the view that you are negatively criticizing an individual can come about only due to a communication gap. Encourage the team to give constructive criticism or inculcate an environment where suggestions replace criticisms. Present criticism as suggestions for improvement and encourage the team to give suggestions for improvement rather than criticism. Criticism should be tempered to state how it could be done better rather than how it was done badly.

e. Involve the team members in target setting and be transparent in setting baselines. This will reduce their resistance to setting tight targets. Regular communication will mitigate resistance when an urgent need arises. Communicate well and regularly.

4. Expectations of the subcontractors:

   a. One of the pet peeves of subcontractors pertains to how they are sometimes treated at the work site. In some cases, subcontractors are not allowed the same common facilities as the project team, making them feel like second-class citizens. Try to treat them as part of the project team and extend to them all the facilities that are enjoyed by the project team.

   b. Accord approvals ASAP. Do not delay them for frivolous reasons.

   c. Payments also should be processed as expeditiously as we demand work from them. It is only reasonable that they be paid on time.

5. Expectations of the suppliers:

   a. Typically, suppliers only complain about inward quality control and unreasonable rejections. When we reject supplies, it should be based on solid reasons and those reasons should be shared with the supplier.

   b. Payment should also be released ASAP and should not be delayed without reason. If we have to delay for reasons beyond our control, communicate it with a profuse apology for the delay.

The best way to manage expectations is to recognize them as early as possible in the project and openly discuss those expectations so they are set correctly.

The second aspect of expectations management is keeping everyone involved and informed in matters concerning them. You might have noticed that in the previous suggestions, communication is the one action that was most frequently mentioned. Excellent communication (defined as providing information that is right for the receiver, timely, and lucid) bridges many gaps and averts many issues. Work diligently on doing your best in the matter of communication. Remember that stakeholders like to know what is happening on the project. They like to have firsthand official and accurate information. Ensuring that you communicate progress is the key to managing expectations of stakeholders.

One communication that is regularly sent out by the PM is the project progress report. It is normally sent every week on Monday or the first workday of the week, if Monday happens to be a holiday. By the time the stakeholders come to their workstations on the first workday of the week, the progress report should be on the table or in their mailbox. This will give stakeholders the necessary information and allow them to plan their activities depending on the progress of the project. It also enables them to make note of their 'to do' items and take the required action. Having them ask for information about the progress of the project and their own action points thereof can be very frustrating. Sometimes it may be unavoidable to delay the report. In such cases, inform the stakeholders that the report is delayed along with the new target date on which it will be received. Not receiving the progress report is bad enough, but not having any information that it will be delayed or when it will be received is like adding salt to the injury.

Similarly for organizational management stakeholders, a regular progress report is a necessity and should follow the same pattern as with customers. It should be noted that the progress report sent to the customer will be slightly different from the progress report sent to our management. We may not like to expose internal issues to the customer. So the progress report to the customer may be a subset of the report made to our management. The progress report to our management will be comprehensive. The progress report to the customer will contain such items that are relevant to the customer.

In short, managing stakeholder expectations can be successfully accomplished by:

1. Recognizing that there are expectations
2. Clear, timely, and the right communications to all stakeholders is the key to handling expectations successfully

3. Meeting and fulfilling all reasonable expectations are a necessary part of project management
4. Setting the right expectations in the case of remaining expectations helps ensure that the stakeholders will not make unreasonable demands

Appendix G

Project Scheduling

Introduction

Scheduling is a very important activity in project management. It is not an exaggeration to say that project planning means just scheduling in quite a few organizations. Those organizations manage their projects based only on the schedule. The schedule is the calendar for the project based on which all the work is carried out. Scheduling, although critical, is only a component of project planning and one of the important tools of the project manager.

Project scheduling in its simplest form of definition is the sequencing and setting of calendar dates for the planned activities to accomplish the goals of the project. Scheduling is deciding the order of execution of project activities as well as deciding which activities can be executed concurrently, in parallel with each other, and which activities need to be executed in sequence, one after the other. It is also determining the type of resources required for performing each of the activities and making a tentative resource allocation to activities. Then all this information is documented in such a way that it can be easily understood and referenced by all stakeholders to carry out their assignments on time. Scheduling is not a routine activity, and good scheduling calls for creativity and human ingenuity. The post-project activities would be planned and scheduled based on the information provided in the schedule.

> *A project schedule is a document that contains the list of all project activities with the corresponding duration, required resources, the starting date, and ending date for each of those activities at a minimum.*

While we might be able to avoid documenting other plans, the project schedule is one document that cannot be left undocumented. When scheduling a project, we have to understand the following:

1. The project consists of a number of activities (tasks), the performance of which would result in completion of the project.
2. The activities consume resources, namely, personnel, material and equipment, money, and time (duration).
3. The project has a number of "milestones," the reaching of which signifies completion of a certain group of activities as well as achieving recognizable project progress.
4. The project has a starting point, a "start" milestone, which is the first milestone. All other project activities or milestones would be its successors.
5. The project has an ending point, an "end" milestone, which is the project's last milestone. No other project activity or milestone would be its successor.
6. All other activities and milestones of the project have to be performed between the start and end milestones.
7. Some of these activities can be performed concurrently (in parallel) with each other.
8. Some of these activities need to be performed in sequence (one after the other).
9. Some activities can use multiple resources and some cannot.
10. We can allocate more resources to an activity in order to reduce the duration for its completion, but there is always a limit to the number of resources we can deploy for any given activity.

A list of all activities (tasks) and milestones needed to execute and complete the project is commonly known as the work breakdown structure (WBS). The first item in the WBS, as stated previously, is the "start" milestone signifying the project start and the last one is the "end" milestone signifying the completion of the project. The remaining activities of the project are embedded between these two milestones.

Let us now see how to perform scheduling with an example project. The example is composed of an abbreviated list of activities and fictitious effort values.

Initial Work Breakdown Structure

The first step in scheduling a project is the preparation of the WBS. It contains the list of tasks that are to be performed in order to execute the project. Table G.1 depicts a brief initial WBS for an IT infrastructure project. All

Table G.1 Initial WBS

Task ID	Task description	Effort in person-days
1	Start	0
2	Feasibility study	2
3	Project planning	5
4	Sizing	10
5	Procurement	4
6	Facility construction	12
7	Development of application software	15
8	Network cabling	12
9	Installation of networking hardware	10
10	Installation of servers	6
11	Installation of workstations	5
12	Installation of system software	3
13	Installation of application software	3
14	Testing of infrastructure	2
15	User documentation	5
16	User training	3
17	Pilot runs	10
18	Changeover to production	2
19	Handover and sign-off	1
20	End	0

activities are embedded between the "start" and the "end" milestones. Please note that the effort required for performing each of the activities is shown only for illustrative purposes and is not based on the actual values.

Work Breakdown Structure with Predecessors Defined

Of course, a real-life project would have many more activities. Having prepared the initial WBS, the next step is to determine the sequence of execution of the tasks listed in it. We achieve this by adding another column to Table G.1, captioned "Predecessor," as shown in Table G.2. Some organizations use both predecessors (the activities that need to be completed before starting the current activity) and successors (what comes next) to define the sequence. Excluding the "Start" milestone, the rest of the project activities should have at least one or more predecessors.

Table G.2 WBS with predecessors

Task ID	Task description	Effort in person-days	Predecessor
1	Start	0	
2	Feasibility study	2	1
3	Project planning	5	2
4	Sizing	10	3
5	Procurement	4	4
6	Facility construction	12	5
7	Development of application software	15	5
8	Network cabling	12	5,6
9	Installation of networking hardware	10	5,6
10	Installation of servers	6	5,6
11	Installation of workstations	5	5,6
12	Installation of system software	3	10,11
13	Installation of application software	3	7,10,11
14	Testing of infrastructure	2	8,9,12,13
15	User documentation	5	7
16	User training	3	15
17	Pilot runs	10	14, 16
18	Changeover to production	2	17
19	Handover and sign-off	1	18
20	End	0	19

Defining predecessors is a process of considering each activity and answering the question, "what activities should have been completed in order to begin this activity?" The answer would be recorded in the predecessor column. The predecessor indicates the activity that needs to be completed in order to begin this activity. The scheduler would walk through the WBS iterating the process of asking and answering the question for each activity. It becomes easier if we begin at the end milestone and move backward to the start milestone. The process ensures that predecessors are identified and recorded for all activities. It is possible that some activities have only one predecessor and some may have multiple predecessor activities.

Looking at Table G.2, we can see the definition of predecessor for each task. A successor is the next task that gets executed upon completion of the present task. The end milestone by definition has no successors.

For Task 2, the predecessor is Task 1 and the successor is Task 3 (Task 2 is mentioned as the predecessor for Task 3). For Task 5, the predecessor is Task

4, and the successors are Tasks 6 to 11. Notice that Task 5 is a predecessor for six tasks. That is, six tasks can start upon completing Task 5. In the example, Task 14 has four predecessors; Task 14 cannot start until all four tasks are completed (graphically this would be shown as a web converging to a single point). A task can have multiple predecessors as well as multiple successors. You can map predecessors and successors for each task typically shown in a Gantt chart or a network diagram. These will be depicted later in the *Graphic Representation of Schedule* section of this appendix. Every task must have one or more predecessors and one or more successors. As pointed out previously, the exceptions are the start milestone, which would not have any predecessor, and the end milestone, which would not have any successor. There can be multiple tasks as successor to the start milestone. Similarly, the end milestone can have multiple predecessors. We can have additional milestones in the schedule and the network diagram to enhance the clarity of the schedule. There is no limit to the number of milestones that can be inserted between the start and end milestones if they enhance the schedule's clarity and understanding.

In our example, analysis of the schedule raises questions about the predecessor relationships. The question is "should the successor wait until its predecessor is completed? Can it not be started some time after starting its predecessor activity?" Yes, it is possible in some cases. There are actually four types of precedence relationships in scheduling.

Look at Tasks 2 and 3 in Table G.2. Task 3 (Project planning) cannot be started unless Task 2 (Feasibility study) is completed. This relationship is called a *finish-to-start relationship.* Task 2 must be finished before Task 3 can be started.

Task 14 (Testing of infrastructure) can start once any one of Tasks 8, 9, 12, and 13 is completed, and can continue as other tasks are completed. Therefore, there is a finish-to-start relationship between Tasks 8, 9, 12, 13 and Task 14. In our example, Task 14 can start when any one of Tasks 8, 9, 12, and 13 is finished but cannot be completed until all Tasks 8, 9, 12, and 13 are completed. The relationship between Task 14 and Tasks 8, 9, 12, and 13 is called a *finish-to-finish relationship*.

Now look at Tasks 12 (Installation of system software) and 10 and 11 (Installation of servers and Installation of workstations). Should Task 12 wait until all the servers and workstations are installed? It can, but it is not necessary. When a server or workstation is installed, its system software can be installed. The relationship between Task 12 and Tasks 10 and 11 is a called a *start-to-start relationship.* Task 12 can be started after starting either of Tasks 10 and 11 with a time lag that is necessary between the installation of the machine and the installation of its system software. Task 12 can be completed only after Tasks 10 and 11 are completed.

There is one more relationship that we need to define to account for all possible relationships, which is the *start-to-finish relationship.* In this type of relationship, a task "n" must be started in order to finish task "m." This type of relationship is not typical in IT projects and is mentioned only for the sake of completeness.

Summarizing, there are four types of precedence relationships:

1. Finish (predecessor)-to-start (successor) or FS-n (with "n" being the hours/days the successor has to wait after finishing the predecessor; if "n" is not mentioned, that means n = 0): In scheduling this is the default relationship. If no relationship is mentioned, we can assume that the relationship is FS.
2. Start (predecessor)-to-start (successor) or SS-n (with "n" being the hours/days the successor has to wait after starting the predecessor; if "n" is not mentioned, that means n = 0).
3. Finish (predecessor)-to-finish (successor) or FF-n (with "n" being the hours/days the successor has to wait after finishing the predecessor; if "n" is not mentioned, that means n = 0).
4. Start (successor)-to-finish (predecessor) or SF-n (with "n" being the hours/days the successor has to wait after starting the predecessor to finish the successor; if "n" is not mentioned, that means n = 0).

For each of these relationships, we can specify a time *lag* (waiting time) before the successor can be started/finished. Here are some examples:

1. Task 3 can be started one day after finishing Task 2. This is depicted as **FS-1**, "the relationship of Task 3 to its predecessor, Task 2, is finish-to-start with a time lag of one day."
2. Task 12 can be started after two days of starting Task 11. This is depicted as **SS-2**, "the relationship of Task 12 to Task 11 is start-to-start with a time lag of two days."

Work Breakdown Structure with Initial Dates

Now that we have completed the second step towards preparing our WBS by defining the predecessors, the precedence relationships, and ensuring that all the tasks have predecessors and successors, we are ready to start assigning dates to the tasks. This is depicted in Table G.3.

Note the following from the schedule:

1. The start date for the "Start" milestone is the project starting date.
2. The end date for the "End" milestone is the project completion date.

Table G.3 WBS with initial dates

Task ID	Task description	Effort in person-days	Predecessor	Start date	Finish date
1	Start	0		3-Apr-12	3-Apr-12
2	Feasibility study	2	1	3-Apr-12	4-Apr-12
3	Project planning	5	2	5-Apr-12	11-Apr-12
4	Sizing	10	3	12-Apr-12	25-Apr-12
5	Procurement	4	4	26-Apr-12	1-May-12
6	Facility construction	12	5	2-May-12	17-May-12
7	Development of application software	15	5	2-May-12	22-May-12
8	Network cabling	12	5,6	18-May-12	4-Jun-12
9	Installation of networking hardware	10	5,6	18-May-12	31-May-12
10	Installation of servers	6	5,6	18-May-12	25-May-12
11	Installation of workstations	5	5,6	18-May-12	24-May-12
12	Installation of system software	3	10(SS-1),11(SS-2)	21-May-12	28-May-12
13	Installation of application software	3	7,10,11	28-May-12	30-May-12
14	Testing of infrastructure	2	8 (FF-2), 9(FF-3), 12(FF-4),13 (FF-6)	29-May-12	7-Jun-12
15	User documentation	5	7	23-May-12	29-May-12
16	User training	3	15	30-May-12	1-Jun-12
17	Pilot runs	10	14,16	8-Jun-12	21-Jun-12
18	Changeover to production	2	17	22-Jun-12	25-Jun-12
19	Handover and sign-off	1	18	26-Jun-12	26-Jun-12
20	End	0	19	26-Jun-12	26-Jun-12

3. Weekends (Saturday and Sunday) have not been counted as working days. We need to exclude holidays also.
4. Notice that Task 3 is starting on April 5, while Task 2 is completed on April 4—the day before. Why so? Because when somebody says that the task will be completed on April 4, it typically means that it will be completed by the end of the working day on April 4. Therefore, the successor could only start the next day.

5. Task 14 (four predecessors) starts on May 29, the day after the finish of Task 12. Task 14 has an FF (finish-to-finish) relationship with Tasks 8, 9, 12, and 13. Task 8 finishes on June 4, Task 9 finishes on May 31, Task 12 finishes on May 28, and Task 13 finishes on May 30. The first one to finish is Task 12. Task 14 can start only after the completion of Task 12. In this case, if two or more tasks finish on the same day, the one with the shortest time lag would determine the day on which the successor can start.
6. Since Task 14 has an FF relationship with Tasks 8, 9, 12, and 13, its finish date is dependent on the task that takes the most time considering the time value associated with it. Thus, the finish time of Task 14 is June 6 considering Task 8; June 5 considering Task 9; June 4 considering Task 12; and June 7 considering Task 13. Here we have to take the greater of all the values and that is June 7.
7. Notice that no precedence relationship is mentioned for many tasks. When no relationship is explicitly mentioned, it is an FS-0 (finish-to-start) relationship with no time lag. Task 17 has two predecessors—Task 14 (completes on June 15) and Task 16 (completes on June 20). Therefore, Task 17 can start one day after Task 16, which completes last in its predecessors.

From these explanations we can draw the following inferences for future use:

1. The start date of an activity depends on its relationship with its predecessors:
   a. In a finish-to-start relationship with its predecessors, the start date depends on the predecessor that finishes last.
   b. In a start-to-start relationship, the start date depends on the predecessor that starts first and has the shortest time lag. If two or more predecessors start on the same day, we need to select the predecessor that has the shortest time lag for determining the start date of the successor. The time lag in this type of relationship is to constrain the start of the successor activity.
   c. In a finish-to-finish relationship, the successor starts after the activity that completes earliest of all its predecessors. It can finish after the predecessor activity that finishes last. The lag in this relationship is to constrain the completion of the activity.
2. The end date of an activity depends both on its duration and on the relationship with its predecessors:
   a. In a finish-to-finish relationship, the end date depends on its predecessor finishing last.
   b. In other relationships, the determination of the end date is achieved by adding the duration to the start date of the activity.

Work Breakdown Structure with Resource Allocation

In Table G.3, the term "Effort" is used synonymously with duration. This allows us, for the sake of illustration, to assume that only one resource is allocated to the project. In most real-life projects, multiple resources are allocated to the project activities. Naturally, the number of resources allocated will determine the duration of the activity. As an example, let's assume that network cabling takes 10 person-days to complete. If one technician is allocated to the task, the duration would be 10 working days, and if two technicians are allocated, the duration would be 5 working days, assuming that all technicians possess similar skill level and put in comparable effort on the job. Please note that the effort is measured in "person-days/hours" and the duration is measured in "calendar days/clock hours." Therefore, we need to add a resource column to Table G.3 and adjust the duration to get a realistic schedule.

Take a look at Table G.4. Notice that the duration (effort/number of resources) is now adjusted for each task taking into consideration the number of resources allocated for each task. Duration depends on the effort in person-days and the number of resources allocated for the activity. The dates in the schedule are recomputed based on the revised duration and precedence relationships. Table G.4 now reflects all of the components needed for a usable schedule. This schedule can be used by the stakeholders. (Figure G.1 is a graphic representation of a sample WBS.)

Scheduling in Practice

In practice, we do not have to iterate so many times. We take advantage of tools such as spreadsheets like MS Excel and fill in the information, column by column. We can take advantage of Excel's capability for date arithmetic for assigning dates to tasks. Specialized software tools such as Primavera, MS Project, and PMPal can assist in scheduling and they take care of weekends and holidays too, while assigning dates to tasks. Most organizations use one of these tools for scheduling projects.

Using an automated spreadsheet or specialized scheduling software makes scheduling and rescheduling easier. When we shift the project start date or change the duration or dates for any of the tasks, the tool automatically recomputes all subsequent dates and provides the new schedule instantaneously.

One other aspect to be noted is that scheduling and the techniques of PERT/CPM (program evaluation and review technique/critical path method) are closely linked. PERT/CPM are techniques to aid the scheduling of the project. Knowledge of PERT/CPM is essential to produce a credible schedule. Appendix D provides an introduction to the techniques of PERT/CPM.

Table G.4 WBS with resource allocation

Task ID	Task description	Effort in person-days	Resources allocated	Duration	Predecessor	Start date	Finish date
1	Start	0	0	0		3-Apr-12	3-Apr-12
2	Feasibility study	2	1	2	1	3-Apr-12	4-Apr-12
3	Project planning	5	1	5	2	5-Apr-12	11-Apr-12
4	Sizing	10	2	5	3	12-Apr-12	18-Apr-12
5	Procurement	4	1	4	4	19-Apr-12	24-Apr-12
6	Facility construction	12	4	3	5	25-Apr-12	27-Apr-12
7	Development of application software	15	3	5	5	25-Apr-12	1-May-12
8	Network cabling	12	4	3	5,6	30-Apr-12	2-May-12
9	Installation of networking hardware	10	2	5	5,6	30-Apr-12	4-May-12
10	Installation of servers	6	3	2	5,6	30-Apr-12	1-May-12
11	Installation of workstations	5	1	5	5,6	30-Apr-12	4-May-12
12	Installation of system software	3	1	3	10(SS-1), 11(SS-2)	1-May-12	7-May-12
13	Installation of application software	3	1	3	7,10,11	7-May-12	9-May-12
14	Testing of infrastructure	2	1	2	8 (FF-2), 9(FF-3), 12(FF-4), 13 (FF-6)	3-May-12	17-May-12
15	User documentation	5	1	5	7	2-May-12	8-May-12
16	User training	3	1	3	15	9-May-12	11-May-12
17	Pilot runs	10	2	5	14,16	18-May-12	24-May-12
18	Changeover to production	2	1	2	17	25-May-12	28-May-12
19	Handover and sign-off	1	1	1	18	29-May-12	29-May-12
20	End	0	0	0	19	29-May-12	29-May-12

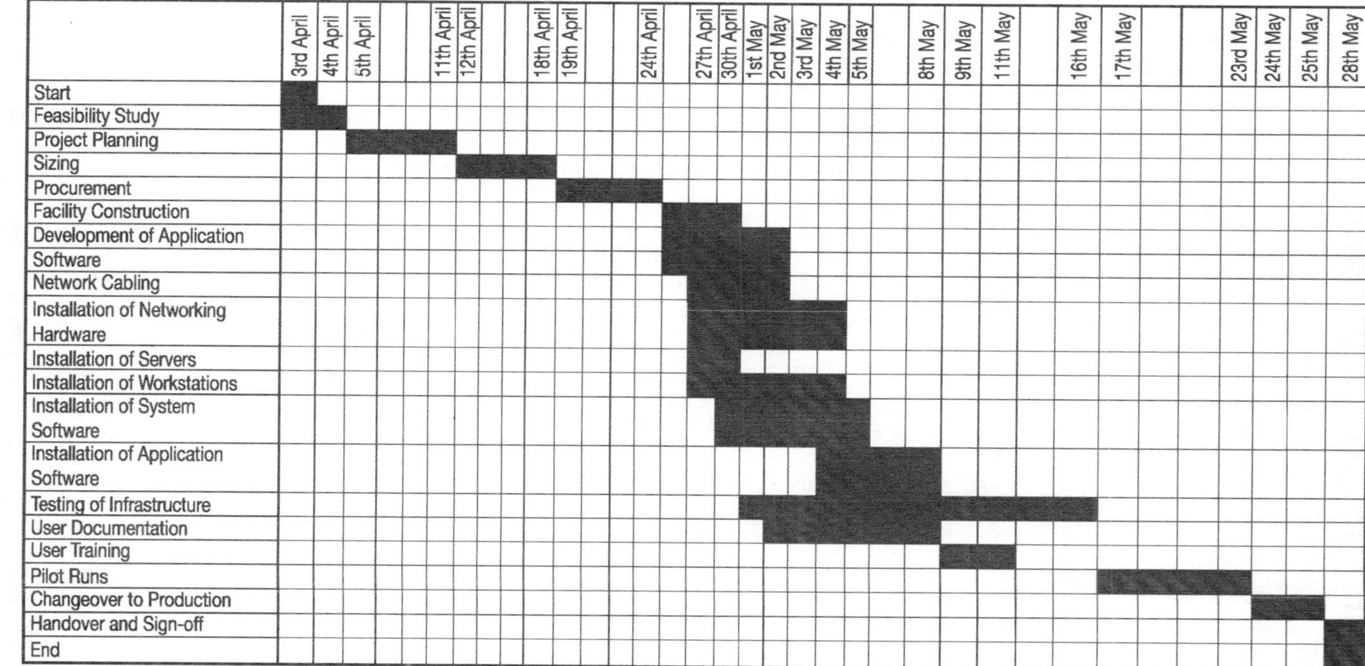

Figure G.1 Bar chart for sample WBS

Graphic Representation of Schedule

Two popular ways of graphic representation are:

1. Bar charts (also called Gantt charts because they were originally developed by Henry L. Gantt)
2. Network diagrams

A bar chart, as shown in Figure G.1, can be produced using MS Excel spreadsheets or scheduling packages like Primavera and MS Project.

Figure G.2 is a network diagram depicting a WBS developed earlier in this appendix. For the sake of brevity, only the task numbers are given in the network diagram. There are various forms of network diagrams. In Figure G.2, the task is depicted in the circle. In more traditional network diagrams, the task is depicted on the arrow of the network, and the circle depicts the milestone. In the form of network diagrams currently being used in the IT industry, the arrow represents only a precedence relationship.

The most frequently used depiction of an activity in the scheduling tools is shown in Figure G.3. It is rectangular in shape and divided into seven sections. Variations of this type of representation are found in different scheduling software tools. Scheduling can be carried out effectively using such software packages as MS Project, Primavera, and others.

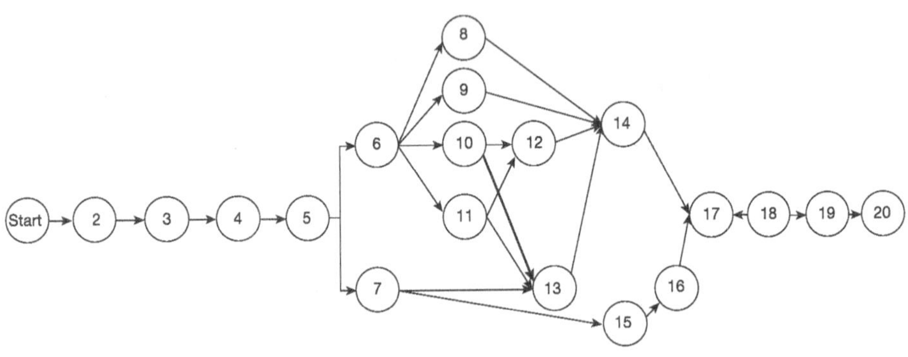

Figure G.2 Network diagram of a WBS

Early Start	Duration	Early Finish
	Task Name	
Late Start	Slack	Late Finish

Figure G.3 Network node

Appendix H

Abbreviations

AC	Alternating current
ACWP	Actual cost of work performed
AON	Activity on node
ASCII	American Standard Coding for Information Interchange
BCWP	Budgeted cost of work performed
BCWS	Budgeted cost of work scheduled
BI	Business intelligence
BPM	Business process management
BPO	Business process outsourcing
BTU	British thermal unit
CADD	Computer aided design and drafting
CAT	Computerized axial tomography
CCB	Configuration control board
CD	Compact disk
CEO	Chief executive officer
CIO	Chief information officer
CMMI	Capability Maturity Model Integration
COTS	Commercial off-the-shelf
CPI	Cost performance index
CPM	Critical path method
CPU	Central processing unit
CRT	Cathode ray tube
CSMA/CD	Carrier sense multiple access/collision detection
CV	Cost variance
DBMS	Database management system
DCF	Discounted cash flow
DLL	Dynamic-link library
DMA	Dynamic memory access
DPI	Dots per inch
DSL	Digital subscriber line
EAI	Enterprise architecture integration
EBCDIC	Extended Binary Coded Decimal Interchange Code
ECG	Electrocardiograph
EDP	Electronic Data Processing
EEG	Electroencephalograph
ENIAC	Electronic numerical integrator and calculator
EVA	Earned Value Analysis
GB	Gigabyte
HR	Human resources
HTML	Hyper Text Markup Language
I/O	Input/output
IP	Internet Protocol
IRR	Internal rate of return

IS	Information systems
ISO	International Organization for Standardization
ISP	Internet service provider
IT	Information technology
ITPM	Information technology project management
LCD	Liquid crystal display
LOC	Lines of code
LP	Linear programming
MBPS	Megabits per second
MRI	Magnetic Resonance Imaging
NC	Non-conformance
NCR	Non-conformance report
NPV	Net present value
OS	Operating system
PC	Personal computer
PCB	Printed circuit board
PERT	Program Evaluation and Review Technique
PM	Project manager
PMO	Project management office
PSU	Project size unit
QA	Quality assurance
QC	Quality control
RAM	Random access memory
RDBMS	Relational database management system
RFP	Request for proposal
ROI	Return on investment
SEI	Software Engineering Institute
SLA	Service-level agreement
SOP	Standard operating procedure/policy
SPI	Schedule performance index
SQL	Structured query language
SSU	Software size unit
SV	Schedule variance
TB	Terabyte
TP	Transaction processing
UK	United Kingdom
UPS	Uninterrupted power supply
USA	United States of America
USB	Universal Serial Bus
WBS	Work breakdown structure

Appendix I

Templates for IT Project Management

I felt that including multipage templates in the text of the chapters would hinder the flow of the material. Therefore, I provided a brief outline of the template elements within the corresponding book chapters. For the reader's convenience, templates were displayed as smaller figures to facilitate discussion of the material. These figures were numbered to correspond with the completed template exhibits presented within this appendix. Figure 3.1 displayed in Chapter 3, for example, corresponds with Exhibit 3.1 and so forth.

Exhibit 3.1	Template for establishing the information-processing needs
Exhibit 3.2	Template for a feasibility report
Exhibit 5.1	Template for a deployment plan document
Exhibit 5.2	Template for a software development plan document
Exhibit 5.3	Template for an installation and commissioning plan
Exhibit 5.4	Template for a quality assurance plan
Exhibit 5.5	Template for a procurement plan
Exhibit 5.6	Template for a risk management plan
Exhibit 5.7	Template for a software maintenance plan
Exhibit 6.1	Template for a handover/takeover format
Exhibit 7.1	Template for a progress report for sub-projects
Exhibit 7.2	Template for an IT project progress report
Exhibit 7.3	Template for recording the minutes of a progress review meeting
Exhibit 8.1	Template for a cash flow statement
Exhibit 9.4	Template for a review/inspection report
Exhibit C.1	Template for a sample resource request form

Information processing needs

Compiled by: Date:

1. Name of the department	
2. Name of the business process	
3. Performed by	
4. Information collected from	
5. Input data received per transaction	
6. Overhead for control data	
7. Total data volume per transaction (sum of rows 5 & 6)	
8. Expected number of transactions per day	
9. Total data volume per day (row 7 multiplied by 8)	

Brief description of the business process:

List the possible days for peak loads:

1.
2.
3.

Period for which the transaction data needs to be online:

Period for which the transaction data needs to be stored offline:

Any other relevant information:

Exhibit 3.1 Template for establishing information-processing needs

<Title page>

Feasibility report

For *<Project ID>*

Revision history:

Date	**Version number**	**Record of changes**	**Prepared by**	**Approved by**

<End of title page>

<Table of contents page>

<Insert table of contents>

<Content pages>

1. Scope of the project.
2. The goals set for the proposed project.
3. Information processing needs to be fulfilled by the project.
4. Deliverables from the proposed infrastructure.
5. Proposed IT infrastructure:
   a. Servers
   b. Workstations
   c. Networking hardware
   d. Networking accessories
   e. System software
   f. RDBMS
   g. Middleware
   h. Webserver
   i. Application software:
6. Proposed support equipment:
   a. Floor space requirement
   b. Electrical power equipment
7. Organizational structure for managing the proposed infrastructure.
8. Security arrangements for the proposed infrastructure:
   a. Physical access security arrangement
   b. Protection against malware (viruses, spyware, adware etc.)
   c. Firewalls
9. Cost estimate for the proposed IT infrastructure (attach a detailed estimate to the report)

Item	Estimated cost—minimum	Estimated cost—maximum
Hardware		
System software		
RDBMS		
Webserver		
App server		
Application software		
Security software		
Administration utilities		
Electrical equipment		
Networking equipment and cabling		
Floor space		
Any other cost		
Contingency/cost escalation allowance		
Total cost		

10. Annual maintenance cost for the proposed infrastructure

Item	Estimated cost—minimum	Estimated cost—maximum
Hardware		
System software		
RDBMS		
Webserver		
App server		
Application software		
Security software		
Administration utilities		
Electrical equipment		
Networking equipment and cabling		
Floor space		
Any other cost		
Contingency/cost escalation allowance		
Total cost		

11. Operational costs for running the proposed infrastructure (attach estimation sheets to the report)

Item	Estimated cost—minimum	Estimated cost—maximum
Salaries		
Power		
Telephones		
Bandwidth for Internet access		
Consumables like paper, ribbons, cartridges, backup media, etc.		
Miscellaneous expenses		
Total cost		

12. Suggested upgrade path and replacement criteria
13. Project management strategy:
    a. Activities that can be outsourced
    b. Activities that are recommended to be performed in-house

Appendices

1. Attach all the information compiled from various sources (primary as well as secondary)
2. Attach/Include the analysis sheets for analyzing the compiled information for deriving the information processing needs of the organization

Exhibit 3.2 Template for a feasibility report

<Title page>

Deployment plan

For *<Project ID>*

Revision history:

Date of release	Release details/revisions	Prepared by	Approved by

<End of *title page*>

Table of contents page

<Insert table of contents>

1. Introduction *<Include a brief overview of the project, its scope, abbreviations, etc.>*
2. References *<Enumerate the list of documents referred. Include the work order, organizational process, standards, guidelines, templates, feasibility report, floor plan, etc.>*
3. Hardware deployment drawing here *<Either include the drawing or give reference to it here.>*
4. Bill of material *<Include the BOM here or give reference to it.>*
5. Schedule *<Include the schedule here or give its reference to it.>*
6. Quality control activities:
   a. Inspections *<Enumerate the proposed inspections and their timing here.>*
   b. Testing *<Include the types of testing proposed as well as references to the test plans and test cases here.>*
7. Handover plan *<Include the people to take over the facility, artifacts to be handed over, references to signoffs, etc. here.>*
8. Waivers *<Enumerate the waivers obtained from an organizational process, if any here.>*

Software deployment plan

Machine	Details of software including OS

Exhibit 5.1 Template for deployment plan document

<Title page>

Software development plan

For <*Project ID*>

Revision history:

Date of release	Release details/revisions	Prepared by	Approved by

<End of *title page*>

Table of contents page

<Insert table of contents>

1. Introduction *<Include a brief overview of the project, its scope, abbreviations, etc.>*
2. References *<Enumerate the list of documents referred. Include the work order, organizational process, standards, guidelines, templates, feasibility report, floor plan, etc.>*
3. Strategy for acquiring the application software *<Describe the strategy proposed for acquiring the application software for the project. This information should be available in the feasibility report.>*
4. Implementation strategy *<Describe the proposed strategy for implementing the software. This information also should be available in the feasibility report.>*
5. Software development life cycle *<Enumerate the software development life cycle selected for (a) the development of fresh software (b) the customization of COTS product, if selected.>*
6. Quality assurance for the software *<Enumerate the proposed quality assurance for the software.>*

Activity	**Proposed quality control activities**
URS	Peer review, end user review, and managerial review
SRS	Peer review, end user review, and managerial review
Software design	Peer review, expert review, and managerial review
Database design	Peer review and unit testing of table scripts
Coding and construction	Peer review, unit testing, and integration testing
Software testing	System testing, load testing, and concurrent testing
Any other activity	As necessary

7. Standards <*Enumerate the standards for coding, software design, database design, testing, formats and templates, and checklists*>

Activity	**Selected standard**
Software design	
Database design	
Coding and construction	
Software testing	
Any other activity	

8. Software maintenance <*Describe the proposed software maintenance strategy. If it is proposed to be outsourced, include the actions planned for outsourcing the work and if proposed to be handled in-house, enumerate the actions planned for effectively handling the activity. Alternatively, give reference to a software maintenance plan if a separate document is available.*>
9. Staffing <*Describe the staffing strategy either for outsourced development and maintenance, or in-house development and maintenance, or a combination of in-house and outsourced development and maintenance.*>
10. Change management <*Describe the actions planned for handling mid-project changes.*>
11. Delivery <*Enumerate all the deliveries planned including their scheduled dates.*>

Delivery	**Deliverables**	**Scheduled date**
Delivery 1		
Delivery 2		
Delivery 3		
Delivery 4		
Delivery 5		

12. Implementation <*Describe the actions planned for implementing each of the deliveries.*>

Delivery	**Actions planned**
Delivery 1	
Delivery 2	
Delivery 3	
Delivery 4	
Delivery 5	

13. Roles and responsibilities *<Describe the roles and responsibilities of all the stakeholders in the project.>*

Role	**Responsibilities**
IT Project Manager	
Software Project Manager	
Quality Assurance	
Configuration Control Board	
Software Project Leader	
Software Project Team—In-house	
Sub-contractor	
Software Project Team—Sub-contractor	
Any other role	

14. Managerial methods, tools, and techniques *<Describe the methodology of managing the project as well as the tools and techniques proposed for use in the project.>*

Activity	**Methods, tools, and techniques**
Work management	
Configuration management	
Quality management	
Productivity management	
Progress monitoring	
Integration management	
Measurement and metrics	

15. Communication *<Describe the communication mechanisms tools and techniques proposed for use in the project.>*

Communication mechanism	**Occasions for utilization**
E-mail	
Phone calls	
Tele/Video conferences	
In-person meetings	
Faxes	
Personal visits	

16. Issue resolution *<Describe the mechanisms to be followed for resolving issues as they arise, including the tools and techniques proposed for issue resolution in the project.>*
17. Escalation *<Describe the escalation mechanism for resolving disputes when they arise.>*
18. Risk management *<Describe the risk management activities proposed for the project. Please give a reference if a separate risk management plan is prepared.>*

Exhibit 5.2 Template for a software development plan document

<Title page>

Installation and commissioning plan

For *<Project ID>*

Revision history:

Date of release	Release details/revisions	Prepared by	Approved by

<End of *title page*>

Table of contents page

<Insert table of contents>

1. Introduction *<Include a brief overview of the project, its scope, abbreviations, etc.>*
2. References *<Enumerate the list of documents referred. Include the work order, organizational process, standards, guidelines, templates, feasibility report, floor plan, etc.>*

Note: Items 3 through 15 must be replicated for all the proposed iterations.

3. Facilities *<Enumerate the facilities covered by this iteration here.>*
4. Hardware details *<Enumerate the hardware items, including the servers, workstations, and networking equipment along with their system software here.>*
5. Software details *<Enumerate the details of the application software that is scheduled to be delivered for this iteration of installation and commissioning.>*
6. Installation team *<Enumerate the team members responsible for this iteration.>*
7. Roles and responsibilities *<Enumerate the roles and responsibilities pertaining to this iteration.>*

Role	Responsibilities
IT Project Manager	
Software Project Manager	
Quality Assurance	
Configuration Control Board	
Software Project Leader	
Software Project Team—In-house	
Sub-contractor	
Software Project Team—Sub-contractor	
Any other role	

8. Installation procedures *<Describe the procedures applicable to this iteration of installation and commissioning. You may give references to organizational procedures if they are being used.>*
9. Quality control *<Enumerate the quality control activities proposed for this iteration.>*

10. User training <*Describe the training proposed for end users including course titles, faculty, facilities, and schedules for conducting the training.*>
11. Piloting plan <*Describe the activities for running the installation on a pilot basis, fixing any uncovered defects and criteria for determining the installation's readiness for cutover.*>
12. Cutover plan <*Describe the activities for cutover of the installation to production use, including the master data preparation, handholding, in-process inspection, etc.*>
13. Handover plan <*Describe all activities proposed to handover the installation including the people designated to takeover, schedule of takeover, documents to be signed, etc.*>
14. Schedule <*Enumerate the schedule of this iteration or give a reference to the sched-*

Exhibit 5.3 Template for an installation and commissioning plan

<Title page>

Quality assurance plan

For *<Project ID>*

Revision history:

Date of release	Release details/revisions	Prepared by	Approved by

<End of *title page*>

Table of contents page

<Insert table of contents>

1. Introduction *<Include a brief overview of the project, its scope, abbreviations, etc.>*
2. References *<Enumerate the list of documents referred. Include the organizational process, procedures, standards, guidelines, formats and templates, and any other relevant documents here.>*
3. Quality objectives for the project *<Enumerate all the quality objectives set for the project. They may include defect density, reliability, cost of quality, response times, load-bearing capability, concurrency control, etc.>*
4. Quality control activities:

Artifact/Activity	Proposed QC activities
Procured hardware	Inward testing to ensure that they are free from defects and conform to their specifications
Procured COTS product for application or other software	Acceptance testing
Application software developed in-house	All quality assurance activities set out in the software project's software quality assurance plan
Application software—outsourced development	Specification of quality assurance activities in the purchase order; verification of quality records; and acceptance testing
Networking	Connectivity, load, and speed testing
Server room deployment	Inspection of equipment for conformance with the deployment plan
Installation of system software on all computers	Cursory inspection; configuration tool testing
Master data preparation	Inspection of quality records; sample testing
System readiness	Beta testing
Any other project specific activity	As necessary

5. Audits <*Enumerate the proposed audits including conformance audits and investigative audits for the project.*>
6. Defect resolution <*Include the procedure, formats, templates, tools, reporting, and escalation etc. prescribed for defect resolution.*>
7. Metrics and measurement <*Enumerate the measurements to be carried out, their periodicity, and the metrics to be derived for ascertaining the quality achieved in the project here.*>
8. Waivers <*Enumerate the waivers obtained from organizational process, if any, here.*>

Exhibit 5.4 Template for a quality assurance plan

<Title page>

Procurement plan

For *<Project ID>*

Revision history:

Date of release	Release details/revisions	Prepared by	Approved by

<End of *title page*>

Table of contents page

<Insert table of contents on this page>

1. Introduction *<Include a brief overview of the project, its scope, abbreviations, etc.>*
2. References *<Enumerate the list of documents referred. Include the work order, organizational process, standards, guidelines, templates, feasibility report, etc.>*
3. List of items decided for procurement *<Enumerate the items or give reference to the BOM.>*

Item description	Required by date

4. Schedule *<Include the schedule of procurement here or give reference to it.>*
5. Waivers *<Enumerate the waivers obtained from organizational process, if any, here.>*

Exhibit 5.5 Template for a procurement plan

Risk ID	Risk description	Risk probability	Risk damage ($)	Risk value ($)	Risk priority	Mitigation actions
IT01	Delayed supply of servers	10%	200	20	3	Regular follow up to ensure on-time supply
IT02	Delayed supply of work stations	5%	100	5	4	Regular follow up to ensure on-time supply
IT03	Delay in network cabling	25%	200	50	2	1) Regular follow up to ensure on-time supply 2) Connect in phases
IT04	Delay in development of application software	30%	1000	300	1	1) Careful planning 2) Regular follow up 3) Iterative development
IT05	Some more risks					

Exhibit 5.6 Template for a risk management plan

<*Title page*>

Software maintenance plan

For <*Project ID*>

Revision history:

Date of release	Release details/revisions	Prepared by	Approved by

<End of *title page*>

Table of contents page

<*Insert table of contents*>

1. Introduction <*Include a brief overview of the project, its scope, abbreviations, etc.*>
2. References <*Enumerate the list of documents referred. Include the work order, organizational process, standards, guidelines, templates, feasibility report, floor plan, etc.*>
3. Strategy for software maintenance <*Describe the strategy decided for carrying out application software maintenance.*>
4. Software maintenance team <*Enumerate the desired skills for the maintenance team.*>
5. Initial training plan <*Include the topics necessary to ramp up the software maintenance team during handover of code to the maintenance team.*>

Training program	Topics	Desired faculty	Possible date
Functionality training	Module-wise software functionality	Development Team—PM	
Software design	Architecture and design of the application software developed	Development team—architect	
Standards and guidelines	Guidelines proposed for the software maintenance project	Organizational process group	
Software quality control	Quality control activities proposed for the maintenance project	Organizational quality group	
Software metrics	Measurement and metrics proposed for the maintenance project	Organizational metrics group	
Any other topic relevant to the organization			

6. Induction training plan <*Include the topics necessary to induct a new resource to the maintenance team after the software is under maintenance.*>

Training Program	Topics	Desired Faculty	Mode of training
Functionality training	Module-wise software functionality	PM of the maintenance team	
Software design	Architecture and design of the application software developed	PM of the maintenance team	
Standards and guidelines	Guidelines proposed for the software maintenance project		Self-study
Software quality	Quality control activities proposed for the maintenance project		Self-study
Any other topic relevant to the organization			

7. Metrics to be collected and analyzed:

Metric	Person responsible	Periodicity
Average time to fix defects	PM	Monthly
Maximum time taken to fix a defect	PM	Monthly
Minimum time taken to fix a defect	PM	Monthly
MTBF (mean time between failures)	PM	Monthly
Uptime of software	PM	Monthly
Cost per defect	PM	Monthly
Any other metric		

Exhibit 5.7 Template for a software maintenance plan

IT Infrastructure handover format

Date of handover:

Handed over by:

Taken over by:

Asset ID	Asset description	Location	Remarks

All the above enumerated assets are verified by me and are in working condition.

Signed:
Name of the person taking over the assets:
Date:

Exhibit 6.1 Template for a handover/takeover format

Progress report for sub-project

Sub-project ID: Date:

Project manager for the sub-project:

Overall progress:

	Planned	**Actual**
Total activities		
Planned for completion by this date		
Resource utilization:		
Expenditure		
Resource 2		
Resource 3		
Resource n		

Activities completed this week:

Activity	**Delay**	**Reasons for delay**	**Proposed corrective actions**

Ongoing Activities:

Activity	**Scheduled completion date**	**Percent completed**	**Probability of success**

Activities proposed for next week:

Activity	**Scheduled completion date**	**Probability of success**	**Any issues**

Issues raised:

Issues	**This week**	**Total**
Raised		
Resolved		
Pending		

Special events:

Event	Significance

Process improvement suggestions:

1.
2.
3.

Any other relevant information:

1.
2.
3.

Exhibit 7.1 Template for a progress report for sub-projects

Progress report for project

Project ID: Date:
Project start date:
Project scheduled completion date:
Project manager:

Executive summary: *<Briefly describe the highlights about the project progress.>*

Overall progress:

Parameter	Planned	Actual
Total activities		
Planned for completion by this date		
Sub-projects on schedule		
Resource utilization:		
Resource 1		
Resource 2		
Resource 3		
Resource n		

Progress of the sub-projects:

Sub-project	Number of activities completed on time	Number of activities delayed	Number of on-going activities

Earned value analysis:

Metric	Value
Budgeted cost of work scheduled	
Budgeted cost of work performed	
Actual cost of work performed	
Cost variance	
Schedule variance	
Cost performance index	
Schedule performance index	

Issues needing management attention:

Description of the issue	Date of origination	Pending with (name of the person)

Project metrics:

Name of metric	Organizational standard	Actual achievement	Explanation for variance
Productivity			
Quality			
Effort			
Schedule			
Cost			

Special events:

Event	Significance

Process improvement suggestions:

1.
2.
3.

Any other relevant information:

1.
2.
3.

Exhibit 7.2 Template for an IT project progress report

Minutes of meeting

Meeting conducted on:

Chaired by:

List of participants:

1.
2.
3.
4.

Highlights of the meeting: *<Describe the highlights of the meeting in this space.>*

Action points:

Item No.	Action item	Date of origination	Scheduled date of completion	Person responsible	Status (open/closed)
1					
2					
3					

Any other items discussed:

MOM Prepared by:

Date:

Exhibit 7.3 Template for recording the minutes of a progress review meeting

Cash flow statement for IT project

Project ID: Date:

Project manager:

Funds requirement:

Nature of requirement	**Earliest date of requirement**	**Latest date of requirement**	**Amount required**	**Minimum amount**
Total				

Notes: *<Explain any special aspects here. There may be assumptions about the dates and prerequisites to be fulfilled, the consequences of not meeting any dates, penalties, etc.>*

1.
2.
3.

Exhibit 8.1 Template for a cash flow statement

Review/Inspection Report

Project name:

Name of the artifact/work being reviewed/inspected:

Name of the lead reviewer/inspector:

Date on which review is conducted:

Type of review/inspection:

Defects uncovered during the review/inspection (use an additional sheet if necessary):

Defect ID	Defect description	Defect origin	Closed on	Status (open/closed)

Signature of the lead reviewer/inspector:
Date:

Closure action by the author:

Corrective actions implemented:

Corrective action implemented	Defect IDs covered by this corrective action	Comments

Preventive action implemented:

Preventive action implemented	Defect IDs covered by this corrective action	Comments

Signature of the person resolving defects:
Date:

Defect closure actions (to be filled in by the lead reviewer/inspector):

I have verified and found that all the defects described above are closed satisfactorily, except the following defects, which are retracted or pending:

1.
2.
3.

Signature of the lead reviewer/inspector:
Date:

Exhibit 9.4 Template for a review/inspection report

Req. No	Resource requested	Resource type	Qty	Required by date	Probable release date by phase
1.	Hardware engineers	Personnel	12	10th Oct 12	1. 5 by 20th Nov 12 2. 5 by 10th Dec 12 3. 2 by 1st Jan 13
2.	Networking engineers	Personnel	2	1st Oct 12	1st Jan 13
3.	Electricians	Personnel	2	1st Oct 12	1st December 12
4.	Networking cable	Material	2 Miles	1st Oct 12	Not applicable
5.	Continuity tester	Equipment	5	1st Oct 12	1st Jan 13

Exhibit C.1 Template for a sample resource request form

Index